FROM OUR OWN CORRESPONDENT

FROM OUR OWN CORRESPONDENT

Edited by Roger Lazar

BRITISH BROADCASTING CORPORATION

This book is based on a selection of the
talks given on the Radio 4 programme
'From Our Own Correspondent' over the
last twenty-five years. The date given refers
to the first broadcast of each piece.
   The programme's present editor is
Paddy O'Keeffe

Published by the
British Broadcasting Corporation
35 Marylebone High Street
London W1M 4AA

ISBN 0 563 17858 2

First published 1980
This collection © British Broadcasting
Corporation 1980

Printed in Great Britain by
Jolly & Barber Ltd, Rugby, Warwickshire

Contents

Preface

By 1955, the BBC had built up a highly-skilled corps of foreign correspondents and diplomatic staff. Their main task in those days was to broadcast brief news reports *in voice* for the programme *Radio Newsreel*, on what was then called the Light Programme, and even briefer news reports for incorporation – very rarely *in voice* – into the regular news bulletins. This was plainly not making full use of their talents; and so it was decided to start a new programme that would. It was called *From Our Own Correspondent* and the first edition went on the air on 25 September 1955.

The programme was an immediate success, both with its audience – at first on the Home Service, later Radio 4 – who wanted to know more about the world outside and what was going on there, and with the correspondents themselves who now had a regular outlet in which to spread their wings as broadcasters.

It was never the aim of *From Our Own Correspondent* just to re-tell the week's news from abroad. Its main object was to provide the domestic listener with a fuller understanding of international events. It tried to do this by dealing in depth with the social and philosophical backgrounds against which they had happened, and with the men and women involved. The correspondents also threw new light on events in Britain by reporting on the attitudes towards them from abroad.

That policy has remained unchanged for twenty-five years; what has changed is the way in which the correspondents' reports reach London. In 1955, the quality of international telephone calls was rarely good enough to allow for re-broadcasting; so a radio circuit to London, usually of better quality, had to be ordered, and this normally needed at least twenty-four hours' notice. The other method open to correspondents was to record their pieces on tape – and for this purpose they were provided with enormously cumbersome tape-recorders – and then to send the tape to London by commercial airline. This took even longer. Now, with the spread of underseas cables all over the world, the widespread use of satellites for telephone communications and the adoption of tiny and reliable cassette tape-recorders, things have become much easier both for the correspondents and for the editor in London.

On its twenty-fifth anniversary, nearly two thousand editions of *From Our Own Correspondent* will have been broadcast – and that makes getting on for ten thousand despatches from the correspondents. This book does not pretend to consist of 'the best' of those thousands, because sometimes what may have been 'the best' when it was broadcast, today makes dull reading outside its context of time and interest. It is a personal selection of pieces which I consider will still be of interest and, perhaps, of enlightenment to the reader of today.

I could not end this preface without saying thank you, first to the correspondents – all of them – who have provided the makings and the quality of the programmes, and second to Paddy O'Keeffe. As my assistant during the years when I was editor, she did all the hard work, and when I passed on to other things in 1969, she took over that editorship with satisfaction even to my ultra-critical ear.

Roger Lazar

Austrian Independence

GUY HADLEY   30 OCTOBER 1955

Austria had just regained her independence, after occupation by British, American and Soviet troops since the end of the war.

On this Sunday morning here in Vienna, the bells of St Stephen's Cathedral are ringing out over a city in a joyful mood. The last foreign soldier has left Austrian soil after ten years of post-war occupation and the national sovereignty has been restored. Parliament has approved the Government's policy of neutrality for Austria and the formation of an Austrian army to defend it. The Chancellor, Herr Raab, has again called for the admission of Austria to the United Nations, and he is seeking from Britain, the United States, France and the Soviet Union a joint guarantee of Austrian integrity and independence.

The Viennese, whose natural gaiety has helped them through so many troubles, are now basking in the glow of this new freedom. They're turning with renewed affection to the historic memories of their Imperial city, and especially to the revival of its artistic splendours from the ashes of war. The famous Burg Theater has been rebuilt; the classical Spanish Riding School is back in its old eighteenth-century home; and the climax comes next week with the reopening of the Vienna Opera.

The atmosphere is like a coronation – a coronation which has no throne, but crowns a spirit which has always drawn the world. To walk through the streets of Vienna today is like watching one of those big operatic scenes when there's going to be a party or a public holiday, and the stage is suddenly full of people and bustle and noise. Hammers and chisels are busy on every side, and you never in your life saw so many men in white overalls – painters, plasterers, carpenters and masons – popping out from scaffolding and piles of timber and stone. They're busy putting the last touches to this labyrinth of Habsburg palaces and courtyards and churches.

But this imposing architecture also reminds one of the economic problems which face an Austria shrunk to so much smaller size. Happily, the present outlook is much better than it was after the First World War. The Austrians have recovered their oil-fields from the Soviet Zone and the output, now running at over three and a half million tons a year, is a rich natural asset. Austria has to provide the Soviet Union with a million tons of oil a year, for ten years free of charge, plus over fifty million pounds' worth of other goods during the next six years. But she's gained two highly productive new oil-fields. The country has a valuable surplus of oil for export, if the Austrian price can be fixed at a competitive level.

Austria is also a big exporter of hydro-electric power and timber, both in demand abroad, and she's in the fortunate position of being largely self-sufficient in food production.

There is another side to all this. The housing problem is serious, especially in Vienna, and the country is supporting a very large number of officials and civil servants in proportion to its population. But from what I've seen and heard, I'd say that Austria faces the future with more confidence than at any other time in the past forty years.

Stalin's Reputation
ERIK DE MAUNY   1 APRIL 1956

Late in February, at the twentieth Congress of the Soviet Communist Party, Khrushchev had astonished the world by making a devastating assault on Stalin's reputation and on the 'cult of personality', which he had established. Erik de Mauny examined the effects that this bombshell had had throughout Eastern Europe.

Well it's clear, I think, that what we've been seeing during the last three or four weeks, is the overthrow of a god, for Stalin was in fact revered as a god in his later years. There's no other way of putting it. Supreme military genius; father of art and the sciences; leader and teacher of mankind – these were some of the praises heaped upon him. But even these are mild – mild when compared for example with the following rhapsodic outburst which appeared in the pages of *Pravda* as far back as 1936: 'Oh great Stalin, oh leader of the people; you who created man; you who populated the earth; you who made the centuries young; you who made the springtime flower.' Or the following extract from an anthology published in 1946: 'Stalin – here in the Kremlin his presence touches us at every step. We walk on stones which he may have trod only quite recently. Let us fall on our knees and kiss those holy footprints'. There's been nothing quite like it since the Emperor Augustus allowed himself to be worshipped as divine among the furthest provinces of the Roman Empire.

Now it's fairly obvious, I think, that such a god can't be overthrown in a day, or even a week, and in fact it's taken the present rulers of the Soviet Union nearly three years to nerve themselves for the final onslaught. For, of course, when such a great idol crashes, a great many other things happen. For example, one of the first repercussions was a report of rioting in Georgia, Stalin's native region; and the Party has admitted to sending out thousands of agitators, or propaganda experts, to explain the new line to the workers. And then, of course, there are all these activities that are not without a certain grimly comic aspect: the quiet removal of the huge portraits; the shrouding of the giant statues; the tremendous labour of once more rewriting all the textbooks and histories of the past twenty years. Indeed, the decision is bound to have its repercussions in every sphere of Soviet life – in education and economics, in art, philosophy and science. For all these things Stalin is now said to have perverted and falsified.

Well, Soviet society has had a long training in not answering back when official policy changes. But, of course, the change has also had profound repercussions among Communist Parties outside the Soviet Union. It's here that the old wounds are being reopened and the stench isn't pleasant. For one important sequel has been a reappraisal of the 1948 split between the Cominform and Tito. And one of the consequences of that break was a wave of treason trials throughout Eastern Europe – in fact wherever Stalin thought he could detect the least dangerous whiff of Titoism.

Well now, already one of the chief victims, the former Hungarian Foreign Minister, Laszlo Rajk, has been posthumously reinstated; for it's now been officially proclaimed, by no less a person than the Hungarian Communist Party leader, Mr Rakosi, that Rajk was condemned and executed on false evidence. And the prime instigator in laying that false evidence, according to Mr Rakosi, was none other than Beria, the former Soviet security chief, himself executed by the present Soviet leaders three years ago – Beria, who, according to *Pravda*, flourished like the green bay tree under Stalin's dictatorship. And of course there were other treason trials – Kostov in Bulgaria, Slansky in Czechoslovakia – it's quite a formidable list. Perhaps we haven't heard the last of them yet.

For now that the process of unravelling Stalin's reign of terror has begun, it's difficult to see where it will stop – or even where it can be stopped – since the Soviet leaders will presumably want to call a halt at some point. Meanwhile there's one interesting and even rather paradoxical fact that emerges from studying the reactions of Communist Parties in Eastern and Western Europe, and that is that their leaders have not by any means all shown the same alacrity to accept the Moscow denunciations. The Eastern Communist leaders have echoed them wholeheartedly enough – at Party meetings, in their own newspapers and radio broadcasts. But in the West, and particularly in Italy and France, the Party leaders have adopted a noticeably more delicate and shrinking attitude. In fact, like the French Party leader, M. Thorez, writing in last Tuesday's *Humanité*, they've tended rather defiantly to lay all the stress on Stalin's positive achievements. And there's the apparent paradox. One might say the ordinary Soviet citizen, in his tightly-policed world, had little option but to acquiesce in what went on under Stalin, whereas the Western party members at least had the advantage of distance, and might have been expected to see what was happening. And, of course, that's just the point. They did see, and they applauded. They even vied with each other in acclaiming Stalin's infinite wisdom and goodness as one carefully staged trial succeeded another. No wonder they're now thrown into some confusion. No wonder they're finding it rather difficult to put the right conviction into their appeals for popular front governments.

Meanwhile, when something as big as this happens – and many observers think it's the biggest thing that has happened since the Revolution – it's just not possible to grasp all the motives and consequences involved. It may seem fairly obvious, for example, that the present Soviet leaders had to destroy the terrible Stalin myth before they themselves could begin to breathe freely. But it's a good deal harder to guess what the full psychological effect of their action will be on a people, conditioned for more than a generation, to worship the very ground that Stalin trod. No one has suggested that the long-term aims of Communism have changed. But at least the new Soviet leaders have shown an apparent desire to ease tension abroad and create a more liberal atmosphere at home. One may say that, in the long run, they had no choice. The really vital thing is that they seem to have breathed a little wind of freedom into the huge prison of Soviet society, and who can say what this may eventually lead to?

The Suez Canal

DOUGLAS STUART   19 AUGUST 1956

President Nasser of Egypt had nationalised the Suez Canal and ordered the formation of an Egyptian Liberation Army to defend it. Britain and France reacted angrily to what they saw as a threat to their communications with the East, and Britain had, indeed, called up some reservists. Douglas Stuart was the BBC's Correspondent in Cairo.

Most days I park the car in the same spot in a back street in the centre of Cairo and then walk to my various appointments. Over the weeks, I've got to know the people near the parking place quite well, particularly the steady customers of the small soft-drinks shop. We smile at each other, say good day and exchange platitudes about the weather; then they sink back into their chairs on the pavement and return to their newspapers and gossip. But I've noticed that the whole street seems to congregate round the door of the shop whenever Cairo Radio broadcasts the news, for popular interest in the London Conference, in fact over every aspect of the Suez crisis, is very great. But the Egyptians, although they consider themselves to be entirely in the right, are not at all bellicose. I've not encountered hostility anywhere; on the contrary, I've found a great deal of friendliness and enjoyment of even the slightest of jokes. For example, there was the time when an Egyptian asked me, 'How are you this morning?' It was just after President Nasser had refused to attend the Conference in London. I replied: 'Still confident,' and this mild witticism was greeted with shouts of laughter and I'm still being teased about it.

On the other hand, the Egyptian Government is doing its best to stir up popular indignation against the West. The newspapers and the radio play up what is termed the 'Anglo-French military threat to Egypt'. President Nasser has coined a new slogan to describe the efforts of the Western Powers to secure international control of the Suez Canal. 'This is collective colonialism,' he says.

Everywhere there are signs of strenuous preparations to meet what's called 'the danger of an imperialist invasion'. The authorities have turned schools into recruiting centres for the new National Liberation Army. This is the equivalent of our own Home Guard. The slogan of the new force is 'a rifle behind every shutter'. Women, too, are being trained in the use of firearms. Every day the newspapers carry pictures of veiled Egyptian damsels holding submachine guns and valiantly trying to hide their distaste. Children are not excluded from the general mobilisation. Boy Scouts are being formed into battalions and I've seen army instructors showing six-year-olds how to drill. There are no longer any playing fields or sports clubs in Egypt; the authorities have turned them all into parade grounds and military training establishments.

The Egyptian Army, Navy and Air Force are fully mobilised; all leave has been cancelled. What's more, President Nasser has signed a decree making it illegal to publish information about the armed forces without special permission from the Minister of the Interior.

Religious leaders have announced their support of Egypt's cause. The Rector of Al Azhar, Cairo's one-thousand-year-old Muslim University, has announced that for a man to defend his country is a sacred duty; he's called for a *jihad* or holy struggle against Egypt's enemies. To show that he meant what he said, this elderly bearded scholar doffed his robes the other day, put on uniform, and accepted instruction from army officers in the use of a rifle.

The authorities have not lost sight of the need for a passive defence; they've opened blood banks, recalled doctors to duty, doubled the number of beds in State hospitals and appealed for gifts of blankets, clothing and medical stores. The principal cities of Egypt have all undergone mock air raids. In Cairo, it took me completely unawares. In my flat the lights flicked off and on twice and then the sirens began to wail; ARP wardens ran down the streets blowing horns and shouting, 'Put that light out!' Within a matter of seconds the city was in darkness; only the light of the moon illuminated the white cliffs of the skyscraper apartment houses along the banks of the Nile.

This then is the paradox of the Egyptian scene. On the one hand, there's what I can only describe as the apathy of the man in the street. He follows the news carefully; he supports Colonel Nasser to the full, but so far, he's not displayed an ounce of jingoism. On the other hand, Colonel Nasser's military dictatorship, with all the skill of modern propaganda techniques, is seeking to create a martial mood among the people. The streets of Cairo are decorated with huge photographs of their leader in army uniform. An enormous silver eagle, the symbol of the revolutionary regime, blazes across the Nile at night in neon-lit splendour. A giant plywood soldier straddles one of Cairo's main shopping streets. In the air-conditioned cinemas the people watch films glorifying the Egyptian Army. From time to time there's a little clapping.

Well, what's the explanation? A British friend of mine asked his servant the other day what he thought of the Suez problem. 'Colonel Nasser's right,' the man replied with conviction. 'Well, will you defend Egypt to the last drop of blood?' my friend asked. The servant's face expanded into a big grin. 'When the first bang comes,' he said, 'I'm off home to Aswan; there'll be no bombs there.' And yet I doubt whether many Egyptians feel this way. Europeans who've spent many years in the country tell me that there's a new spirit abroad, a spirit of resolution, and men of resolution do not need to be jingoistic.

A Modern Peasants' Revolt

THOMAS BARMAN 28 OCTOBER 1956

Eastern Europe was in turmoil. In Poland, there had been rioting in the city of Poznan and it seemed that the country was on the verge of full-scale revolution. However, firm action by President Gomulka took the strain. In Hungary, though, students, workers and much of the Hungarian Army did revolt against the Communist regime and the presence of Soviet troops. Mr Nagy was swept to power and, for a time, it looked as though the revolution had succeeded. Tom Barman was Diplomatic Correspondent.

It is tempting to see, in this Hungarian insurrection, an analogy with the events of 1849, when the Russian Army was called in to put down a patriotic revolt against the Government in Budapest. But I am not sure that the analogy with 1849 is a good one. For the events of 1848 and 1849, when so many Governments in Europe were shaken to their foundations, were the outcome of a burst of optimism and self-confidence. They grew out of a ferment of hope.

And I do not think it is possible to argue that either the riots in

Poznan, or the insurrection in Hungary are grounded in hope. It seems to me much nearer the truth to say that they are the wild acts of brave men driven beyond endurance into desperate courses. So the analogy is not with the stirring events of 1849, but with the endless and hopeless revolts of the European peasants in the fifteenth and sixteenth centuries. The appeals and manifestos of the time strike the same chilling note of despair as emerged in Poznan a week or two ago.

Now the authors of the Russian Revolution, like the most heartless type of feudal landlord, feared and despised the peasant. There was Trotsky, for example, who once described the peasantry as a shapeless remnant of medievalism in contemporary society. There was Stalin who, as Mr Khrushchev has told us, got all his knowledge about farming and the countryside from the propaganda films that were produced to hoodwink Western audiences. And however much the Russian Communist leaders may have disagreed among themselves about aims and policies, they did agree on one thing: that the peasant must be prevented – so long as he remained a peasant – from having any substantial influence upon the work of the Party.

It was with the support of the Party that the Russian leaders embarked upon their war against the peasants. It was a war that started some years after they had taken over. Its aim was to coerce the peasant into producing plenty of cheap food for the towns without giving him anything in return; or, in other words, to squeeze all the funds required for an over-ambitious industrial programme out of the peasant – out of his standard of subsistence. No one knows how many people lost their lives in this Communist war against the Russian peasant – I don't suppose anyone ever will – and it isn't over yet.

When the Russians moved into Eastern Europe, they brought the peasants' war with them. They introduced the same policies and made precisely the same costly mistakes as they had made at home. The industrial plans they forced upon Poland and Hungary – which looked so fine on paper – were little more than hand-to-mouth expedients. Their main purpose, it now seems, was to conceal the fact that the peasants were resisting the efforts of the authorities to take their crops and their cattle from them. Their resistance turned out to be sterner and yet more resilient than that of the Russian peasant, because it drew comfort and consolation from the Roman Catholic Church. So the Church, too, came under attack.

The men who are now returning to power in Eastern Europe have told us something of the desolation that the planners have left behind them. In Poland, as one would expect, the collective farm experiment has been an utter failure. This rich farming country is now an importer of foodstuffs. From Hungary there comes the same story; and people in the towns now face the winter in the knowledge that they are standing on the very edge of famine. The food shortages in the towns are a direct consequence of the peasants' war, and it is against that consequence – among others – that the people of Budapest have now revolted.

All these privations and shortages might perhaps have been tolerable if they had been suffered in the national interest. They weren't. They were the consequences of Russian exploitation – of the Russian insistence that every phase of life in Poland and in Hungary and elsewhere in Eastern Europe must be subordinated to the rapid industrialisation of the Soviet Union. And now, in 1956, as the Poles and the Hungarians have shown, the strain has become unbearable.

Israel Attacks Egypt
PETER FLINN   4 NOVEMBER 1956

Things had come to a head in the Middle East. In collusion, some suspected, with Britain and France, Israel had responded to threats from President Nasser by attacking Egyptian-occupied Sinai. Douglas Stuart, in Cairo, had been interned by the Egyptians and couldn't report. But Peter Flinn, in Tel Aviv, was able to.

The fighting in Egypt began on Monday and finished on Friday – four days – and even the Israelis who had been so cocksure can hardly believe in their success. Four days and so many worrying thorns plucked out of their Egyptian flank! No more infiltrators crossing the practically unmarked border from the Gaza Strip or out from the Sinai Desert; no more worries whether their old British and American-made tanks would be a match for the new Russian tanks delivered to Egypt, and – this was the worst threat –

no question of the crowded cities of Tel Aviv and Jerusalem being bombed. And yet they're still taking the conflict – the word 'war' just doesn't exist in official language – they're still taking it seriously. The blackout is just as intense; the blood donors are still volunteering in hundreds; every car driver keeps his tank topped up when he can, for petrol has been like gold in the last week. Half the buses and cars have disappeared from cities. I saw them in the hands of the Army, camouflaged with daubs of mud, carrying Egyptian prisoners who looked as if they were ready to fall in on parade – so neat and ungrimed. And here and there on the well-kept roads of Israel you see vehicles with Arabic number plates, smart little Egyptian ambulances or well-worn green jeeps.

In the settlements, the farm colonies which Israel deliberately built up all along her borders to emphasise that she would never give up an inch of land, the ploughmen still take their rifles along with them on the tractor, possibly by force of habit. But, of course, there is a difference this weekend in the settlements along what was the border with Egypt. The settlement children – there are always lots of children in settlements – the children have been taken down to look at the miserable little ditch that marked the Gaza Strip; not too close, because mine clearance parties are out. Israel wants to get the new land ploughed as soon as possible, ready for the winter rains which are already overdue.

But the great difference in the settlements is at night. The years of night watches are over and the children no longer need to sleep in the shelters and, whatever they do in the towns, the settlers ignore the blackout.

In the towns the men left in civil life have worked enormously long hours – they certainly couldn't have kept up this pace for long – but there was little grumbling. Shopkeepers became short-tempered at the end of the day's efforts to work out a private rationing system of their own among the hoarders who descended like vultures. The Israeli prefers to live at the top of his voice, and some of the shops have been babel.

The Army has been fanatically silent. The Chief of Staff – General Moshe Dayan – I saw him for a fleeting moment outside Gaza, with his piratical black eyeshield. He lost an eye serving in the British Army. General Dayan has a motto: 'We don't fight to provide a good story for journalists', and all the Israeli moves have been made swiftly and secretly. After the almost bloodless capture of the Gaza Strip, the fighting troops were whisked out to re-form elsewhere. The infantry went off in buses on which they chalked 'Tel Aviv to Cairo' on the destination boards. They might have been going in that direction, but it's been officially announced that the Israeli Army will not cross the Canal.

As to other borders, Israel's border with Jordan alone is twice as long as the border with Egypt. And facing Jordan, Syria and the Lebanon, the settlements remain on the alert. This may be one reason why the Israelis remain earnest and intent listeners rather than talkers – their usual role is that of a talker. Now they listen to every news bulletin they can. And in this polyglot country no language is incomprehensible. All the Arab world broadcasts, all the foreign language and English transmissions of the BBC, they all have their listeners, who put out the news again by word of mouth.

One last word. Only a minority of Israelis are strict orthodox Jews. As they say themselves in one of their shorthand jokes, 'Most Israelis eat Kosher food as well.' But there are hundreds and thousands of Jews here who came to Israel to find a safe home, and in the synagogues on this Sabbath, the prayers were not of thanksgiving for victory but for peace.

Suez: the American View

CHRISTOPHER SERPELL   4 NOVEMBER 1956

The day after the Israeli attack on Egypt, Britain and France gave the two sides twelve hours to stop fighting; to withdraw their troops ten miles either side of the Suez Canal; and to allow Anglo-French forces to occupy key points at Port Said, Ismailia and Suez. The twelve hours elapsed and British bombers attacked Egyptian airfields, while Anglo-French invasion troops sailed to the area of conflict. Resolutions condemning this action were supported in the Security Council by the United States, but vetoed by Britain and France. The United States was angry, as Christopher Serpell, based in Washington, reported.

It's not been a pleasant experience for an Englishman among Americans during the last few days. If you turned on the radio, you heard sombre or melodramatic voices announcing the latest developments as if they were the end of the world, with the British to blame for it. Oh, and the French, too, as an afterthought. The broadcasting air was full of the crash of broken treaties and crumbling alliances, so you turned it off and you opened the newspaper, and that was just as bad. At least it was in Washington where the local newspaper, usually a critic of the State Department, had rallied to its side in this grim moment. On the front page, a man who had dined with Mr Dulles the previous night was writing that the British and French had not only failed to inform the United States Government of their plans, they had supplied deliberately misleading information instead.

So you went outside to rake the falling leaves off the garden and up came your neighbour, with his face set in the grave, sad lines of personal bereavement, to ask you what you made of it all. You murmured something about the crucial importance of the Suez Canal to Western Europe – at least, I did – and the neighbour said hastily, 'I'm absolutely sure you're right, only – well – let me help you rake those leaves.' It was almost a relief to take off for New York in air as thick as warm, wet cotton-wool.

When I asked the taximan at La Guardia, New York, to take me direct to the United Nations he said, 'Yes, sir – the Assembly. You've certainly got a mess on your hands there. I only hope you can make something of it.' And as we wove swiftly in and out of the galloping lines of horsepower that were crossing the Triboro' Bridge, he resumed his train of thought. 'Yes, sir,' he said, 'I certainly hope that while they're talking in there tonight, they remember people are being killed. Gee, that's a terrible thing,' he went on, cutting sharply across the bows of an enormous lorry, 'people getting killed out there while we sit talking here.'

On the whole, I've found the atmosphere here in New York more relaxed than in Washington. Perhaps that's because people get used to the world being turned upside-down; perhaps it's because New York is further away from officialdom. Certainly the huge and independent-minded Jewish population of this area is delighted at the apparent victory of the Israeli forces and in no mood at all to call it aggression. 'You gotta put things in a nutshell,' said one. 'A feller keeps picking on you and you gotta finally swing at him.'

The reactions of New York and Washington give one little clue to the general reactions of this huge country. And what will all the comment add up to in the end – the casual remarks over mint juleps in the shady courtyards of New Orleans; the heated arguments in the cosy bars of San Francisco; the laconic utterances of men in high-heeled boots in the poolrooms of Gillette, Wyoming; and, in Chicago women's clubs, the carefully prepared impromptu speeches by members who have made at least one trip to Europe? Some people think it will lead to a revival of isolationism; certainly Mr Nixon seemed to be banking on that last night with his ingenious interpretation of events as a new American revolution against the outworn forces of colonialism.

The Invasion of Hungary
PETER RALEIGH   11 NOVEMBER 1956

The people of Hungary were still fighting. The Russians had struck to suppress the revolution and they did so ruthlessly. Budapest was bombed and occupied by Soviet tanks. Mr Nagy had been forced out of office. Foreign correspondents in Hungary, including the BBC's Ivor Jones, were unable to get their stories out. Refugees were streaming over the frontier bringing the news with them. Peter Raleigh was in Vienna to meet them.

It's a little difficult to report from Vienna at the end of a week such as this with detachment. It seems sometimes like waiting outside the hospital ward in which a friend lies desperately ill and fighting for life. The doors are closed; the news is meagre, and the outlook grave. And I think I can say that this feeling is shared by nearly all Austrians. I exclude the few Austrian Communists who had to bow down to considerable popular hatred this week.

We've had to wait this week, fearing the worst and moved by the sight of thousands upon thousands of men, women and children tramping across the frontier to safety, or waiting patiently in the tall rooms of some camp, their homes and friends behind them and a difficult new life ahead.

As the fighting flickered and coursed through an isolated Hungary this week, Vienna has been inevitably a prey to rumour and contradictory reports. For it's a week since Western correspondents in Budapest, among them the BBC special correspondent, Ivor Jones, who would otherwise be talking to you, filed their last reports to Vienna and the outside world. Most of these correspondents we know to be in safety in the legations of various countries in Budapest. It's a week since the Russians marched on Budapest and sent their armour running through the streets. It's a week since the last moving appeal from the Hungarian Prime Minister, Imre Nagy, for help from the United Nations, from the great powers. Then silence came down on the true state of things in Hungary, and fact and fiction mingled together have trickled at intervals through this curtain.

Inevitably many of the reports reaching Vienna are exaggerated, perhaps false. But through these mists of uncertainty you can still see the outlines of the almost unbelievable fight for freedom which the people of a small country, badly armed and badly fed, have made against an overwhelming military strength. Last Sunday, few observers gave the Hungarian Resistance Movement more than a day or two. The Russians themselves were soon asserting over Moscow Radio that resistance had been crushed, but it was not so. Day by day, at least some reports of fighting came into Vienna – fighting in the narrow streets of the old part of Budapest; in the main industrial districts; fighting from Nationalist strongpoints in the bigger buildings. Men of the Resistance have been bombed at least once. They've faced the attacks of tanks, but they've held out. Reports of fighting have come from outside Budapest, for example from the neighbourhood of the uranium mines near Pocs in the south. One refugee told me, by the way, that these uranium mines had only just been got ready for production – a production destined, he said, wholly for the Russians. Reports of fighting have come from north-western Hungary – from the Gycer area – where the Nationalists had one of their main military headquarters.

That the unequal battle could last so long as it has seems to afford proof of the stories of incredible gallantry reaching Vienna – stories of gallantry to the point of death on the part of young boys, sometimes armed, as in the days of the first uprising three weeks ago, with little more than bottles of petrol with a primitive fuse. One story, which may or may not be true, tells of a Russian tank unit which was attacked by three boys with bottles of petrol. One by one the boys were shot down. And then the Russian tank commander surrendered – surrendered because, he said, such gallantry showed that he was meeting a genuine resistance of the Hungarian people.

But for that one report of a Russian being moved to surrender, there are others which speak of the complete ruthlessness and disregard for life shown by the Russian soldiers. When the Russians offered an amnesty recently and some few Hungarians accepted it, they were shot at once. The loss of life cannot be gauged. The most conservative figures I've heard, mention three thousand dead and seven thousand wounded, and casualties are thought to be in fact far higher. And all this week the International Red Cross units here have been unable to get from Austria into Hungary to carry out their neutral, their humanitarian task. If and when they do get into Hungary, the Red Cross teams will take with them food as much as medical supplies, for they'll find starvation and hunger and devastation, a land without much transport or fuel. For three weeks there's been a general strike in Hungary. Radio Budapest has told of districts without electricity; shops looted; houses burned down; queues for food. There have been urgent appeals to workers to return to work, threats and promises of bonus pay, but the latest reports are that few of the workers are yet at work.

If in this last week the International Red Cross has been unable to help those inside Hungary, it's done much to help the Austrians care for the seventeen thousand refugees who've arrived here. I've seen these refugees in so many places, crossing the frontier – sometimes with a small paper parcel, sometimes without one – in clothes that make one realise that at a given moment they'd dropped what they were doing and came over, just as they were, to safety. A man who came over the border on a motor bicycle was lucky; he still had on his old leather jacket. I've seen the faded yellow buses provided by the Austrians driving the refugees to the reception camps. I've seen the battered barracks where those children – luckily few – who are all alone in the world were being cared for. I've seen the peeling Army cadet school at Traiskirchen, the main reception camp, where hundreds stood, pallid and weary in a greasy November rain, exchanging news or standing silent looking into space. I've seen the families lying on the straw-filled mattresses, holding their children. Sometimes the children were crying in these strange surroundings.

I've heard doctors talk of the tiny children, weak and thin for want of food when they arrived; of the older people whose hearts could hardly stand the strain of their scramble to safety. Some of these refugees I've talked to were bitter. 'You can't fight tanks with bare hands.' 'Why don't you send us arms as well as penicillin?' 'Why did Suez have to happen now so that we were forgotten?' Others are content to have found refuge, saying, 'I've been waiting to escape the Communists for years.' And then they may talk about what they want to do next, but often they will ask for news of what is happening in Hungary, and then they are clearly thinking of their friends or relatives and the sad prospects before them.

Escape from Budapest
IVOR JONES   18 NOVEMBER 1956

After a week trapped in Budapest by the fighting there, Ivor Jones, together with a number of other correspondents, managed to get out.

Reporters are notorious individualists but, five days after the Russian attack started, we in Budapest found ourselves almost spontaneously working together. We had to get out to tell our story. There were no normal communications, and we thought that the bigger our convoy was the better our chance would be. So early in the morning of Friday the ninth, we began to form up outside the American Legation.

It was an amazing collection of cars – more than thirty of them – some barely roadworthy, some elegant enough for a glossy advertisement, but nearly all plastered with the flag of some Western nation. We set off. We had no papers allowing us to go. Some of us hadn't even got visas allowing us to be in Hungary. But we set off. There was still some firing going on.

We crossed the Danube by what seemed the easiest bridge. There were Russian tanks at either end, but the sentries let us pass. Beyond, in the suburbs, the debris of fighting was as heavy as in the city centre. Wrecked Hungarian guns lay beside the road; walls and the sides of houses had been shot away.

About ten miles out we reached a big barracks held by the Russians. We were stopped at a check point outside it. There was already one tank there and some tommy-gunners. Another tank came up and I spent most of the next few hours looking down its gun-barrel, which seemed to be trained directly on my car. Our spokesman sought out the barracks commander, a Russian colonel.

He was correct, almost affable. He said that, unfortunately, he had no authority to let us pass and, since we had no documents – well . . . We asked him to do something about it; to ring the Foreign Ministry; to do anything. He said he'd try, but nothing happened.

We sat and watched Soviet troops coming and going and, with them, small groups of AVH men – Hungarian security police. The AVH were an aristocracy of sadists that kept such Stalinists as Rakosi in power. I'd met men who'd been obscenely tortured by them. Others showed me perjured documents and bogus confessions from the AVH files. Well, when the Russians arrived the remnants of the AVH came out of hiding. And there some of them were, outside these barracks. It wasn't a comforting thought for those of us whose passports weren't in order.

We stayed until mid-afternoon and then went back to Budapest, to the Foreign Ministry. We stood in the hall there, a frustrated rabble, calling for the Minister, for senior officials, for anybody. The Minister appeared – at least I think it was the Minister. He said yes, he thought he could arrange for us to have a safe-conduct to the Austrian border. We settled down again to wait while permanent officials came and went. They were quite friendly. It turned out that we were to be given a document in Hungarian and Russian and signed by the Deputy Prime Minister of Hungary – but not, unfortunately, till the next morning.

Next morning we were back at the Ministry. The documents finally arrived. But by this time we'd learnt that the Russians weren't willing to accept these pieces of paper, even though they were signed by one of their puppet ministers. He's probably well used to such humiliations.

So we started all over again by going round to the Soviet headquarters, the Kommandatura. This is housed in a curious pink rococo mansion surrounded by tanks, armoured cars and troop-carriers. We stood around in the hall, an immensely tall room painted white and decorated with plaster roses. At the corners of the walls were coy statues of naked girls. And everywhere were tough-faced, square-built Russians armed with pistols and tommy-guns. Around the edge of the room, halfway up, ran a gallery from which Soviet secret police in plain clothes looked down on us.

Finally we got a sort of assurance that we'd be given passes. But not until tomorrow. Next morning we actually did get them. They were blurred and untidy and I don't know what magic formula was written on them, but they got us past the Russian check-points, about a dozen of them, between Budapest and the frontier. Anyway, we reached the border.

As we crossed there was some small-arms fire in the distance. We were told that it was by AVH men firing at Hungarian refugees – some of the millions who were less fortunate than ourselves.

American Oil Sanctions
CHRISTOPHER SERPELL   2 DECEMBER 1956

America's anger with the British over Suez had led her to cut off oil supplies to Britain – oil supplies desperately needed because of the closure of the Suez Canal. Relations had almost reached breaking point. Christopher Serpell reported from Washington.

Diplomats here believe tomorrow will be face-saving day, both in London and in Washington. In the House of Commons, Mr Selwyn Lloyd is expected to announce the 'phased withdrawal' of British and French forces from Egypt in terms which do not sound too much like an unconditional surrender to orders from the United Nations and pressure from the United States. Washington is expected to hail Mr Lloyd's statement as a capitulation to world opinion, due to the wide influence of the United States. Washington's attitude will, of course, be struck mainly for the edification of Asian and African countries, but it will also derive from the need to save official faces inside the Administration.

Last weekend, the British and French Governments, already sent to diplomatic Coventry, were being made to feel the cane of American oil sanctions. Acting on the principle of refusing to discuss any serious matter with Britain and France until after these Governments had unconditionally withdrawn their forces from Egypt, officials were saying, more in sorrow than in anger, 'This hurts us more than it hurts you.' By the end of the week they were beginning to wonder whether this traditional formula might not in fact be true.

It was being pointed out to them that the consequences of their 'one-eyed moral bias', as the columnist Mr Walter Lippmann

28

called it, might include either the downfall of the British Conservative Government and its replacement by a Socialist administration, or, if the British Government stood firm in isolation under pressure from its right wing, an oil shortage in Western Europe, followed by desperate economic depression and unemployment. If the second of these alternatives were realised it would mean that the post-war American investment into European recovery might well be wasted. It would almost certainly involve the political break-up of the North Atlantic Treaty Organisation and the extension of Soviet influence in Western Europe. It might result in the denial to the United States Air Force of the British bases on which its Strategic Air Command at present depends.

When Mr Selwyn Lloyd spoke at the English-Speaking Union in New York last Monday, just before leaving for Great Britain, perhaps one of the most telling phrases he used was his reminder that 'we in the United Kingdom have stood almost alone before, and we have not always been proved to be wrong'.

This picture of renewed British isolation seems to have impressed at least one man in the United States Administration, a man with particular reason to remember Anglo-American co-operation. On the following day, from the golf course at Augusta, Georgia, where he's been studying international affairs between morning and afternoon nine-hole rounds, President Eisenhower issued a significant statement through his Press Secretary. Announcing that Mr Dulles, only five weeks after his operation for cancer, would fly to Paris for the Ministerial meeting of NATO, the President recalled publicly that NATO was, as he put it, 'a basic and indispensable element of American defence alliances', and went on to argue that 'differences between the United States and its allies over a particular international incident in no way should be construed as weakening or disrupting the great bonds that have so long joined the United States with the United Kingdom and France'.

This view, now expressed by the President, had, for many previous days, been ventilated by American political commentators on foreign policy and also by a number of State Department officials on the working level. But these voices from below have not been heeded by high policy-making officials, such as Mr Hoover, the Acting Secretary of State in Mr Dulles' absence. Mr Hoover, who is said to have been in frequent touch with Mr Dulles in Florida, perhaps reflected the high tone of moral indignation against what was felt to be an Anglo-French transgression, a transgression which some officials evidently felt merited discipline and punishment.

By the end of the week it was clear that the President's warning had taken effect on policy. First, officials merely allowed it to be known that a statement of British and French intentions to withdraw would immediately be rewarded by oil for Western Europe. Then, when the British Foreign Secretary had delayed his definitive statement till after the weekend consultations with France, and when American correspondents in London were predicting that it would, in any case, precipitate the Government's downfall, the decision was taken on Friday to put the emergency plan for supplying oil to Europe into immediate operation, without waiting for British and French declarations of policy.

The United States had, apparently, received the necessary assurances in private, and it was hoped that a public diplomatic withdrawal in Washington might make military withdrawals more palatable to London and Paris.

Italy's Intellectual Climate
ROBERT STIMSON   27 JANUARY 1957

With the coming of 1957, the Russians had crushed the Hungarian revolution and the crisis over the Middle East had eased. The programme was able to take a breather after the two stories which had entirely dominated it for months. The BBC's Rome Correspondent, Bob Stimson, discussed the intellectual climate in Italy.

I've recently met some British and American expatriates who used to live in France but have now made their homes in Italy. They agree, so far as I can judge, that, while France is more stimulating intellectually, Italy is more comfortable because – and this is, of course, a very broad generalisation – Italians attach importance to the purely cerebral processes only if these add to their enjoyment of living. This may explain why, in Italy, stomach ulcers are comparatively rare.

Philosophical ideas that run counter to the teaching of the Roman Catholic Church don't easily take root here. I've never met an Italian existentialist, for example. Even those Italians who vote Communist describe themselves, almost without exception, as Roman Catholics. So you see, habits of thought here tend to be traditional.

Italians are highly intelligent, but they instinctively follow the advice of the American wit who told his friends to leave their minds alone. On the whole, they read very few books. The novels and short stories of, say, Alberto Moravia are more widely read abroad than they are here. Italy publishes only about half as many books each year as the United Kingdom, although their populations are roughly the same. Moreover, Italian editions are comparatively small. Average sales for good novels are only two or three thousand; a novel selling five thousand copies is in the bestseller class. There are no big subscription libraries in Italy and although there is a fairly good network of public libraries, the books they provide are limited almost entirely to those of a specialist or technical kind.

Italians aren't even very great readers of newspapers. Circulation figures show that. But they certainly know what's happening. They're indefatigable talkers and they pass the news on by word of mouth.

As for the arts, the Italians know what they like and what they like is what they're used to. Any Italian errand boy can whistle every aria from almost every opera by Verdi or Rossini, but there's probably not one Italian in a hundred thousand who knows or cares about modern experimental music.

It's much the same with painting. A maid-servant will ask her mistress for time off to go to an exhibition of paintings by Fra Angelico; but when a year or two ago someone organised an exhibition of modern painting in the Via Margutta (the artists' quarter in Rome), only the foreign community was really interested.

The Italian theatre in the seventeenth and sixteenth centuries had immense prestige all over Western Europe. Today it's in a very sad state. The great Italian playwrights of the past, such as Goldoni, no longer capture the public imagination, nor do contemporary Italian playwrights have much of a following. The comparatively few Italians who patronise the theatre prefer Shakespeare, Shaw and Chekhov, or Thornton Wilder and Noël Coward.

What all this means is that those who come to Italy hoping to find exciting new art forms and to hear new daring ideas being discussed may be disappointed. But what Italy does offer to an unrivalled extent is a superb tradition of craftsmanship. It's a revelation to come across a little town like Volterra, for example, in Tuscany, and find almost every man, woman and child producing lovely things from alabaster. If you want anything from a handsome cigarette box to an exact replica of Michelangelo's 'Pietà', they'll make it for you.

It's an unfailing delight to wander round the back streets of, say, Florence or Naples, and watch men and women, who are scarcely able to read, working lovingly with wood, or metal, or leather, or straw, or almost any other material you can think of. When they put their minds to it, Italian craftsmen are incapable of producing anything ugly. This may not be a tribute to modern Italian culture but it surely suggests that the Italians are highly civilised.

On Being a Foreigner
CHRISTOPHER SERPELL   22 SEPTEMBER 1957

What's foreign about a foreign correspondent? Is it the correspondent himself, or is it the people he's working amongst? Christopher Serpell had discovered that it was both.

Recently in Washington I had to tell a lady canvasser at my front door that I couldn't give money to the political cause she represented because I wasn't an American citizen – only a foreign resident. Rather heatedly she replied: 'And you ought to be darned glad you got in here.' Her attitude seemed vaguely familiar, and then I remembered the time in Rome when I had complained to my landlord, the Count, who lived in the flat upstairs, about his mid-Lent party which had kept us awake all night. With an aristocratic disregard for the gigantic and illegal rent he got out of me he remarked, 'Sir, you abuse your position as my country's guest.' And then there was an echo from the further past.

Back in 1946, in Paris, I had made a 'démarche' to the moustachioed old beldame who ran my hotel, protesting with some passion against her practice of letting my bedroom during my working hours to transient guests. Her answering tirade was in the great classic tradition. Beginning with expressions of doubt about the authenticity of my ancestry and the validity of my claim to any education, she passed on to a prediction – well-founded, as it turned out – of the bad luck that would haunt my steps in Paris. And then she reached her grand climax. 'Monsieur,' she declaimed, 'vous avez insulté la France.'

I'm not sure what moral you can draw from this recurring situation, except perhaps that a foreign correspondent ought not to take himself too solemnly. One respected member of the profession recently defined us as 'highly qualified snoopers', and I remember another colleague who in convivial moments would address us as 'Fellow bog-rats' – a poetic phrase not always appreciated by the more dignified members of the company. But he was right and they were wrong; once a correspondent becomes pompous, he starts drawing self-portraits against an exotic background instead of dealing with that background itself. I liked, when I began the job, to say that I was 'interpreting' one country to another. Now I know that claim went much too far; all you can really do is to illustrate the ways in which a foreign country differs from your own and to explain and justify them. This 'justifying them' is important because it is a basic human instinct to resent the 'difference' of the foreigner.

The French are the most direct about this; they often seem to feel this difference as an outrage against good taste, whereas Italians merely regard it with a pitying wonderment. The Englishman rationalises the difference of foreigners by regarding them all as more or less unsuccessful imitations of himself; and the American draws a veil over it by immersing mankind in a warm bath of 'human nature', which immediately qualifies all and sundry for American-style democracy. But you can't be a foreign correspondent and not relish this difference between nation and nation, between continent and continent. So, if I had now to talk about my 'mission', I should say it was the almost impossible one of persuading one people not merely to forgive other peoples for being foreign and different, but to rejoice in the fact that they really are.

Of course, relishing the foreign-ness of another nation doesn't mean that living out your life among foreigners is particularly easy; in one sense it is a great strain and it should be so. If I ceased to be aware of the foreign-ness of my American neighbours, kind and civilised though they are, I should become one of them and disqualify myself for my job. In fact, in spite of the common language, I now feel them to be considerably more 'foreign' than the people of other European countries. In Italy, I used to relax in the company of my fellow English; in Washington, I can relax in the company of my fellow-Europeans. Their ways of thought, regardless of their languages, are generally closer to my own, than the American.

Let me illustrate how a European man can drop an American brick. The train in which I was once travelling through an autumnal countryside in the state of Illinois came to a stop between stations and didn't move again for almost an hour. When we asked the ticket collector for an explanation, he said that on this particular day the hunting season had opened and some s.o.b. had shot away the signal wire, so that they didn't know whether the line ahead was clear or not. In Europe, a mildly humorous incident; and that was how I told it to my American hosts when I apologised for my late arrival. But to them it wasn't at all funny; it was, as they put it, profoundly humiliating that this should have happened to an otherwise fine railroad on a day when a foreigner was travelling by it. And it took several fine martinis to wash away my host's embarrassment at this technological failure, and my own embarrassment at ever having mentioned it.

Tiger Hunting

GERALD PRIESTLAND   7 DECEMBER 1957

Gerry Priestland was the BBC's Correspondent in India and he took a little time off to go tiger hunting.

Apart from being the story of how I went on a twenty-minute safari, this little episode will always be to me 'India, my India'. It began when an Indian friend of mine said that if I wanted to shoot tiger, he had an uncle in the Kumaen Hills, the Jim Corbett country, you know, who would arrange everything. It would, he said, take little more than twenty-four hours. All we had to do was to drive up there in the morning; sit in a tree over a water-hole; shoot the tiger that night, and be back for lunch the next day. So, a couple of days later, after phoning his uncle, we set out for the hills.

I'd equipped myself with a pocket first-aid outfit, a fur hat which was once condemned by Mr Khruschchev as 'impolite' – that was in Burma – and a medicine bottle of vodka donated by an aquaintance in the Soviet Embassy to commemorate the Sputniks. Quite how this story got such a Russian angle I don't really know.

Well, to begin with, it took eight hours to get up to the hills instead of the four my friend had promised, and then we ran up against the holy River Ganges. There was, of course, no bridge, there never is in India, but there was an ancient ferry modelled on the Kon-Tiki raft and navigated in much the same way. We had to wait two more hours while an American missionary was ferried across with his jeep. He was on a tiger hunt as well.

Inside the jeep he had two darling baby buffaloes for the tigers to kill and on the outside was painted 'God is Love' and 'Suffer Little Children'.

By the time we got across, it was pitch dark and the people who'd been waiting to take us to the water-hole had given up and gone home. We drove thirty miles along a sinister jungle track to the nearest resthouse. It was pouring with rain and my Indian friend said complacently: 'It is good we did not get here on time, we might now have been up a tree,' to which there really was no answer.

We passed a miserable night in the resthouse with no lights and the wind blowing the doors open. If the tiger had been hunting us, it could have walked in and helped itself. Next morning, it was time to go home. We drove back along the jungle track, past notices saying 'Beware of Elephants' and 'Night driving forbidden'. I felt I had to be able to say I'd been out after tiger, so we stopped the car and plunged about in the undergrowth for a bit with shot-guns – all we had, by the way. The jungle was thick and menacing; we saw a tabby cat, two man-eating rabbits, and some dangerous looking peacocks; also a great deal of rather ostentatious elephant dung. In the end, my friend lost his temper and shot a sitting snipe – poor thing, it practically disintegrated. His gun was loaded for tiger.

Nostalgia

THOMAS BARMAN   25 JANUARY 1958

Tom Barman in a nostalgic mood.

There isn't very much scope nowadays for the old-fashioned kind of journalist, for the man who goes plodding away quietly at his facts without any fuss, who doesn't want glory or power or even the acclamation of the public.

There seem to be arc-lights all over the place these days, with advertising specialists organising vast Press conferences. Why, at the last meeting of the North Atlantic Treaty Organisation, there were nearly two thousand journalists in attendance. And as I recall that gloomy arena, where we waited to so little purpose, my mind goes back to an old-fashioned journalist I used to know in Sweden – a man who'd never attended a Press conference in his life.

His name was Stridsberg, and he was the principal writer on foreign affairs on the staff of the leading Conservative newspaper in Sweden, the *Svenska Dagbladet*. He died – well, it was early in 1945, I think. He was always an old man. I cannot imagine what he would have looked like in his teens, or even in his early thirties. He wore the sort of coat you see Prince Bismarck wearing in all those stock pictures of the Iron Chancellor. And it was always fastened so near the chin that you could never be sure of the sort of collar he was wearing – it might have been a clerical collar for all I knew. He was short and almost square, with one shoulder rather higher than the other, and with something more than a hint of the hunchback about his appearance. His voice was edged with sandpaper when he got excited or angry, and when he was amused the flow of words would break against a heavy chuckle that was laced with acid. I used to spend hours talking with him in his flat in Stockholm, where he lived alone with an old rocking-chair as his constant companion.

He was one of the best-informed people I'd ever met on all sorts of topics, ordinary and extraordinary. I don't think I ever caught him out on a question of fact, or on a quotation. So far as I know he had never travelled outside his own country, except for an occasional week's holiday – in Estonia, I think. He had never had any formal education. He'd been a sickly child, and there had been no question of his going to school. His mother had laid the foundations of his vast knowledge – the rest he'd done himself. He could read all the main European languages with the greatest of ease – French and German and English and Italian and Spanish and Portuguese – and his desk at the office was stacked high with all kinds of exotic newspapers. When he took a day off, he often stayed in bed in order to enjoy a little quiet reading. He told me once that the Oxford English Dictionary was one of his favourite works – the big one, you know, running to some fourteen volumes. He read it, he said, page after page, out of sheer enjoyment.

He was a mine of information about the politics of almost every

European country – and, above all, of England and Germany. And when he talked to me of Lord Palmerston, or Lord Curzon, or about Mr Gladstone, or Mr Ramsay Macdonald, I had the feeling that he really knew them – had known them for a long time and intimately – and that he understood the motive that inspired them.

About Germany – well, there was almost nothing that he did not know. He knew that something horrible was stirring in Germany, long before the so-called experts had any inkling of it.

He had an enormous regard for the political maturity and good sense of the English people. He was always so certain that so long as they were left to themselves, without any pressure or misinformation, they would do what was right and sensible. And all the mistakes that were made in British policy towards Hitler shook him. I can still see him, in his agitated rocking-chair, shaking a finger at me, his voice echoing harshly through the room.

And one day he was invited to lunch at the British Legation – as it then was – in order to meet Mr Anthony Eden who, as Lord Privy Seal, was on a short visit to Sweden. In 1934, I think it was. And I remember how Stridsberg got himself involved in an argument with Mr Eden about the nature of the German danger. No, it wasn't an argument; he seemed to be making a speech, in an accent that was almost unintelligible. And then suddenly we all realised what it was. He was quoting something from Heinrich Heine, from an article that that greatest of German poets had written in 1832, and which had only just been reprinted. It warned Europe of the evil spirits that had gone to earth in the forests of Prussia. One day, Heine had prophesied, they would emerge; and then, 'the old stone gods will arise from the accumulated rubbish of the past and rub the dust of ages from their eyes. You will hear an explosion such as never yet occurred in the history of the world.' So there was Heine's forecast of the German revolution.

Well, it seemed to those present that the quotation was a new one to Mr Eden. At all events, it seemed to make a considerable impression upon him. And Stridsberg, I know, hoped that Heine's words would be reported to the British Government and have their effect upon British policy. He was very much moved – I could see that – but he was desperately afraid lest any information about his part in this affair should leak out. He didn't want to pose as a statesman, he said, or as one who advised the great. He was only a journalist with his ear to the ground. I do not imagine for one moment that he would have approved of my talking about him in this way.

And I don't think he would have fitted into our world of advertising and self-glory. Certainly, I cannot see him scribbling away at a meaningless Press conference in the company of two thousand other journalists.

The Senate Rackets Committee
GERALD PRIESTLAND   21 FEBRUARY 1959

Gerry Priestland had moved from India to the United States and had attended the hearings in Washington of the Senate Rackets Committee.

The scene was a Brooklyn snackbar; the characters: the manager of a chain of jukeboxes, the organiser of a crooked trade union, who wanted him to sign on, and two other men (one a convicted murderer) who wanted a seventy-five-per-cent share in the jukebox chain. To the appropriate strains of one of his own jukeboxes, the so-called union official beat the manager semi-conscious.

I heard the victim of this shake-down describe his ordeal to the Senate Rackets Committee. After some hours of evidence, I came away with two burning impressions. First, that however small a facet of life they may represent, American TV crime shows and films are little more than the truth, and second, that there is something appallingly wrong with the administration of justice, when men like these can be arrested on a dozen or more charges and yet so often escape conviction.

The Senate investigation does nothing to dispel this cynicism. The exposure of rackets is a perennial Senate activity. Very little gets done as a result of it. Hearings are conducted with a showmanship as much designed to cast credit on the exposers as discredit on the exposed. I saw thug after thug shuffle to the witness table, most of them so sinister-looking that a television casting director would have turned them down for overdoing it. One after another, they swore to tell the whole truth, gave their names and addresses and then, like well-trained prisoners of war, fell back on the Fifth Amendment – 'I respectfully decline to answer, because I honestly believe my answer might tend to incriminate me.' And they answered this even to questions like: Were they married? Had they a father and mother? Had they ever done a decent thing in their lives?

The witnesses smirk as they answer; the Senators grin; the public galleries titter; but the Committee is powerless. It is not a court of law – indeed the courts are suspicious of it – and the most it can do is to charge a witness with contempt of Congress or perjury. Of the seventy so charged over the past eight years, only two have got as much as ninety days in prison. A Fifth Amendment man runs little risk from the law.

The jukebox racket is being investigated as part of the wider trade union racket. Here, one of the rare co-operative witnesses can be quoted as saying: 'Someone told me how much money there was in the union business, so I sold my restaurant and started a union.' No one suggests that all the unions are corrupt. Most of them are as monumentally respectable as the giant business corporations with which they deal. Their parent body, the AF of L – CIO, has been exercising its own internal discipline on some of the offenders, six of whom have been ejected; the longshoremen, bakers, jewellery, laundry and distillery workers, and teamsters. Some of these are being rehabilitated; but in the teamsters, the union mainly involved in the present scandals, the AF of L – CIO sees no evidence of progress. The union itself boasts that since it was expelled, its membership has gone up by a hundred and thirty thousand. Such unionism, if it can fairly be called that, is part of the same gangsterism which flourished in the roaring days of Al Capone and Prohibition. Today it battens on such varied trades as garbage collection, catering, second-hand cars, moneylending and even the stock market. Some of these serve only as fronts for dope and vice traffic, but the jukeboxes are a racket in their own right, yielding a direct cash dividend and opening a door into the record companies and the plugging of selected crooners.

The gangsters get into the business in one of two ways. Either they install their own machines and bully the snackbar proprietors into accepting a very low percentage of the takings, or they intimidate established jukebox chains. This is where the crooked trade union comes in. If the chain doesn't sign an agreement with the union, its premises may get picketed and pickets are liable to get rough. The chain may also be persuaded to buy union labels to stick on its machines. These will magically protect them from damage by hooligans. Incidentally, the union may have no card-holding members at all. The employer pays all the dues and the organisers get all the benefits.

The retired sales manager of a jukebox firm, on being asked whether he liked this form of salesmanship, told the Committee, 'We didn't, but we had to sell jukeboxes.' 'Even if it involved murder?' he was asked. 'That,' he replied wearily, 'is one of the liabilities of the business.'

The enormities seemed infinite. We heard police evidence of how sixty of the country's leading gangsters held court to hear the appeal of one of their number against a gangland death sentence on him. They commuted it to a fine. We heard of a gangster benefit show to raise money for two wanted murderers to flee the country. Nearly all of those involved were Italian or Sicilian by birth. We met Joey the Blond, Harry the Hawk, One-Armed Louie and Flip Flop Salardino.

How can such things happen? At best, one can put it down to a series of conditions that permit it. The militant freedom of enterprise; the hatred of government control in the United States; the filling by election of so many local offices with the opportunity that provides for corruption; the lack of prestige for the police and the frontier tradition of anarchy; toughness and gun-toting; the localisation of rackets in a few big centres so that most of the country is not affected by them; and the astute victimising by racketeers of the unloved middle man rather than the general public.

Khrushchev in America
CHRISTOPHER SERPELL   25 SEPTEMBER 1959

Mr Khrushchev made a whirlwind tour of the United States,
accompanied by Christopher Serpell.

Mr Khrushchev's tour round the United States, outside Washington, lasted exactly one week by the calendar; but for those who followed him it was an indefinite and incoherent lapse of space and time; punctuated irregularly by staggering runs across airfields with a suitcase; by telephones shrilling the alarm in the small hours in strange hotel bedrooms; by furious arguments in chaotic hotel lobbies about accommodation; and by everybody asking everybody else all the time what they thought of it.

And there was this continuous effort to keep an eye on the doings of this strange troll-like figure and, at the same time, to keep contact with one's own base on the other side of the Atlantic, and almost on the other side of the clock. It was like taking a series of snapshots on the deck of a liner in a hurricane and then getting them developed and printed in the ship's wireless cabin. Not surprisingly, the pictures that came out were disjointed and even contradictory.

Here, for instance, is an old warrior, belligerent and badgered by a Hollywood magnate and a Los Angeles Mayor, showing himself a dirtier in-fighter than either of them. As he said to us in the train after Los Angeles: 'When they stick the needle into me I hit back,' and he illustrated his words with a gesture that went well below the belt.

Here is an outraged puritan, patently shocked by what he and other people called the pornography of Hollywood's version of the Can-Can, but inhibited by the presence of his own wife and a lot of pretty girls on the film set from saying what he thought.

Here again is the universal canvassing politician, standing bare-headed in the Californian sunshine, responding delightedly to a cheerful crowd and, with tears in his eyes, uttering the most appalling sentimental clichés about a baby that waved to him from its mother's arms. And here's the conquering hero on his hotel balcony on the summit of one of San Francisco's highest hills, waving triumphant acknowledgment to a large crowd whose excited curiosity he had misinterpreted as enthusiasm.

Here he is at a banquet in San Francisco, evidently expecting criticism; on the alert for veiled insult, and gradually realising that he's getting nothing but compliments and homage delivered in the most cordial American tradition of making the foreigner feel good; and then gradually relaxing and expanding into an almost patri-archal benevolence as he responded to this constructive approach.

Here again is the clown-like peasant, munching a sausage in the stink of a slaughterhouse; tramping through piles of silage; patting fat farmers on the stomach; urging his host to set the bull on the photographers, and keeping an appreciative twinkle for the girls.

Well, if he bewildered the reporters, it was equally clear that he took the American authorities by surprise. I was reminded of the old fable of the competition between wind and sun to make the traveller take off his cloak. Before he arrived, the official plan was to demonstrate reserve; to receive him with dignity but no cordiality, and to make him understand the American point of view as well as the American way of life. But the more the chill wind of criticism blew, the more defiantly Mr Khrushchev clutched the cloak of intransigence about him. If the head of the Soviet government and his mission were not to be treated with due respect, he indicated, he was ready to go home and extort that respect with weapons rather than diplomacy. But already by this time the American government had become convinced that Mr Khrushchev did have a peaceful mission and was not here mainly to make propaganda. With considerable alarm, they tried to reorientate public reception of the visitor and it was noticeable that American hosts, as well as the people in the street, reverted with some relief to their natural friendliness. Operation Sunlight went into effect. Every American speaker started to accentuate the positive and eliminate the negative, and Mr Khrushchev responded by dropping his cloak and adopting the shirtsleeves of good humour.

To us who accompanied him, the barometer – the official barometer – was Mr Cabot Lodge, whom the President had appointed as his escort. Beforehand, it was realised that Mr Lodge had been appointed because of his well-known reputation for answering Soviet spokesmen back, and Mr Lodge's own spokesman indicated he would be ready with rebuttals of Mr Khrushchev's misleading statements. But from New York onwards – as soon, in fact, as he came into personal contact with the Soviet Prime Minister – Mr Lodge's own public utterances were uncontroversial. It may or may not be true that he encouraged the tough attitude of the Mayor of Los Angeles, but by the time we reached Iowa, we were being informed that Mr Lodge's relations with Mr Khrushchev were as cordial in private as they were in public.

I suppose I'd better end with my own answer to the question: What good did the tour do? I think it gave Mr Khrushchev a chance to appreciate the reality of America and Americans the chance to appreciate the reality of Mr K.

Civil Rights in America

GERALD PRIESTLAND   3 SEPTEMBER 1960

*In the United States, the nineteen sixties saw a gathering momentum
in the negro civil rights campaign. Gerry Priestland went south from
Washington to the State of Louisiana.*

Two questions have brought me to New Orleans, and both of them
involve Negroes. The first is this: are Negro children going to be
integrated into white schools here this autumn? And the second:
what's going to be done about twenty thousand or so Negro children
in this state of Louisiana who have been struck off the poor-relief
books because of the alleged immorality of their mothers? On the
spot everyone regards the schools as the major issue. I'm going to
leave them till last – they won't come to a head for another ten
weeks – but the problem of the pauper children, between five and
six thousand of them in this city, that is desperate now. Yet few
white people here seem to think it's noteworthy, and still fewer
Americans outside Louisiana have even heard of it.

First of all I must fill in some of the background of this state.
Despite its very deep Southernness, it is probably the nearest thing
to a welfare state in the USA. People are relatively poor, but the
state gets a considerable revenue from taxing the oil companies,
which it redistributes in the form of pensions and welfare benefits.
This began under the reign of the fabulous Governor Huey 'King-
fish' Long, and continued under his brother, the hilarious Governor Earl Long. But this year the Longs went out of power, and the
new Governor is Mr Jimmie Davis, best known to the world as the
composer of that wartime favourite, 'You are my sunshine', and
himself the favourite of the extreme white supremists. One of their
first moves was to begin trying to eliminate Negroes from the state
voting registers; their next was to pass state laws designed to
frustrate the efforts of the Federal Courts to integrate the schools.
And the next again was to pass a law depriving these pauper
children of their relief benefits.

Now, it's only too easy to interpret this move as a political one,
designed to put back in their places those Negroes the Longs had
encouraged, and to punish them for demanding integrated schools
and the right to vote. But Governor Davis and his friends have a
different and, to some extent, quite plausible explanation. They say

43

it's become a matter of course for Negro women to live in sin, giving birth to a new child every year, and living on the welfare grant. One white politician told me: 'We have been subsidising prostitutes to produce black bastards' and, making allowance for language, this is quite true.

I've just spent most of the day visiting emergency relief centres in New Orleans. The following is, I swear, typical of more than twenty conversations I had. I am speaking to a twenty-seven-year-old Negro woman who is obviously pregnant.

Question: 'Are you married?' Answer: 'No, sir.'
'How many children?' 'Seven, and one due next week.'
'When did you last eat?' 'Day before yesterday.'
'Have you any money at all?' 'Ain't even got my bus fare home. Anyways, I'm two months behind with the rent, and landlord says he throw me out tonight.'

This woman had her last welfare cheque, a pitifully small one, seven weeks ago. Her case, as I say, was typical.

I met other unmarried women with ten children; few with less than four. About half were pregnant. 'Do you see what we mean?' say the whites. 'This must stop. All a woman has to do to get back on relief is to get married, or otherwise prove she's given up her immoral life.'

Unhappily it takes time to satisfy the Welfare Officer that there has been this change of heart; and nothing is done to tackle, or even diagnose, the causes of the degradation. In the meantime, voluntary relief bodies are scraping the bottom of their meagre barrel – the Federal Government and the Red Cross are so far paralysed by the legal and political aspects of the case, and the City Council has run out of funds and passed the baby, or the babies, back to Louisiana, which abandoned them in the first place.

Let's now return to the schools. Here again Louisiana has had an excellent record, according to its lights. The doctrine of 'separate, but equal' has been applied conscientiously. As buildings, the Negro schools are quite as good as the white, but they are segregated, and it can be argued that of course Negroes will have low social standards so long as it's made impossible for them to join those who have higher ones. If you are not allowed to eat at table, what incentive is there to learn good manners?

It would take hours to explain why the vast majority of Southerners are vehemently opposed to any form of integration whatsoever. Their motives are indescribably tangled – historic, political, economic and sexual. And with them there goes a complete inability to analyse the situation objectively. Politicians here will go on record with such hair-raising remarks as, 'The Negro is still in the jungle.' 'If it weren't for the police there'd be as much rape here as in the Congo.' Suggest to them that their attitude is a disaster for the United States abroad, and they will accuse you of being a Communist. And yet, here in New Orleans, there are responsible, fair-minded people – for example, the Mayor, the Roman Catholic Archbishop, and the owner of the biggest local TV Station – who can think straight and are prepared to integrate, slowly, for slowly it must be if violence is to be avoided.

The Soviet Union and China
ANTHONY LAWRENCE   10 SEPTEMBER 1960

There had been much speculation about a possible rift between the Soviet Union and China. Tony Lawrence, based in Hong Kong as the BBC's Far East Correspondent, gave his view of the situation as it looked then.

If it is true that the Soviet Union and China, the two biggest countries in the world, have started a real quarrel, and that their alliance is in danger, then, of course, this is one of the great events of modern history, and we're all likely to be affected by it sooner or later. Russia is already one of the world's strongest powers; in another twenty years China will also be a world giant in terms of industrial strength. And long before that – most experts think in about five years – China will be producing nuclear weapons. So, there isn't any doubt that the relations between these two countries – one of about two hundred millions and the other of more than six hundred and fifty millions – must oblige the Western world to make some very careful assessments.

If these two giants continue in alliance, and if leadership is maintained by a Soviet Union which doesn't like the idea of a nuclear war, then the future might not seem too perilous. But, if the leadership of the Communist camp is in dispute; if the Chinese refuse to recognise the Russians any more as their elder brothers and leaders of the great revolution; if they produce nuclear weapons by their own efforts, while declaring that imperialism can be conquered only through armed struggle, then it may seem that the future is far less bright. That's how it looks from out here in the Far East.

But what is the state of the Russo-Chinese alliance? Is it breaking down? Evidence seems to be far from conclusive. It is certain that there have been differences in thinking – they have become known to the outside world through careful study of speeches and articles in official newspapers and magazines in Moscow and Peking. They concern the possibilities of peaceful co-existence and the need for so-called 'just wars' to protect Communism from the imperialist powers, with Peking taking the more belligerent line.

But, mostly the criticisms and the differences have been indirectly expressed. More concrete have been the reports of Russia withdrawing unknown numbers of technicians who've been in China helping build new factories, and the closing down of two Chinese-Soviet magazines, called *Friendship* and *China*. And, at an important congress of orientalists in Moscow recently, it was reported that no Chinese delegation put in an appearance.

All this may well be evidence of serious differences between the two governments. Differing attitudes have long been apparent. It's well known, for instance, that Mr Khrushchev has not at all approved of Chinese actions in the frontier dispute with India. Soviet attitudes towards the United States are far from the state of almost hysterical belligerence that's revealed daily in the Chinese press and radio. Russia is becoming one of the 'have' nations, while China, with its grievance over Formosa and entry to the United Nations, and its terrible food problems, is very much a 'have-not'.

But the main cause of difference, as seen from this part of the world, often seems to lie in the minds of the Chinese leaders themselves. There's good reason to believe that, in some ways, like the Nazis in the thirties, or indeed the rulers of any totalitarian state who never travel abroad, they're becoming cut off from reality. They may well be believing that it's because of the Communist influence of the new and vigorous China that Syngman Rhee was driven out of Korea; that President Eisenhower was kept away from Tokyo; that the regime in Turkey was overthrown, for it's very unlikely that much factual reporting is going back from abroad to Peking these days, either from Chinese embassies or from Chinese correspondents. Instead, the legend is being fostered that the United States is on its last legs – a paper tiger – and that the triumph of the Communist world is imminent. Khrushchev has shown too soft an attitude towards these dying imperialists, and it's time the super-race – the Chinese – took over leadership of the Communist camp.

In a country like China, facing terrible internal problems, it's always dangerous when the leaders lose touch with the real facts of the world situation and begin to believe their own propaganda. It leads to trouble, not only with the outside world, but with their own allies. It may well be that Moscow has been withdrawing technicians to bring home to the Chinese just how much they do depend on Russian aid in building up the country. But most observers here agree that it's unwise to go too far in assuming a real break between the Soviet Union and China.

The Chinese leaders are undoubtedly critical of much of what Mr Khrushchev has done and said, and would like a much tougher line towards the West, but they still depend, to a tremendous extent, on Russian help. They still, at least in press and radio, speak of Russia as the leader of the Socialist camp. If the struggle for world Communist leadership is really on, then it would still appear to be in its very early stages.

The Congo

RICHARD WILLIAMS 10 SEPTEMBER 1960

At the end of June, the Congo became independent, but, within a week, mutiny had broken out among the armed forces and, a few days later, the wealthy mining province of Katanga declared itself independent, electing Mr Tshombe as president. United Nations troops were flown in in an attempt to keep the peace, and the BBC sent Dickie Williams to Katanga to report on the situation there.

We landed slap in the middle of the enemy camp. At Elisabethville, Mr Tshombe's military commander, Major Crevecoeur, a Belgian officer, had assured us that Bakwanga Airport was in friendly hands. He was positive that Mr Kalonji's troops had recaptured it the day before and United Nations troops were there too. So, we took off in a tiny aircraft with Alan Kearn, a British pilot, to fly across the desolate Congo landscape to Bakwanga, five hundred miles away.

The countryside and the few villages we passed over seemed peaceful enough, but we knew that the Africans who lived there were locked in a ferocious battle. We located Bakwanga by the great open-cast mine on the outskirts, where sixty per cent of the world's industrial diamonds are produced. That day, the mine was shut and deserted. We discovered later that the four thousand Africans who work there, mostly from the Baluba tribe, had all fled in fear of their lives. £10 million worth of diamonds were still locked in the strong rooms. We circled the rough airstrip once and saw black faces under steel helmets staring up at us. The blue berets of the United Nations troops were evident, too, and that seemed good enough. We came down steeply and in no time at all we were churning up the red dust of the Kasai, the most stormy province in the Congo.

As soon as we clambered off the aircraft, we knew that things were different from what we had been led to believe. A United Nations officer, a Tunisian, approached. Behind him, glowering and staring at us, stood a large group of Mr Lumumba's Force Publique, all heavily armed. They came from the notorious Thysville garrison, the first one to mutiny in the Congo. After years of special training by Belgian officers, they've been completely brutalised. We were to get much better acquainted with them later that day.

An aura of deep suspicion divided us from them, but for the moment, our story that we had come from friendly territory was accepted. We drove into town with a UN commander, a brave and friendly Tunisian, whom I remember very warmly. We owe him a great deal. Among all the officers in the Congo, his task in this remote and cruel town of Bakwanga was perhaps the most difficult. He took us to the mining club, where a hundred-odd Belgian men – the only Europeans left – were living in a dormitory under UN protection. They were technicians from the diamond mine. There we met the devoted Australian team of the Red Cross and they recounted the horrors of the previous day, culminating in a massacre of the innocents at Bakwanga church, where seventy African men, women and children had been shot to pieces. The only sur-

48

vivors were six babies and a small, bright-eyed golden rhesus monkey, whom they adopted as a pet and called Ossi. The four doctors had been burying bodies all day. Their leader, Dr Fox, told me sadly: 'I came here as a medical man, not to be a grave-digger.'

Well, we decided not to hang about and drove back to the airport for a quick get-away. But by now suspicion had deepened into open hostility. The sergeant-major of the Force Publique came up and barked at us that we were under arrest. We were bundled into a truck and driven, under heavy escort, to the African quarter of Bakwanga. They placed us in a small guard room, with two armed soldiers at the open door. By this time we were hungry and thirsty and we were very glad when the Red Cross man brought rations and a supply of soda water. The city water plant was not working.

After he'd gone, the sergeant-major returned, scowling heavily. I got the impression that he didn't like white people very much. He started shouting again, and we remained silent. 'You will be sent to Luluabourg,' he said, 'where you will be shot.' These words were to have very serious consequences for us, which we did not foresee at the time. They were heard by a large group of soldiers who had gathered outside.

As soon as the sergeant-major left, they began to crowd the small room, their tommy-guns and rifles clattering. We were sitting down and we were allowed to smoke. Without warning, one soldier snatched the cigarettes from our lips with a cry: 'Spies can't smoke!' Another poured the precious soda water over us. They took our chairs away and they removed the Red Cross rations. We asked to see the Commandant and they laughed. It seemed odd to hear laughter in that hot and crowded room.

Two more soldiers arrived, one carrying a long stick, the other with an evil, black truncheon. The atmosphere was heavy with menace. By this time we were four frightened men, trying hard not to show it. We watched discipline and the thin crust of civilisation crumple in front of our eyes. The soldier with a truncheon struck a ferocious blow at pilot Kearn. We stood together in a corner, while the soldiers screamed threats and imprecations. The shouting became a meaningless chant. A guard tried to protect us with outstretched arms. It didn't help very much, but we were grateful. The mob – it was nothing else by now – continued to surge forward. Several pairs of hands clawed at my watch. They tore my suit in a frantic search for valuables. They took all I had – documents, money, sunglasses, pen. My companions were treated likewise. Then, they dragged off our shoes and threw them away.

Fortunately, the Commandant of the Force Publique arrived soon afterwards and the crowd fled. He realised at once what had happened. He said quietly in French: 'You've been very lucky.' Then he told us that we'd be handed over as prisoners to the United Nations. The deep-set eyes of this soldier, trained in the North African desert, looked at us gravely as he said: 'They can be very dangerous, you know. They kill easily.' We were the UN Commander's guests for three days, while he and two hundred Tunisian soldiers did their job fearlessly and well: the thankless task of keeping the peace in a most unhappy country.

The Cuban Revolution

ERIK DE MAUNY   13 MAY 1961

Anti-Castro refugees from Cuba had sailed to the island from the United States in a spectacularly unsuccessful attempt to overthrow the regime – the 'Bay of Pigs' disaster. Erik de Mauny had been sent to Cuba to examine the situation following the attempt, and had then returned to Washington.

'*Que Felicidad*,' 'What happiness to be here at last,' murmured the well-dressed, middle-aged woman, as we stepped down from the plane at Miami Airport. It was eight-thirty in the evening. All around her other faces were beginning to lose their taut, watchful look. For them, for the refugees from Fidel Castro's Cuba, it had been a trying day: more than four hours' delay at Havana Airport while Security officers checked and rechecked the passenger list; and before that, how many hours of anguished family consultation. Dr Castro had said that all who wanted to leave could go, but what if he should change his mind at the last minute? I could imagine all they were feeling as they set foot at last on United States soil. And yet, at the same moment, another image came into my mind: of a girl I had talked to only the day before in Pinar del Rio province, on one of the new farms. Her name was Noemie Garcia. She was eighteen years old and she was one of three hundred young voluntary teachers sent to that particular farm to teach its peasant occupants to read and write. For in Cuba, this is not only the year of the anti-Castro invasion, it is also the year of education, and a year of new hope for many thousands of Cubans who, before the revolution, lived in conditions of virtual slavery. And this was the feeling that Noemie Garcia radiated – a feeling of hope and of absolute faith in the justice of the revolution.

I spent more than two hours on that farm because it is here that one touches the heart of the Castro revolution, in a so-called Granja del Pueblo, or state farm, of which there are now about three hundred and fifty spread across the island. This one – El Rosario – was one of the first to be started, and some peasant families had already been in occupation for more than a year. Their houses were not luxurious: simple three- and four-roomed brick bungalows. But to appreciate the contrast, it was enough to drive northwards to the coast to a newly formed fishermen's co-operative, where people still live nine or ten to a room in squalid huts.

With Government subsidies, they have almost finished building a fleet of twenty deep-sea fishing boats – incidentally, with British marine engines. Before the revolution, not one of the fishermen of Puerto Esperanza had his own boat. He had to hire it from one of three rich local boat-owners who are now all in exile and probably clamouring for some new campaign to restore freedom to Cuba.

One can't help feeling that, in the eyes of its United States detractors, the one unforgivable thing about the Castro revolution is that it's a success. Cuba is the first Latin-American country to put through an agrarian reform programme which has actually increased production, and it's also the first in which the professional army has been eliminated as a factor of power. It was the militia who raised the alarm when the anti-Castro forces landed in Southern Cuba and who, in three days of hectic fighting, pinned the assault force down to a narrow coastal strip. It is, in fact, a genuine people's army, whose fighting ability and devotion to the regime seem to have been completely overlooked by the exiles and the CIA.

For other outside observers, however, there is some excuse for feeling mystified by the Castro revolution. The State Department has bluntly labelled it Communist, but it is certainly like no other Communist revolution ever staged before. For one thing, there is a total lack of the puritanism one associates with Communist regimes. I can still see the look of blank incredulity on the face of a

Polish miner as he sat with other visiting delegates at the May Day parade and watched a huge float roll by adorned with some of Havana's most alluring and scantily-clad showgirls. It was as if the *Folies Bergère* had suddenly erupted into Moscow's Red Square.

But on a more serious level, as I discovered in long talks with the President, Dr Dorticos, and with the Minister of Industrialisation, 'Che' Guevara, the Castro regime is completely unmoved by labels. It has set out to do what it thinks is best for the Cuban masses, for the rural proletariat of the great sugar estates; and if the result approximates to a Marxist formula, it sees no reason not to acknowledge it. Soviet and Chinese influence is indeed evident on the bookstalls and in the presence of technical advisers. But the regime still insists that it turned to the East for help only after it had been rebuffed in the West.

The revolution has its sinister aspects. The execution of some six hundred people in the months immediately following the overthrow of Batista has left its mark. Further mass executions are unlikely. But G2, the Cuban Secret Service, still maintains a whole street of villas in which it interrogates suspects, and many thousands more are still being held for screening in makeshift prisons. On the other hand, the regime has, without doubt, been immensely strengthened by the abortive anti-Castro landing, and feels indeed strong enough to be able to afford clemency, which is what Dr Castro has virtually promised most of the captured invaders.

The Inside Story

DOUGLAS WILLIS   15 JULY 1961

There was a short-lived crisis in the Sultanate of Kuwait in the Persian Gulf, which was under threat from Iraq. The Sultan called on Britain, under her treaty obligations, to help defend his country. Doug Willis was the BBC's East Africa Correspondent, based in Nairobi, and how he became involved was the subject of this report.

One of the reasons I can consider myself to be the best informed correspondent on military affairs in East Africa is that the Army Public Relations Officer lives across the road from my house, and had no telephone until a couple of days ago. This has meant that I've been able to eavesdrop on matters of great import, and that my small sons have been able to play a leading part in the Kuwait crisis by running across the road with the message: 'Tell Major Dodman that the army wants him.' It also meant that none of the other correspondents could communicate with him except through me, and this is the stuff of which scoops are made. Philip Gibbs and Edgar Wallace in their heyday would never have approved, particularly when I was without messengers and fired a toy machine gun in the direction of the Major's house to bring him running in his dressing gown from his bath.

Well, the pace of our Intelligence, faithfully reported to the BBC, increased until one Saturday a fortnight ago, when the Army, on orders from London, had been draping what is known in the trade as 'a veil of secrecy' over troop movements from Nairobi. This veil had been penetrated only by the local press, several thousand passengers at Nairobi airport and, of course, myself. Well, my son Douglas and I were driving along the Mombasa road, which goes in the direction of the airport, when we found ourselves beside an Army lorry filled with troops carrying automatic rifles, and wearing expressions suggesting that they were not going on leave. I said to my son, 'Ask them if they're going to Kuwait.' He opened the window and shrilled the question, and one of the happy warriors replied: 'Yeah.' Here at least was official confirmation, and I drove off home to Major Dodman who was out doing the shopping but, in no time, assisted by boys on bicycles, contact had been made.

The task now was to put myself in the company of the Army, which was being flown to Kuwait by the Royal Air Force. The Ministry of Defence in London had signalled that all correspondents had to find their own way to Kuwait, and one or two of the more energetic had taken off by commercial airline to Beirut; one had even gone to Athens. As a firm believer in the direct approach, I phoned Major General Goodwin, GOC East African Command, who phoned his Chief of Staff, who phoned Air Commodore MacDonald of the Royal Air Force, who must have phoned a whole lot of other people at the same time as I was phoning the BBC, who were phoning the Ministry of Defence. And at the end of all this phoning it emerged that I was to be put on board a troop transport plane leaving on Sunday.

At the airport, there developed one of those situations the reason for which only became clear to me when I'd been to Kuwait and returned to Nairobi. A flight lieutenant, bearing a strong resemblance to one of Jon's 'two types' in the Eighth Army News, resolutely refused to allow me to board the plane, and said that I had to wait four hours for the next one. Air Commodore MacDonald was fortunately available to countermand the refusal, and off I went. And it was only later that I discovered that there was a general feeling that I should not be flying with the Royal Rhodesian Air Force, as indeed I was, as nobody was supposed to know that the Rhodesian Air Force was involved in the operation.

Anyway, we were on our way, with the troops carrying automatic rifles wrapped in sacking to protect the upholstery in the plane. We stopped at Mombasa to refuel, then went straight on to Aden, keeping out to sea – presumably to avoid offending the Ethiopians and the Somalis. At Aden the plane was said to have broken down, and I spent a night in a brightly-lit tent with a motor generator next to my right ear. Total sleeping time was about one hour or perhaps less. Then we foregathered in the NAAFI passenger lounge, which was filled with tired troops, a thick haze of smoke, a battalion of beer tins and the dying gasps of eight air-conditioners engaged in a hopeless struggle with the heat and the smoke. The campaign was beginning to lose its glamour.

But eventually we took off in a Britannia and flew to Bahrain where I was entertained by the Royal Air Force; took my shirt off in a bath house; found that all the baths were filled; was taken to another bath house, and left there. And when I came out, I was unable to find the first bath house, and finished up in the mess kitchen without my shirt. The problem was solved by a friendly correspondent, whom I had last met at a cage-bird show in London in 1949. He organised a search of the station's eighteen bath houses until the shirt was found.

At the risk of becoming monotonous, we took off for Kuwait and arrived at the new airport, which had not yet been finished. The RAF there was sitting on bags of cement amidst stacks of sand, and conducting operations with the aid of an oil company map. The only items of furniture were three cots and a refrigerator filled with beer supplied by the oil company. Anyway, we'd arrived. A Kuwaiti motor cycle policeman rode out to the main road and came back with a taxi, and in this I drove off towards the front.

The 'Twist' Hits New York

JOHN CRAWLEY   4 NOVEMBER 1961

John Crawley was New York Correspondent with a brief wide enough to cover everything there from the meetings of the United Nations to the following.

New York has recently taken leave of its senses over a dance called the 'Twist'; and not only over the 'Twist', but over the small and medium-squalid dance café called 'The Peppermint Lounge' which is the high temple of the cult. It's jammed with people every night, from nine in the evening till four in the morning, and there's always a long queue outside.

The crowd is an extraordinary cross section, from teenage beatniks through the suburbanites to the famous. The night I was there the celebrity was President Kennedy's sister. Other scalps have been Noël Coward, the Duke of Bedford, Elsa Maxwell, Tennessee Williams and Greta Garbo. There's somebody every night and the place is haunted by press photographers.

I described the 'Twist' as a dance, but that's in dispute. The vast and popular dance hall, New York's Roseland, has banned it on the ground that it isn't a dance. Roseland's manager adds, 'It's lacking in true grace.' Well, in the American phrase, 'Brother, you can say that again.' I watched it for a couple of hours and I had a shot at it myself, and you might call it dynamic, erotic, athletic, primitive, anything except graceful. The music is a very strong rock and roll beat, blasted at you with stunning force by a five-man combination that bounces it off a low ceiling. And the dance consists in shaking the shoulders and swivelling the hips. You swivel pretty fast, like a speeded up golf swing, and I've no doubt it's very good for you. I suppose it's a distant descendant of the 'Shimmy'. What you do with your feet doesn't seem to matter. Certainly it doesn't at the Peppermint Lounge where there's no room to move on the dance floor anyway. Nor do you bother about your partner. You don't touch and you seem to vary your routine independently. Those who were getting the most out of it were the very young – girls with shaggy hair, baggy sweaters, toreador pants and flatties. Some of them who couldn't get near the floor were just twisting away alone in the free square yard by their table and evidently thoroughly enjoying it.

What's the secret of its attraction? Well, it's primitive; it's sensual in an energetic way, and, in the jargon of today, it's a good way to work off tensions. In other words, it's a dance of oblivion. It translates into movement that complete surrender to jazz rhythm that's called 'getting sent'.

Friends who've lived in Africa told me it's strikingly like the West African dance called 'High Life'. It seems a natural development. Our basically Negro music has for years been matched with dance steps from many Latin American and West Indian sources, and now with one that is nearer the African than any before.

Is there a connection between the desperate state of the world and the popularity of this frenetic dance? I think there is. Certainly one can't imagine such a dance getting widely popular in a time when people felt satisfied and confident in the future. Is it going to prove just a New York fad that'll die out, or a nation-wide craze, or perhaps one that will sweep Europe, too? It's hard to tell. But there's one feature about it that seems to belong particularly to New York: that is the way Café Society has gone slumming again as it did in the twenties, when it was smart to be known in the lowest dives in Harlem.

As for its future. Well, the Twist has already spread into the expensive night clubs, and one of the big schools of dancing is taking space in the papers, saying, 'Quite frankly, the Twist is not our favourite dance, but we will teach it to you in six easy lessons for twenty-five dollars'.

The Young Men of Africa

LIONEL FLEMING   7 APRIL 1962

A Fabian Society pamphlet had been published which drew attention to the alarming number of young men, mainly from West Africa, who came to Britain under their own steam in the hope of improving their education, and found only suffering and failure. The BBC's Commonwealth Correspondent, Lionel Fleming, examined the problem.

I have seen few more touching sights in Africa than the young men leaning against the lamp-posts after dark. By their light, they are studying their text-books, a thing impossible to do in the noisy, overcrowded shanties where their families so cheerfully live. The text-books, they feel, will lift them above that, into the world of cars, decent clothes, office jobs – perhaps even political power.

It's hard to give an idea of the passion with which education is pursued out there. The mothers of Eastern Nigeria, for example, nearly brought the Government down a few years ago in a series of dangerous riots, because they felt their children weren't being given proper benefits at school. In any big bookshop in Lagos or Accra, the young Africans who wander in won't be found examining the paperbacks. They'll all be fingering the 'Do-it-yourself' books – on electrical engineering, or building, or business management. On the outskirts of the town, queer so-called 'colleges' display badly-painted signs, in semi-literate English, in an attempt to cash in on the universal hunt for knowledge.

And in this atmosphere, where education is almost considered as a form of magic, nobody has a higher reputation than the 'been-to'. What, you may ask, is a 'been-to'? Well, he is simply a person who has been to England, and who has, at least in theory, come back with the deep learning, the expertise, which this country alone is thought to give. Many indeed are highly qualified, and get enviably good jobs as a result. Others at least put a good face on it, and stories of their splendid life in England quickly circulate in the townships and villages. And some haven't come back yet.

This is where the tragedy lies. What are called the 'recommended' students are usually safe enough. They are pre-selected, officially sponsored by their own countries, and assured of a place either at a university or some other kind of training centre. But the 'unrecommended' student – the boy for whom his village has enthusiastically subscribed, or who has scratched up enough fare money on the strength of what his 'been-to' friend has told him – he may be a very different case.

Such a boy arrives in England with an innocent and sometimes quite misplaced confidence in his own capacities. He feels sure of getting into Oxford or Cambridge. If this proves impossible, which it generally does, he settles for some kind of technical school – and the extent to which he does so is revealed by some of the figures given in this Fabian pamphlet. In one such place in south London, eighty per cent of the students are African, in another place, seventy-three per cent.

I don't want to exaggerate the plight of these boys. A lot of them, it appears, do make good. But undoubtedly, a lot of them don't. Hopelessly under-qualified, they can't cope with their training course, and make matters worse by having to take part-time jobs in order to pay their way. They don't dare to tell their parents of their failure, and keep strictly away from any of the bodies in this country which might be able to help them – for the shame of being perhaps sent home. An unsuccessful 'been-to' is more than they are willing to risk. England, itself, may have proved a cold and unfriendly place after all the grand tales they'd heard about it, but in England they stay, just hoping for the best. It is not surprising that some of them go out of their minds.

Their problem is a very difficult one, and probably can only be solved by stricter control in the African countries to ensure that only qualified people do arrive here. But something should be done. The young men by the lamp-posts deserve better than this.

Report from Leopoldville
DANIEL COUNIHAN 19 MAY 1962

Affairs in the former Belgian Congo were still in a state of upset and Dan Counihan had been sent to the capital, Leopoldville, to cover events from there.

The Congo, which rushed so headlong into independence, prefers, in the mechanics of everyday living, to make haste very slowly indeed. This isn't something that the European, fresh to the scene, notices at once, for noise and confusion so easily convey a superficial impression of busyness, and Leopoldville, the Congo's hideous, sweating capital city, is very noisy and very confused.

In Brazzaville, in the former French Congo, on the other side of the river, life is essentially quieter, and the Africans there tend to look sniffy as they gaze across the water, and like to refer to their Belgian-reared neighbours as 'les sauvages'. But always the steamy feckless vitality of Leopoldville reaches out, and it is the former Belgian Congo that impresses itself at the Brazzaville ferry, where the little steamers leave every half hour to chug through the drifting clumps of river-choking water hyacinth to Leo, as everyone calls it.

Noise – brain-battering Belgian Congo noise – surrounds you as you line up for your ticket in a queue most variously composed. Hausa men, the itinerant traders of all West Africa, will always be there, lounging and looking remotely superior in their coloured, cassock-like gowns, their little decorated skull caps, and their heel-less slippers. And there will be African women, anarchistically incapable of keeping in line, swathed in bright-patterned cotton gowns and headcloths, boxes, bundles and babies. Wrist watches of anxious Europeans tick relentlessly towards the time for the boat's departure, but no African woman will be hurried, nor be able to find her money at once, still less have it ready in her hand, nor accept the price of a ferry ticket as something not open to bargaining.

Many words are said in a splendid salad of Lingala, Swahili and local French, and not one of them in anything softer than a scream. The men yell, too. The children cry. Only the Europeans are patient, relatively silent and scrupulously anxious not to be seen jumping the queue, for independence on both sides of the Congo is self-conscious and quick to take offence. At the ferry, the last trace of vanished European supremacy is in the fact that a white hand is automatically given a first-class ticket.

When the boat completes its passage, Leo greets you with more noise – a sudden shock of noise like a train emerging unexpectedly from a tunnel. This time, the African women have lost their tickets, or cannot understand why their various bundles – and what bundles of mystery they are – should need to be opened and looked into by the Customs. And all the yelling begins again. It's added to by the hordes of young Africans who want to persuade Europeans to enter their taxis, who fight, kick and quarrel for the privilege, and who seem united only in the belief that anyone with a white face is both a millionaire and a cretin.

The European must be on his best behaviour with the Customs and Immigration officials, for here again independence is hyper-sensitive. The experienced begin by smiling broadly and shaking hands with any official in sight. They then stand quietly while every single word on their passport, visa, or whatever document they are showing, is read aloud and with agonising slowness. It's not unkind to say that reading is still an accomplishment in the Congo and something to be demonstrated as a status symbol.

A quick and exact knowledge of simple arithmetic is a much more common gift, if the hordes of money changers who surround the

European on every Leopoldville corner are anything to judge by. And even with these one must be patient – and patient, too, with the waiters who take orders and then go away and forget about them, so that a restaurant meal can seldom be completed in less than two hours, and is as often as not abandoned half eaten, to rot in the sun on the table amid the flies and the dirty pile of relatively worthless currency left to pay the bill.

He must be patient, again, with the telephone operators, who never find any number unoccupied and, if he is a journalist, he must be patient with the innumerable people in positions of responsibility who have either no information at all about anything, or information so inexact and unlikely that every statement must be checked and checked again.

Patience, a little understanding if you can manage it, a lot of self-control, these are what are needed for day-to-day living in the Congo, as well as for a workable solution to its baffling and foot-dragging politics: patience all the time and a good set of earplugs.

'Five Days that Shook the World'
ERIK DE MAUNY   3 NOVEMBER 1962

Late in October, President Kennedy of the United States announced that the Russians were building a missile base in Cuba and he immediately ordered a blockade of the island. For five days there were fears that the situation might lead to war between the two Great Powers. Then, Mr Khrushchev agreed to dismantle the Cuban base. Erik de Mauny looked back on the crisis from Washington.

'Five days that shook the world.' This is how one American news-paper headline sums up the Cuban crisis. Well, the dust hasn't settled yet, and I find that many of my American friends are even more shaken now, as they look back on it, than they were in the hour of greatest danger, when the whole country behaved with a moral fortitude that isn't usually regarded as one of the leading American virtues.

But although, as I say, the immediate future in the Caribbean is still uncertain, one thing does already stand out with stark simplicity from the confusing flurry of moves and counter-moves – a new pattern of power relationships. Indeed, it's so large, simple and obvious that a number of people are still rubbing their eyes and questioning the evidence of their senses – like Lilliputians surveying one small fraction of Gulliver's anatomy.

And yet, to see this new pattern, one has only to examine what President Kennedy really did when he took his command decision over the Soviet nuclear missiles in Cuba, and then ask oneself what this action implies for the future. And the answer, it seems to me, comes in two parts.

First, the President finally achieved what he had been trying to do in all the frustrating months since his meeting with Mr Khrushchev in Vienna last year. He finally persuaded the Soviet leader that, on grounds it considered vital to its survival, the United States would stand and fight rather than temporise or withdraw. Mr Kennedy also, of course, persuaded some of his own countrymen of this same fact, and that was so much pure gain.

And then, secondly, but just as importantly, the President served notice on the Western allies that, when it came to the crunch, the United States was prepared, if necessary, to act alone. It's true that Britain and the other NATO partners were politely told of the Cuba blockade decision in advance, but it was only a matter of hours in advance – there were no consultations – and it's unlikely that any objection raised at that moment would have deflected the President from his course.

Now, I suppose from a European angle it may appear that Mr Kennedy has put himself into the position that Mr Khrushchev had been angling for all along – that is, of entering into a direct dialogue between Washington and Moscow over the heads of friends and allies who might otherwise raise difficulties. No doubt the Soviet Prime Minister had been looking for such an opportunity, but on his own terms; and now in Washington's view the boot, or the shoe – to mention Mr Khrushchev's favourite oratorical device – is on the other foot. And this is clearly going to have a far-reaching effect on a whole range of other problems, from Berlin to South-East Asia, but especially with regard to Berlin. In short, instead of merely reacting to Soviet pressures, the United States have seized the initiative and the face of the Cold War has been drastically changed as a result.

Now, this clearly may involve fresh dangers. The Western position in Berlin, for instance, is a good deal more vulnerable than was the American position over Cuba, but at least there's a healthy chance that the dialogue between the two great nuclear powers will, from now on, be conducted on a much more realistic level. Indeed, looking back on it, perhaps the most striking feature of President Kennedy's speech announcing the blockade of Cuba was its total absence of ideological overtones; there was no Cold War rhetoric, no crusading talk of making the world safe from Communism. It was one Great Power talking to another in the sober language of power. But the further consequence of this is that Britain and the other Western allies of the United States are going to have to adapt themselves to a new role.

It's not that the allies are being left out of the picture. Indeed, there have already been extensive discussions of each vital issue, and for each – Berlin is the prime example – contingency plans are already in being. What the United States is insisting on is that, once these contingency plans have been agreed, there must be no vacillation when the moment of critical decision arises. The decks must be left clear for action. It's the firm belief of officials here that if the Soviet missile build-up in Cuba had not been unmasked, within these next few weeks they would have been confronted with an ultimatum from Mr Khrushchev over Berlin.

They hope never to come so near to such a danger again.

'Cablese'

LIONEL FLEMING   16 FEBRUARY 1963

Lionel Fleming was in what was then called Southern Rhodesia, from where he lifted the veil on one aspect of the correspondents' craft.

Scholars have done a good deal of research into the origins of queer languages like pidgin English; but so far as I know, few have paid much attention to the extraordinary language that passes between foreign correspondents and their London editors. This is cablese, and I'm in a position to give its origin straight away: the desire to save words, and therefore money, in telegrams and cables. There is a certain old-fashioned charm about this language; in some ways it goes straight back to the Middle Ages. 'Canst', for example, is cheaper to say than 'Can you?'; and the same goes for 'wouldst' and 'couldst'. A lot more money-saving discoveries have been made as time went on, including the very valuable prefix 'un' which does for any kind of negative.

Let's take an imaginary example. The editor wants to tell his correspondent that, according to reports on the news agencies, serious riots have broken out near Timbuktu. He wants to know if the correspondent can book an air passage there, without delay, in order to investigate the situation for himself. So he cables: 'Agency-wise riots reportedly outbroken Timbuktuwards canst proceed airwise query'. The reluctant correspondent, who is having a high old time in Cape Town or somewhere, will be all against Timbuktu-warding. He will cable back: 'Viewing story upfolded Tuesday unthink coverage newsworthy'. This, I hardly need explain, means 'In view of the fact that the whole affair ended last Tuesday, I really think there's not very much more I could say about it now'. This never gets him anywhere, and the next cable he gets is always 'Proceed soonest'. If he wants to fire a final shot, he can only say: 'Send a hundred pounds urgentest'.

The classic exchange of cablese – I'm afraid it's a cliché to all journalists – concerns a very lazy correspondent who received the cable: 'Why unnews query'. Cynically he cabled back: 'Unnews good news'. His office replied: 'Unnews unjob'. Unfortunately, the correspondent's final cable was too rude to be reproduced here – he lost the job anyway!

Then there's the story of the London editor who noticed enviously that the reporters of the rival papers had all been getting into fearful trouble and were cabling back hair-raising accounts of their misfortunes. He asked his own correspondent: 'Why unarrested?'

One of my friends, isolated in some dim spot where there was no news, could get no answer to his urgent pleas for recall. He let another week go by in total silence, and then suddenly cabled the one word: 'Boo'. That woke them!

Their instant reply was 'Boo or unboo you onstaying'.

But my favourite example concerns another friend whose paper asked him for the age of the Governor of a colony that we were visiting at the time.

'How old Brown', it read. He was furious. He said they could easily have got the date from the Colonial Office list in London. So he cabled back: 'Old Brown fine how are you'.

Kim Philby

DOUGLAS STUART   6 JULY 1963

Kim Philby had just defected to Moscow, joining Burgess and Maclean there. Douglas Stuart had known Philby well when he was in the Middle East.

I remember that it was a very hot day in Beirut – a Sunday in the spring of 1958. My wife and I had agreed to meet Kim – that was Philby's nickname – at a swimming club on the beach. We brought air mattresses and sat out on the rocks; bathed; sunned ourselves and drank beer. Kim was a very good talker, although he stuttered a good deal. When he stuttered badly, he would draw his hand across his chin. It was my wife who said: 'Kim, tell us about the Third Man.' He took a lot of coaxing, but eventually began talking.

He said that he had known Guy Burgess at Cambridge before the war. Burgess he described as a man with a brilliant mind, but incapable of application. They were not friends but – Kim said – on friendly terms when they met. He claimed that he saw nothing of Burgess during the war. This was the time when Philby was starting to make a name for himself in a branch of the British security services. He also claimed that he never knew that Burgess was a Communist. And in this connection, Kim made no secret of the fact that he was a child of the thirties: that's to say that he personally hated Nazis and Fascists and supported the democratic forces of the Left. 'But,' he added, 'everything that I wanted for Britain was accomplished by the first and second Labour Governments after the war.'

When Kim went to Washington in the late forties, he was – and I quote his own words – 'On the road to a knighthood'. He was good at his job, he said, and the Americans liked him. It was at this time that it became obvious that there was a security leak high up in the Foreign Office. Kim claimed that it was he who narrowed the suspects down to Maclean. At this point, he said, there was a battle between his department and the British security officials. The latter wanted to arrest Maclean at once. Kim and his bosses wanted to let Maclean alone in order to get on to others in the spy ring. Eventually, it was decided to compromise. Maclean was to be shadowed and top secret papers were to be withdrawn from him. Kim told us that this made him furious. Maclean, he said, would immediately realise that the game was up.

In the meantime, Burgess, who had been given a temporary appointment at the Foreign Office, was sent to Washington for a last chance to make good at the Embassy. He and Kim met at a cocktail party, where Kim, who was living alone, invited Burgess to stay with him. 'It seemed a simple gesture of kindness,' he told us, 'the sort of gesture that anyone would make to an old undergraduate acquaintance.' Burgess didn't do well at the Embassy and, in addition, he received three tickets for speeding in the neighbouring state of Virginia. The Governor of Virginia complained to the Secretary of State in Washington. 'Keep your damn diplomats in order' was the gist of his message. The Secretary of State passed on the complaint to the British Ambassador, who, not unnaturally, lost his temper with Burgess and sent him back to London.

Kim's reconstruction of what took place in London was that Burgess went to see Maclean, knowing nothing of the latter's spying activities. The two men had been friends at Cambridge, fellow communists and members of the select Apostles Club. Maclean used Burgess to arrange his getaway, insisting that Burgess should come with him because he had no future in Britain anyway.

After the flight, Kim said that he was recalled to London. The Americans would not talk to him. They believed that he had tipped off Maclean. He claimed that his office at home was convinced of his innocence. But this, he added, was not true of Security. He told us that he was interrogated for three days almost continuously. He described the chief interrogator, a giant of a man, he said, with a face of cement and steel. He told me his nickname but that I can't tell you. After the interrogation, those who had thought Kim guilty, still thought him guilty, and those who had thought him innocent were unchanged in their opinion. He resigned from the service. 'My usefulness was at an end,' he said. Afterwards, there were the attacks in Parliament and the official clearance by Mr Macmillan. It was almost impossible to get a job, Kim said, until the *Observer* hired him to go to the Middle East where his father lived.

Well, that was Kim Philby's story. I don't think that he told it to many people. Was he telling the truth? I don't know. And immediately I say this, I feel disloyal. Of Burgess, he once said, 'I am not a fair weather friend.'

'Suitable Virgin Wanted for Healthy Industrialist'

IVOR JONES   30 NOVEMBER 1963

Ivor Jones had been appointed Delhi Correspondent. He found that with the cooler weather, the marriage season was beginning.

Amongst my most interesting weekend reading, are the matrimonial advertisements in the press here, and especially in the Sunday edition of the conservative and respectable *Hindustan Times*. There are two hundred and fifty and more a week, filling column after column. And, because of them, innumerable young men will find themselves loaded with silver ornaments and riding on white horses to marry embarrassed girls they've scarcely met, if at all.

Most come from the middle classes and the *nouveau riche*. As a New Delhi hostess once observed to me: 'The best people do not advertise.' And the style is usually direct and factual. A typical example starts: 'Suitable Virgin for healthy industrialist'. There's no place for the coy chatter about temperament and personality found in the West. These either don't matter, or will be looked after later by the families concerned.

Girls are often described as 'pretty' or 'beautiful', though, and young men as 'handsome'. Another boast on behalf of prospective brides is that they're 'fair-skinned', or have a 'wheat-coloured complexion'. Many Indians are more colour-conscious than they or their Government choose to admit. Clearly, any father advertising for his children isn't under oath; but obvious handicaps have to be admitted. So, at the end of a catalogue of virtues, may come 'has slight physical defect, but hardly noticeable', or, 'unfortunately blind'. Almost everyone marries here, whatever their disabilities.

An essential part of any advertisement is what the man's job is, and what he earns. This may vary from two-pounds-ten a week to two hundred pounds. The same's true of girls, if they have a job. This is important, because there's a tendency, say, for doctors to marry doctors. They can then run a joint practice. Family background matters, too, both socially and professionally. A man who's well placed in the civil service or business can be expected to do more for his son-in-law here than in most countries.

Most advertisements, however, have as little embellishment as posters at a cattle sale. But there are exceptions, especially in those from Indians living overseas who are seeking brides from home. A recent one from two young men in Canada – said to be handsome ranch owners – asks for girls who are convent-educated, fluent in English and preferably knowing Indian dances and music; 'Western dance also desirable', it says. And there are others that go to great lengths in establishing what a good catch the man concerned is. There are claims such as: 'Income running into five figures'. 'Much property'. 'Millionaire family'. Such efforts usually end: 'Only families of status need apply. Decent wedding'.

'Decent wedding' is part of the jargon. It means one to which, say, five hundred guests are invited; where at least two bands play, and where the bride's loaded with jewellery. Another favourite expression, used of girls, is 'homely'. It means domesticated. And to say that a man is 'a reputed doctor' means he has a good reputation, not the opposite. Then there's 'no C and D bar'. This means the bridegroom doesn't mind from what caste the girl is, and doesn't ask for a dowry.

This kind of offer is rare, though. Dowries still matter greatly, though it's illegal to ask for one directly. And so does caste. Take this fairly typical case: 'Match sought for Bisa Aggarwal Manglik Goel Gotra virgin'. The starting point here is 'Aggarwal'. It's a caste in the Vaishya, or merchant group, which ranks third after the Brahmins and Kshatriyas, or warriors. 'Bisa' is a sub-caste of it; so the bridegroom should be a Bisa. As for 'Goel Gotra': a Gotra is a kind of clan inside the sub-caste, usually claiming the same ancestor. Members of a Gotra shouldn't marry each other: it's what's called an exogamous group; so the bridegroom mustn't be a Goel. 'Manglik' means something different – that the girl was born under a strong constellation. And most Hindus – who are still very astrology-minded – strongly believe that disaster awaits a marriage between a girl who's Manglik and a man who isn't.

There are other signs, too, in the matrimonial columns that India's not changing as fast as some people think. I've never seen a widow on offer – though some do remarry now. And, of course, they confirm the fact that almost all weddings here are still arranged. As one old Brahmin said to me: 'We in India hold that love begins with marriage, not ends with it.'

1963 – The Year of the Assassin

DOUGLAS STUART   28 DECEMBER 1963

With the New Year approaching, correspondents had been asked to look back on 1963 – the year that had just passed. This was Douglas Stuart's contribution from Washington.

It was a year that began in hope and ended in tragedy. It was a year of protest and of violence. It was a year of death and of private and public grief. It was the year of the assassin.

Death, sudden and violent, came for three men in the United States during 1963 – a postman, a politician and a president – and each time it came from a rifle. An assassin killed the postman, Mr William Moore, on a public road in the State of Alabama. It was a warm spring day, and his victim was walking to Mississippi to implore the Governor of that State to be tolerant in his dealings with the Negroes. A motorist found Moore's body in a ditch at dusk. There were two rifle bullets in his head. An assassin killed the politician, Mr Medgar Evers, just as he was entering his home. He waited for his victim that hot summer night in a honeysuckle hedge, squinting down the telescopic sight of a rifle which he rested on a steel fence. The bullet hit Evers in the back and it ripped through him tearing out his chest. He was a Negro, and he lived and worked in Jackson, Mississippi. A few hours earlier, President Kennedy had told the nation over television: 'We are confronted with a moral issue, a moral crisis, as a country and as a people. It is a time to act in the Congress, in every state and local legislative body, and, above all, in all of our daily lives.' An assassin killed the man who said that, as he rode, smiling, by the side of his wife through cheering crowds in the city of Dallas, Texas. It was high noon in the late autumn, but the rifle shots in Dallas rang round the nation and the world bringing winter to the hearts of men.

Many things bound the three murdered men together besides the act of assassination which ended their lives. They were young. The postman was thirty-five; the politician was thirty-seven; the President was forty-six. They had all served in the armed forces of their country; the postman in the Marines; the politician in the Army; the President in the Navy. In their different ways each wanted to change the world for the better. The postman sought a Utopia of brotherly love; the politician worked for a racially-integrated so-

68

ciety based on equal rights; the President strove for international peace and an end to hatred and fear at home and abroad. Looking back it seems to me that the widow of the postman spoke not only of her murdered husband, but also of the other two men, when she said: 'I don't know why anyone would want to hurt him – he was so kind.'

Why? That's the question so many people are asking at the end of this tragic year. Why? To some people, perhaps, the answer may lie in a passage I found recently in one of Henry Miller's novels. Writing some thirty years ago, this American author described his country as lawless, violent, explosive, demoniacal. 'The whole continent,' he said, 'is full of buried violence, the bones of ante-diluvian monsters, and of lost races of man; of mysteries which are wrapped in doom. Everywhere there is the same fundamental urge to slay, to ravage, to plunder.' And of the Americans themselves, Miller went on to declare: 'Outwardly they seem like a fine, up-standing people, healthy, optimistic, courageous – inwardly they are filled with worms.' But the bitter savagery of this polemic brings no comfort, and as this year of the assassin draws to a close, I prefer to remember the words of the murdered Negro politician's widow. 'I grieve,' she said, 'but I do not regret. Some people are left with nothing. I have magnificent memories. He didn't belong just to me; he belonged to so many, many people everywhere. I feel,' Mrs Evers said, 'his death has served a certain purpose, and when I find myself in pits of depression, I remind myself that fulfilling this purpose is what he really wanted.' It is an epitaph for all three men – postman and President, as well as politician; and perhaps as the old year dies in tragedy, we can still look forward to the new with hope.

Revolution in Zanzibar

ANGUS McDERMID   25 JANUARY 1964

There had been a revolution in Zanzibar and the rebels had banished the Sultan and declared a republic. Angus McDermid, who was across the water in Tanganyika, felt he had to get there.

There was nothing for it but a dhow; and the best dhows, they said, were forty-five miles down the coast from Dar-es-Salaam at the old

German capital of Bagamoyo, twenty-five miles across the strait from Zanzibar. It was dark when we got there. The breakers tumbled into the shore; the palm trees curved over the sand. This was not one of the luxury dhows that take tourists up the east coast of Africa, nor was it one of the ocean-going cargo variety. This was the humblest kind – say forty feet long; built of rough-hewn timber bolted together; much of it salvaged driftwood, and no deck, but for a few square feet at the stern, where the helmsman perched and the skipper stood in a kind of cockpit. His main duty seemed to be to empty out the bilgewater in a biscuit tin, which needed doing every two or three minutes. The four of us had to fend for ourselves, if possible to keep out of the boiling sun. The estimated time for the voyage was three hours. It took that time to catch the right wind and tide, but at last the sail was changed, all three of the crew hauling it over, and the passengers and sacks of mud ballast changed with it. It was the first of many many such changes, but at last we were on the right tack for Zanzibar.

The sea grew choppier, the sky grew dark. We were clearly not going to get into Zanzibar that night, and the crew were perhaps fearful of their reception. So we cruised round through the night, uncomfortably clinging to the rigging. A doze and a sudden awakening as the boat lurched; the crew cooking a fish in the early hours; the helmsman singing little songs about Muslim heroes; the skipper performing his morning devotions at dawn. Finally we hoisted the Tanganyika pennant; then a police launch with a young man with a revolver at the bows hailed us, and we were soon ashore surrounded by gunmen in scraps of uniform and civil defence helmets.

We'd been nineteen hours on that dhow, without lifebelts, navigation lights, radio, of course, and virtually no food or water, but we'd made it. The young man took us straight to see the President. The President was cordial enough, but had other things quite clearly on his mind. He was in the radio station, by now the revolutionary headquarters – a fantastic place, piled high with looted furniture, clothing, and fifty sewing machines laid out neatly on the grass. People with guns, people shouting, pushing, crying; and outside, thousands of Arabs being interrogated; being marched away with hands raised – excited teenagers and bearded old men bearing this burden of their race together.

But how to record all this? How to tell the world? There were no radio communications, but the cable office was working hard and for a while it was easy to drive round the town in a taxi, provided by the revolutionaries with an armed guard, but costing us ten pounds a day, the guard included. Then some more reporters came in by dhow and spy mania set in.

The telephone to Dar-es-Salaam was cut off; and while the suspected journalist spies were being expelled, we others were confined to the hotel, where the splendid Scots proprietress cooked and baked and coped – where a tall African said: 'Welcome to Zanzibar, I am a plain clothes detective,' and where a young revolutionary, when not in solemn conclave with the Chinese News Agency men, spouted Karl Marx, or spoke in Russian to the three other Communist journalists.

Then there was the censor. He was in fact the young man, with a Leningrad badge in his lapel, who'd welcomed us off the dhow. The cable office had two armed guards at the door; the censor had another one at his side, and on his desk was a revolver and a hand grenade. He weighed every phrase of our cables carefully, but, alas, inconsistently. 'Did he say this?' he asked incredulously about a statement which a government press officer had made. Well, it may have been coincidence, but the press officer didn't show up for his next conference that afternoon.

One correspondent piloted his own plane in and the guards greeted him with the words: 'You can't possibly be a pilot and a journalist, there's no such thing.' Well, Zanzibar, like the Congo, will be a place for journalists to reminisce about.

But the moment came, as seemed inevitable, when the censor refused to accept my messages 'after,' as he put it, 'what the Field Marshal said about the BBC last night.' So there it was – no telephones, no cabling.

It was a good time to leave. There was a plane. I took it. Next morning at Dar-es-Salaam airport, I was told quietly: 'There are spies all around us.' And that night the Tanganyikan army mutinied.

'Uncle Nehru is Immortal'

GERALD PRIESTLAND   13 JUNE 1964

Gerry Priestland had been revisiting India when Pandit Nehru, who had been Prime Minister ever since India achieved independence, had died.

'You must be mad to go on that train,' they said. 'Why spend twenty-four hours in a cattle truck when you can fly there in just over one hour?'

Well, that train was the funeral special taking the major remains of Mr Nehru for immersion in the holy Ganges at Allahabad. I'm glad I went on it, not because it wasn't uncomfortable – it was – but because it reminded me of what India's really all about. As we rumbled across the sandy flatness of the North Indian plain, bleached and corroded by the sun, people came down to the side of the line to have *darshan*, to be vouchsafed vision of the sacred relics. This was the heartland of Mr Nehru's Congress Party, and they came down from villages that one could see were still untouched by the first, second or third Five Year Plan. They stood among fields where peacocks strutted in flocks as evening gathered; they packed on to the platforms of country stations to bathe in the reputation of a man whose constant urgings to become scientific, secular and socialist they must have considered far above and beyond them. Such advice was for the learned, for them there remained the spiritual emanations from his ashes.

In the press coaches it was suffocating. Officialdom did its best. There were free issues of explosive fizzy lemonade; in every compartment there were earthenware crocks of drinking water; sweepers crawled on all fours mopping up the dust that swirled in; and at one stop great blocks of ice were dragged aboard in galvanised baths and set under the ceiling fans, so that the blast they circulated would become a little less searing.

At every stop it was like the rush hour on the London Underground. Those lounging on the seats inside stared with wonder through securely barred windows at the shoal of humanity pressed against the outside. Once the Indian reporters in my compartment told the curious peasants who peered back at us that a French correspondent was President Nasser of Egypt. The peasants replied that they were grateful for the honour His Excellency was doing them. They meant it, and I'm glad the Frenchman gave dignity to a bad joke by bowing in reply.

It was impossible to get on to the platform to make one's way to the white funeral coach where the urn was displayed on its floodlit pedestal. But at Cawnpore, I managed to climb out on to the roof of my coach and stumble along the top of the train, jumping the gaps till I reached it. It was one of the most enthralling sensations of my life, one that invaded every physical sense. I squatted there, wedged between the roof of the station and the roof of the coach. Below, the crowd surged to and fro like a heavy sea against a cliff, uttering a continuous wordless roar. They were men – all of them men – not a woman in sight. I was battered by the sound; stifled by the heat that rose up with a strange mixed aroma of sweat, spices and flowers – the flowers they'd brought to toss before the urn. I was rocked by the beating of thousands upon the side of the heavy coach.

It was like observing the very bloodstream of India, hot and throbbing – every head below a human corpuscle.

Then on through the night, with every now and again a chant of 'Chacha Nehru amar hai' – 'Uncle Nehru is Immortal' – swelling up and tapering off from the trackside. The final scenes at the confluence of the Ganges, the Jumna and the invisible Sarasvati River, the holiest of Hindu ends for this agnostic Westernised leader, hammered it all home – the unalterable Indianness of India. As one Indian pointed out to me, it was inevitable that Mr Nehru, despite his wishes, should have had a religious funeral. The New Delhi electric crematorium still isn't operational after eight years' work on it, and the priests are the only people who know how to set about a cremation.

And so Hinduism took its wandering son back to its bosom, with the Indian Army amphibians handling the transport, and the Indian Air Force scoring one direct hit and two near misses with showers of rose petals. On shore, a million people joined in the public holiday. There was hardly a wet eye to be seen, and the weird triangular banners of the holy men fluttered over their encampment on the sandbanks like a goblin army ready to invade the nation.

A Long Hot Summer

ANTHONY WIGAN   25 JULY 1964

New York, and the long hot summer was bringing the threat of new violence in the negro districts. Tony Wigan was then New York Correspondent.

Some years ago now, a student of the American racial situation likened the Negro in the North to some tragic people of mythology – a people which aspired to escape from its unhappy homeland to the apparent peace of a distant mountain, but which by some fatal error of judgement fell into a great chasm of maze-like passages – passages that promised to lead to the mountain but always ended against a wall. When, over the years, the Negro migrated north, his painfully acquired peasant cynicism – the thing that enabled him to live with the familiar brutality of the South – gave him no guiding lines for the competitive life of the individual in the great unknown cities. He had no skills to offer, no master interested in the man-power he had once provided – interested, in fact, in whether he lived or died. He wasn't unique; other immigrant groups found themselves in very similar situations. Like them, the Negro tended to herd together for all the human reasons. Like them, he created slums, and these, like all slums, became and remained concen-trations of crime and vice. But because of the fatality of colour – the label that follows him as a police record follows a man trying to go straight – his particular slum became a prison rather than the bottom rung of a ladder which those who tried hard enough could climb.

That's Harlem today, and not only Harlem. There are other ghettoes as bad, and perhaps worse, even in New York City. But Harlem is the prototype. Unable to get out, the Negro there must conform. There's a rough brotherhood about the place in the face of the common white enemy; not in normal times an active enemy, perhaps, though there are those, too, but passive, impervious, careless of any man's hate or prosperity beside his own interests and his children's – especially their education – an enemy which calls it charity and self-sacrifice to do for the black man what he wouldn't think twice of doing for the white.

The few Harlem Negroes who escape feel too often that they do so on sufferance to prove their worth in outside society; they become whiter than white themselves. The meanest cops in Harlem are found among the Negro officers because they feel like traitors to their own race, or, if they don't, they know that this is felt about them. In a clash, their need to demonstrate what good policemen they are can lead them to stronger methods even than those of their white colleagues. There are excuses, of course. Harlem is an uncomfortable, jittery place for a white man these days. I wouldn't be a cop there for all the tea in China.

It's hard to know where to begin on the vicious circle in which the people of Harlem spend their life, and why the outbreak that has just come was so thoroughly expected and so unavoidable. Something – call it progress – unlocked Pandora's box; the temptations of this absurdly wealthy city have been dangled equally before the Negro and the white.

At the same time, the Negroes have heard the prison doors creak. They've been told that they not only should, but must work for the fulfilment of what they once knew to be hopeless hopes. Their enemy, the white man, has himself given official assent to an armistice, though one he may be unable to enforce. But at street level, gutter level, nothing happens. Frustration and despair, tolerable when there were no far horizons, have been replaced by frantic impatience. The leaders who counsel continued moderation and warn of the dangers of a white backlash against extremism, these men are losing power as they move on to serious negotiation and compromise. The violence in the streets elects its own leaders – spokesmen might be a better word – for pace and direction and anger are dictated from below.

I've spoken of the Negroes of Harlem as an entity, as people do here. I've done so for simplicity. But, like any other community, Harlem is not only the thousands of unemployed – the blood brothers sworn to kill a cop; the drug addicts, the habitual criminals and the growing band of those who believe that extremism in the cause of liberty is no vice. It's also the churchgoers, the churchmen, the elderly and patient, the middle-aged who have something to lose, especially through their children who here must be restrained from what in other places would be normal youthful experiments. These things, too, make up the cross-currents of Harlem. We've yet to see which way the tide will set.

Russian-style Leadership

ERIK DE MAUNY   12 DECEMBER 1964

Mr Khrushchev had fallen and, at a meeting of the Supreme Soviet, he had been accused of trying to run everything his own way without consultation. Erik de Mauny had been appointed the BBC's first resident Correspondent in Moscow and he discussed how the leadership principle worked in Russia.

It's sometimes been said that *War and Peace* is a great novel marred only by its last hundred pages or so, by that final section in which Tolstoy abandons the novelist's role for that of the didactic philosopher as he examines the problem of whether it is the leader who creates history by his shaping will or whether it's the interaction of blind anonymous forces which merely thrust up a leader at the appointed hour.

Now, I apologise for giving such a rough paraphrase of an argument that Tolstoy develops with the tenacity of genius. All the same, I think it would be no bad thing if this closing section of *War and Peace* were made required reading for anyone planning to come and live in the Soviet Union, because in no other country I know of does the argument still present itself so vividly. That's not to say, of course, that this problem of the leader and the masses is peculiar to Russia. One might suggest present-day France as another example. All the same, the whole of Russian history seems to exist as a tension between two opposite poles. On the one hand there is the *Vozhd*, the big chief, who may sometimes be called the Tsar and at another time Stalin. And at the other end of the spectrum, there's the basic unit of communal rule by consent, the village *Mir* or council of elders.

It was partly because of the existence of this and similar institutions with their roots far back in the Russian past that Communism was able to take – as a vaccination takes – on the body of Russian life. But this didn't mean, as people no doubt fondly imagined it did in the early years of the October Revolution, that the opposite principle of the omnipotent ruler had finally ceased to operate. On the contrary, the emergence of Stalin proved that it was capable of returning with full and savage vigour. Stalin did many things for Russia, not all of them bad and many of them certainly necessary, and people wept when he died. But it is the bad things that are all lumped together now when Russians use the phrase '*kult lichnosti*', the cult of the personality. It's a phrase that's worth pondering on if only because, when one knows the things it covers – the purges and the fake trials, the denunciations and judicial murders – it sounds so astonishingly inoffensive. But it's perhaps just because these experiences are still so vivid in the recollection of many Russians that it was necessary to try to contain them within a deliberately flat clinical-sounding description. In any case, if you hear those words on the lips of a Soviet citizen, you know that he knows full well what they mean.

And it was for that reason at lunch the other day with a Soviet journalist friend, and discussing the October switch in leadership, that I suddenly found myself growing indignant. 'I couldn't understand,' I said – and that went for many of my Western colleagues – 'how it was possible to lump a man like Khrushchev together with Stalin by accusing him of setting up a renewed cult of personality? Surely, if anyone had led the country back to sanity out of the excesses of Stalinism it was Khrushchev?', and so on. But I'd hardly managed to state the argument before my Soviet friend began ardently refuting it. 'Look at every word that's been written in *Pravda* and *Izvestia* and elsewhere,' he said. 'There are plenty of criticisms that apply to Khrushchev: that he took overhasty decisions; didn't consult his colleagues enough; made mistakes in agriculture and other fields. But nowhere will you find him accused of creating a cult of personality. At the very most, it's been said that by some of his more thoughtless actions, he was creating conditions that could pave the way for a return to the *kult lichnosti*. But that's a very different matter. No, by the *kult lichnosti*, we mean quite simply what happened in Stalin's time, not in Khrushchev's, and no Soviet citizen is in any danger of confusing the two.'

Is there any encouragement for the future to be drawn from all this? I think there is and it's certainly not hard to find a ready example. Let's take just one of the crucial issues in the Sino-Soviet dispute. The Chinese Communists have said all along that they flatly disagreed with the Soviet repudiation of Stalin, and some of their angriest taunts at the Soviet Union have been at the expense of the de-Stalinisation campaign which no one waged more vigorously than Mr Khrushchev. Now, the present Soviet leaders would undoubtedly like to mend the quarrel with Peking – but not at any price. And far from restoring Stalin to honour, they decided to take action against Mr Khrushchev when, according to the official argument, there was only the merest hint of a danger that the personality cult could ever return.

Now, I don't want to make too much of all this. There's still something deeply disquieting in the way Mr Khrushchev was dropped with never a word of gratitude for his positive achievements. I put this point, too, to my Soviet journalist friend and this time he didn't refute it. Instead, he shrugged and said, 'No doubt our methods and yours are still very different. Perhaps it could have been handled differently, you can't change everything all at once. Perhaps,' he said after a pause, 'it will be done differently next time.'

Civil Rights in the Deep South
CHARLES WHEELER 14 AUGUST 1965

In the southern United States, thousands of Negroes had become eligible to vote under the new Civil Rights Act. In many parts, where the Negroes formed a majority, the benefits to them were immediate. But it was to other parts of the South that Charles Wheeler travelled from Washington.

Outside the Sheriff's office, a recruiting poster for the Ku Klux Klan. Next to it a drinking fountain, curtly marked 'White'. The door opens and there appears a tall figure in a Texan hat and cowboy boots, with a star on his chest and a pistol in an open holster, and a face that's vaguely familiar.

No, it's not a film; it's last Wednesday at the County Court House in Philadelphia, Mississippi, and the man in the doorway is Deputy-Sheriff Price, who, with his chief, Sheriff Rainey, and seventeen other citizens, faces charges in connection with last summer's murder of three young Civil Rights workers, two of them white New Yorkers and the third, a local Negro.

The three were arrested by Price for speeding; were held in the local jail until night time, and then, according to Price, were released. Forty-four days later, after a search by hundreds of Federal agents and troops, their bodies were found eighteen feet below the surface of a newly-constructed dam.

Price, Rainey and the rest are on bail pending the resumption of their trial before a Federal Court on charges of conspiring to deny the three victims their civil rights by killing them. And there, for the present, the matter rests.

In the meantime, life in Philadephia goes on much as before. I called on the Deputy-Sheriff. 'I wonder who killed those men,' he said, and grinned. He and his Chief still run the town. A local doctor, who suggested they be suspended from their law-enforcement duties until the trial is over, lost too many patients and has moved his practice to another county.

I went to see the Mayor. 'I never hear anybody talking about that case,' he said. 'Do the Negroes talk about it?' I asked. 'Oh, we never have trouble with the niggers here,' he said, 'not now.'

Which is, broadly speaking, true. Philadelphia is not part of what is called 'the black belt' in Mississippi. In this town the whites heavily outnumber the Negroes who are among the poorest in the State. Even getting the vote won't enable the Negro community on its own to elect another sheriff, or even force the local council to give some of the jobs it controls to the Negroes – jobs like postmen and garbage collectors. Not in Philadelphia.

Yet, even this sad little backwater isn't quite as backward as it was last summer, for others have come to the town to replace the three who were shot and the local Negroes are starting to respond to their leadership, beginning to win their first elementary rights.

In the heart of the Negro quarter in Philadelphia, in a shabby wooden house across the road from the local Civil Rights Head-quarters, there lives a certain Mrs Jones. She's a widow in her late sixties with nine children, all of them living in the North. And from all of them she gets letters. But because Mrs Jones is black, her letters are not delivered. If she thinks there may be a letter for her, she has to walk a mile to the Post Office and ask. Or rather, she and the rest of her community did have to walk. It was the Civil Rights people who suggested that something might be done. Money was collected and Mrs Jones flew to Washington. She took a bus to the Department of Justice and there she told the story of the non-delivery of the Negro community's mail. This was a year ago and the Federal machine moved slowly. But last month the Negroes got their postal delivery and outside each house there is now a brand new letter box perched on a pole.

And this isn't their only gain. For as long as anybody in Philadelphia can remember, the Negro community has been subjected to an unofficial, but strictly enforced, curfew. The Sheriff, or one of his men, would chase any Negro off the streets after dark. The present Sheriff and his deputy went further. They used to patrol the Negro area by car and when they saw a Negro sitting, after dusk, on his own verandah, they'd order him or her inside the house. Until last summer. Soon after the discovery of the three bodies in the dam, Sheriff Rainey and Deputy-Sheriff Price stopped patrolling the Negro area after dark. They haven't been back at night for months now; and in their own quarter, at least, Mrs Jones and her friends can cross the road to spend an evening with a neighbour. And if it's a hot evening, they can gossip on the porch if they like. It's an elementary right, but it's a start.

The American Shareholder

GRAHAM TURNER   11 JUNE 1966

The BBC's Economics Correspondent, Graham Turner, took a trip to the United States and, while there, examined one aspect of capitalism in New York.

Ask practically any taxi-driver in New York what shares he's got, and he'll run through the list for you. He may also have the latest edition of the evening paper on the seat beside him, with the page open at the stock-market prices. If you ask him how it comes about that he's such an ardent investor, when he's got over his surprise he'll reply that though he never expects to make a fortune as a taxi-driver, he might make one if he plays the stock-market shrewdly enough.

Now it isn't simply that American taxi-drivers are particularly share-minded as a class. There's the same absorption in the doings of the stock-market among secretaries in an office or sales girls in a department store. America as a nation is investment-minded – or, as they might put it, business-orientated – acknowledging instinctively, as we so often don't in this country, that it's business on which their fortune depends.

There are something like twenty-one million shareholders in America, compared with the two and a half million who invest on the Stock Exchange in this country. So, since they've backed it with their cash, very large numbers of people are deeply interested in how industry is performing, and many of them regard the stock-market as the centre of a very high-powered and reasonably respectable game.

Go into a big stockbroker's office in New York at any time during market hours, and there might be perhaps a hundred and fifty or two hundred ardent investors glued to the ticker-tape screen. You wonder how they find the time – and perhaps some of them ought to be doing other things, to judge from the speed with which they disappeared when we tried to film a group of them for a television programme – but there's no doubting their passionate interest.

Naturally enough, in a game where rewards can be so high, everybody wants to play it as well as he can, and a great many investors are prepared to train arduously to do so. For instance, the world's largest stockbroking firm reckons that something like a hundred and sixty thousand people will attend the investment forums they'll be giving during the course of this year all over the United States. Other stockbrokers do much the same thing, though perhaps not on the same grand scale. They may take a commodious salon in one of the big department stores and invite interested women to come along to a ladies-only series of seminars on such subjects as the Fundamentals of Securities Investments. Suffice it to say that the good brokers rarely have enough room for all the worthy ladies who want to come.

The longer you are in America, the more you get the feeling that investment is something for everybody, and not just the lucky few who happen to have a thousand or two lying idle and who know a good stockbroker. You can start an investment account with the biggest firm of stockbrokers if you only have two dollars a month to spare – that's less than fifteen shillings – if you happen to work for a company which has an investment-plan arrangement with them. And this particular stockbroking firm is currently spending something like two million pounds a year on advertising – which British stockbrokers, of course, aren't allowed to do.

But then investment and banking and the whole business of money doesn't seem, in America, to be the affair of one particular class of people. The boss of the biggest firm of stockbrokers is a man who went straight from high school – missing out college – into a chain store, and then on to Wall Street the hard way. In the merchant banks, it's much the same. A senior partner in one of them told me that when he went to college in California, he was so poor that his net expenditure for the first six months was just seven dollars and ninety-two cents. He lived almost entirely on stale bread – at five cents for two loaves. In Wall Street, on the face of it at least, no doors are closed to ability.

Even the banks, which in Britain remain a trifle aloof even if they are more determinedly avuncular than they used to be, sell themselves as hard as any supermarket. While I was in New York, I was given an invitation by one of the big banks to the opening of a new branch in the suburbs. It was in the form of a letter from the manager and began: 'Here's your chance of a lifetime!' If you went along, you could win a free television set, or automatic record players or picnic sets. And, even if you didn't win a prize, there were free balloons for the children and what were enticingly described as 'handy pocket secretaries' for the fathers.

This, then, is the American version of people's capitalism. To someone from Britain it's all perhaps a shade alarming, but there's something natural and healthy about it too. After all, which stock-broking firm in this country would dare to call their house magazine – as one American firm does – simply *We the People?*

Looking Back
THOMAS BARMAN   31 DECEMBER 1966

With the last day of 1966, that most respected of diplomatic correspondents, Tom Barman, retired. He had been a Paris correspondent of The Times *before the War; he had served in Moscow for the Foreign Office during the War, and since then for the BBC. This edition of From Our Own Correspondent was given over entirely to his musings.*

When I look back upon the forty years or so that I've spent in the trade of journalism, I find that what springs to mind are not so much the great events that will ultimately be recorded in the history books, but the footnotes to them. I do not regard these footnotes as mere additions to an exciting story; they have an identity and a meaning of their own. They often record the personal interventions or interpretations that affected its course. They may throw fresh light upon something that at the time seemed inevitable and even ordinary.

In diplomacy, too, it is often the footnote or the casual aside that clothes an abstract argument with the flesh and blood of practical politics. And let me add here that after spending the war years working in different departments of the Foreign Office at home and abroad, I have discovered that the rules governing some aspects of an ambassador's work are not so very different from those that guide the activities of a foreign correspondent. But an ambassador has one great advantage over a journalist; in the ordinary course of events, his reports are not published until after his death, so that when his errors are revealed, they can no longer embarrass him. The journalist's report, on the other hand, is published at once and such mistakes as he may make are made known on the instant. This fact does not lead me to support the argument put forward by many distinguished historians that Foreign Office documents should be made available much sooner than they are. The immediate effect of such a change in present procedures would be to tempt ambassadors to write for an audience rather than for their government. Even now, with the existing restrictions on publication, there are some who do write for the sake of effect, in the hope that their words will look rather nice in the history books or even better in the newspapers, rather than with the determination to tell a round unvarnished tale.

In journalism, as in diplomacy, the changes that have taken place during the past forty years are enormous. There were hardly any press officers in the years before the war; the Foreign Office, it is true, had its official spokesman, but he was so close to the seat of power that he could with justice be regarded as an ultimate source. I do not think my colleagues and I attended any kind of press conference before the war. The press conference, like the public relations officer, is a post-war development designed in the main to prevent journalists from becoming too troublesome. And the trade of journalism, which was once a highly individual affair, has now become a sort of mass movement, a mass pilgrimage to the source of news. The audiences at press conferences get bigger and bigger, but the information that comes out of them becomes less and less significant.

When a British Foreign Secretary attended an international conference before the war, he might be accompanied by a handful of journalists, all of whom were personally known to him. Now, there is a vast migration. At the Summit Conference in Geneva in 1955, there were some two thousand of us – journalists and leg-men and cameramen and radio technicians and teleprinter operators – not to mention the leader writers and commentators. Keeping the press informed was a sort of mass-production job, with press officers working in relays. And inevitably, all this rush and excitement has its comic aspects. All the normal rules of diplomacy get to be broken even by the most experienced politicians. Take the meetings of the North Atlantic Council, for instance. Its proceedings are supposed to be private and sometimes even secret. And yet it's a common sight to see an excited minister rushing out of the conference room into some dark corner – rather like a hawker of questionable postcards – and offering specially selected extracts from his latest speech to journalists representing newspapers published in his own country, in the hope that his name will appear in the morning papers once again. There is nothing like publicity for keeping a politician's liver in good working order.

In the world of diplomacy, there's been the same inflation as in journalism. Some thirty-five years ago, the office hours of British legations in minor European capitals were from 10 a.m. to 1 p.m. Now, the staff toil all day. I remember, in particular, an occasion when I passed on a piece of gossip to the British Minister in Stockholm. We had few ambassadors in those days, since ministers were regarded as quite good enough for the minor places. Anyway, I thought my story might be of interest in the light of some curious remarks that had been made by the then Swedish Foreign Secretary. 'I'll let the Foreign Office know,' the Minister said, 'they'll be amused.' I said I supposed he would be telegraphing the information to London. He looked at me with astonishment. 'Certainly not,' he said. 'I won't do anything of the sort. If I were to send more than a dozen telegrams a month from this post, I'd have a Treasury Inspector in my Chancery asking why we were wasting the taxpayer's money.' Now, thirty-five years later, the telegrams and despatches pour in upon the Foreign Office in interminable floods of paper. Yet I very much doubt whether the Government are better informed today than they were in the more economical days before the war. It is impossible to believe that any one person could read, let alone digest, the vast cargo of material unloaded into Downing Street at all hours of the day and night. There is certainly no evidence to justify the belief that the Foreign Office is better informed than the conscientious foreign correspondent.

If the worlds of journalism and diplomacy have undergone vast changes in the past forty years, the problems facing us in Europe are not so very different. In essence, they turn upon the position of Germany – the problem child of Europe. It arises out of the presence in the heart of Europe of an exceedingly powerful nation – of an industrious and disciplined people who have yet to find a place in the world that satisfies them without harming others. It is evident that their future lies within a European framework which does not upset the present balance of power between the Soviet Union and the United States. But I do not think this can be achieved without a complete British involvement in the affairs of the Continent. If I have become convinced that the British Government should accept the Common Market Treaty in full, without any reservations, in spite of all its drawbacks and disadvantages, it is because I believe that British membership will act as an essential balancing factor. It will reassure the smaller powers of Europe who do not want to be dominated either by France or by Germany or by a Franco–German condominium. It will provide that vast market for foodstuffs without which the farm problem in Western Europe cannot be solved. And it may make possible, in due course, a wider European political and economic partnership. Without the active and wholehearted British participation in European affairs, a European settlement that does not harm British interests, that is supported by the United States, that does not offend the Soviet Union, that does not frighten the smaller powers – such a settlement is out of the question. And those who have reservations about this should be asked to explain why it is reasonable for Britain to undertake an unlimited European commitment in time of war, but must be careful not to lift a finger in days of peace.

If the tragedy of the thirties is to be found in the failure of British politicians – with one or two notable exceptions – to grasp the nature of the German problem, the tragedy of the late forties and fifties is that the foreign policy of British Governments was blown off course by Stalin's follies. As a result of the fears generated by his disastrous mistakes, the Western Powers gave priority to the German national question over the problem of European security. Insistence upon German reunification as the precondition for any kind of rapprochement with the Soviet Union became the touchstone of Western orthodoxy. And when, in 1955, the then Prime Minister, Anthony Eden, suggested a thinning-out of forces in Central Europe as a first step towards disarmament, he was greeted with a howl of rage from Bonn on the ground that he was changing the order of priorities – an order that by then had acquired an air of sanctity. The inevitable effect of this policy has been to widen the breach with the Soviet Union, and also, of course, with the countries of Eastern Europe – particularly the Slav countries which have suffered so terribly under German tyranny. And so, most of the European conferences held after the end of the war have ended in a failure that was inevitable.

This dangerous development of the German problem gave rise to a dramatic incident at a dinner party given during the course of the Summit Conference in Geneva in 1955. With only a handful of guests left in the room, Mr Khrushchev rushed towards the French Foreign Minister and held on to his arm. 'We shall never, never, never change our minds about the German problem,' he shouted. 'We shall never change our policy.' And then he left the room in silence. Although it was always hard to tell if Mr Khrushchev was putting on an act or not – one recalls such ill-mannered affairs as the shoe-banging incident at the United Nations, or the attack on President Eisenhower in Paris – I believe that he was genuine on this particular occasion. It seems to me that Western Governments – our own included – have not paid enough attention to the deep scars left on the Russian people by their appalling sufferings in two world wars. The famine in Leningrad, the slaughter and destruction in Stalingrad and many other places, are still fresh in their minds.

This lack of sensitivity, of perception perhaps, was particularly noticeable at the four-power conference held in Moscow in the spring of 1947. The Russians, as so often before, were bad-tempered and ill-mannered. Mr Molotov was at his worst. The presence of Vishinsky, whose abominable record of bullying and lying was known to everybody, did not help matters. A press conference that he gave had disastrous effects. He had failed to master his brief and responded to questions put to him by British journalists – very reasonable questions they were – with insults and abuse. He behaved in the same overbearing way when he came to the British Embassy in the autumn of 1944 on the occasion of Winston Churchill's dinner party for Stalin. The Russians had turned the Embassy into an armed camp: there were armed Soviet security officials everywhere and all of them in brand new uniforms and clean white gloves in honour of the occasion – in the corridors, on the stairs, with their backs to the dining room. They were everywhere. As he came in, Vishinsky turned to us with an unpleasant grin and said, 'This must be the first time that the British Embassy has been occupied by Soviet troops.' It is only natural that Western Ministers and officials reacted with anger and impatience to this sort of arrogance and tactlessness.

At the 1947 conference then, even the French delegation, who had attended in the hope of doing a deal with the Russians – even the French delegation lost patience. What was not adequately realised at the time was that the Russian people were still living on the very edge of famine. There was only one hotel in the whole of Moscow where white bread was to be had; and even the members of the diplomatic corps, who at times enjoyed unusual privileges in the Soviet capital, had to make their way to this one hotel if the urge to eat white bread came upon them. Some elderly people I saw were obviously starving. And if there were fewer beggars and down-and-outs to be seen than a few weeks earlier in the year, that was only because many of them had been taken out of Moscow in army lorries and dumped some fifty miles outside the capital to make their way back as best they could.

Incidentally, it was at this time that the then British Ambassador found himself in difficulties with the Soviet customs authorities. They had been holding up a consignment of supplies for himself and his staff. The Ambassador called upon Vishinsky and asked for his help. There was no response. 'If I can get this stuff through quickly,' the Ambassador said, 'I shall be delighted to give half of it to the poor of Moscow.' Vishinsky was furious. He rose from his chair to indicate that the conversation was over. 'There are no poor in Moscow,' he said. So, as I've just said, the Western Ministers were both angry and impatient.

But against the background of famine and privation, it is not surprising that Mr Molotov made a demand for reparations from Germany. He insisted upon ten thousand million dollars-worth – clearly an impossible sum. And, of course, the British and United States Governments rejected his demand. They themselves were pumping their own resources into Germany in the hope of getting the machinery of orderly government into working order again. But when the Soviet people read the accounts of the conference in their newspapers, they can hardly fail to have formed the conclusion that only two years after a costly victory, the Western Powers were resuming their pro-German and anti-Russian policy. As they saw it, a starving German was given a higher rating than a starving Russian.

Some twelve years later, in 1959, when Mr Macmillan visited the Soviet Union, a good deal of that uncouth arrogance that was so fashionable in Stalin's day had gone. The Soviet officials I met on that occasion were willing to discuss things and to listen to arguments. There was one reception, I remember, where a Soviet official took me by the arm and drew me into a quiet corner of the room. I'd known him well during the war. He began by saying, 'We cannot understand the foreign policy of your Government. The Soviet Union,' he explained, 'is an enormous country; so is the United States. We can afford to make mistakes, even more than one mistake in our foreign policy, but you – you live on a small and overcrowded island. In a nuclear war you would disappear without a trace in a few minutes. You cannot afford to make one single mistake; you have to walk delicately, so as not to antagonise those who are more powerful than you are. Why then do you join in this anti-Soviet coalition of which Germany is the corner-stone?'

In 1947 then, as in 1959, there was this obsession with Germany and what the Russians regard as the German capacity for mischief. Only the other day, Mr Kosygin, perhaps the most reasonable leader the Soviet Union has ever had, told the representative of a minor power that his people would never forget – they could never forget – that the Germans had got as far as Stalingrad.

Of course, I am not arguing that the Russians should have been allowed to have things all their own way after the war and that the policy of British and other Western governments has been mistaken. The fate of Czechoslovakia is the strongest possible argument in favour of a policy of resistance. Although the Communist coup there did not take place until 1948, it was evident already in 1945 that some of the Czech defences had fallen. In that year President Benes and Jan Masaryk passed through Moscow on their way to Prague. Jan Masaryk made it clear to me that the intriguers were at work. I asked him how he was getting on with the Soviet leaders. He used some unquotable expressions, so I shall have to paraphrase his words. He made it abundantly clear that he'd had enough, that he was not prepared to tolerate any more interference and that within a very short time, within the next few weeks perhaps, he would resign and tell his story to the world. As we all know, he changed his mind. No doubt he thought he could serve his country best by going back and guiding his people out of the labyrinth of treason. Stalin destroyed him, as he destroyed so many others. And it was about this time that Stalin was giving the most solemn assurances to the United States Government about the future of Poland. There was no intention on the part of the Soviet Union, he said, to interfere in Poland's internal affairs. Poland would live under a Parliamentary regime, Stalin added, of the same type as that which existed in Czechoslovakia and Belgium and the Netherlands. Any talk of an intention to Sovietise Poland was stupid.

In spite of these and other Soviet crimes, I still believe that failure to understand the fierceness of the Russian reaction to many aspects of the German problem – like the failure to identify the German problem itself – has added to the vast range of misunderstandings that have separated us from the Soviet Union.

If, at this point, I bring in the name of Anthony Eden, it is because he's always been regarded, and quite rightly, as among the foremost champions of firm policy against the Nazis, and when he resigned in 1938, his attitude was very clearly defined. We all knew what he stood for and what his resignation meant. Winston Churchill has told us how despair overtook him when he heard the news of the resignation. He was not alone in this feeling. Those of us whose job it was to report on Continental affairs felt about Eden's departure as they might have felt about some great personal disaster. I came back to London from Paris a day or two after the event. In Paris, of course, all the anti-British elements were delighted with the turn of events. A friend of mine took me across to the House of Commons to see the Leader of the Opposition, Mr Attlee. He thought that Mr Attlee might like to have a first-hand account of

Continental reactions. I told him how people felt, especially our friends; I told him also of how the hopes of holding the Nazis in check were fading. Mr Attlee made no comment; he made me feel that I had trespassed into a field where I'd no right to be.

Some months later Anthony Eden's resignation came up in rather a different way. It happened when Lady Oxford – better known as Margot Asquith – paid one of her regular visits to *The Times* office in Paris. I can still see her, sitting comfortably in the one safe easy chair we had. What she had to say about Anthony Eden was said in a very few words. 'When we were Prime Minister,' she said tartly, 'young men never resigned.'

I suppose most of us working journalists like to feel that their work will influence the policies of governments, either directly or indirectly, by rousing public opinion for or against some act of policy. This was something of which I was particularly conscious when I was writing for *The Times*. I am sure that the editor, Geoffrey Dawson, one of the ablest journalistic craftsmen I've ever known, regarded himself as more of a statesman, a policy-maker, than a journalist. It can be dangerous, this attitude, because it can lead to the suppression of news in what comes to be described as the national interest. And I know that some members of *The Times* staff, notably that most distinguished of foreign correspondents, Norman Ebbutt, suffered badly owing to the view taken in London that the publication of his despatches in full was not always in the national interest. Politicians who use this argument are the worst enemies of the press. What they say appears to be so very reasonable, until it's closely examined.

The other type of politician who is a nuisance to the journalist is the one who's always trying to please. They strive to please, not of course as an end in itself, but in the hope of getting what they call 'a good press'. Lord Simon, probably the worst Foreign Secretary in recent history, is a case in point. Whenever the press failed to give him the whole credit for any favourable development in foreign affairs, and heaven knows there were not many in his time, he felt himself badly done by. He would accuse his unfortunate officials of falling down on the job. And President Eisenhower – Eisenhower the politician, I'm thinking of now, not Eisenhower the Commander-in-Chief – is another leading figure who failed to establish the right atmosphere with the press.

At the other extreme is Mr Molotov, who does not care about the press at all. I don't suppose he ever gave a press conference in his life. I do not believe that he ever worried about his public image. This became clear to me in an incident in which I was involved during the war. I'd been working in Moscow for some time as the personal assistant to the British Ambassador and I'd been told to give all the help I could to the British correspondents who were reporting the armistice talks with Finland, in September 1944. They ended late in the evening and it was agreed that publication of the terms should be made in the early hours of the following day. There was no question of getting it out on the BBC's nine o'clock news, of course. The Government then always wanted to reserve such news as they had for the morning papers – they did not want the story broken on the BBC first.

Unfortunately, the time that had been fixed for publication was even too late for the morning papers. I complained to the Ambassador. 'Don't tell me,' he said, 'tell Mr Molotov.' And, as usual, Mr Molotov began by saying 'no'! It was obvious that he did not care either way – newspapers did not matter in his life, least of all the foreign press. As an afterthought, he added, 'The procedure has been fixed by Mr Stalin.' I persisted. Eventually he agreed to advance the publication time by two hours. 'I don't think that will make much difference,' I told him, 'it will still be too late.' I reminded him that all press telegrams had to be passed by censor. I told him that the censorship people were far too slow and too cautious and that there were very often long delays. 'Very well,' he said, after a pause, 'I'll put you in charge of the censorship for the next twelve hours. Every press telegram to London carrying your signature will be transmitted without delay.' And then he smiled. 'If you make a mistake we'll exile you to Poland.' At this point he looked at the British Ambassador out of the corner of his eye and repeated – 'We'll exile you to Poland, we have plenty of friends over there.' Of course it was all humbug. The arrangements had already been made with the censors to clear all telegrams, but it was a nice trick, it made me feel happy, and it enabled Mr Molotov to get some remarks about Poland off his chest – as a sort of warning, I suppose.

Now Mr Molotov has always been regarded as a hard and insensitive man, a man who delighted in saying no. Yet those of us who heard him making semi-public speeches at the Peace Conference in Paris in 1947 realised that he was very sensitive, very sensitive to atmosphere. As the Foreign Ministers in the Conference Hall stiffened after some remark that Mr Molotov made – you could almost see them drawing back their shoulders – Mr Molotov developed a painful stammer and at times he was almost unintelligible. It seemed to me that he suffered from this hostility; it disturbed him.

And his reaction to the death of President Roosevelt was highly emotional. He called upon the United States Ambassador in Moscow to express his Government's regrets, and he seemed to be on the edge of tears. A look of sympathy flashed across his face as he shook hands with the Ambassador. 'There are difficult times ahead for your country,' he said, 'we will do all we can to help.' The last words came out with a rush. He knew that with the death of Franklin Roosevelt the world had changed course. The year 1945 was, in fact, a watershed in history.

And now, at the turn of the year, we've come to another watershed. The post-war world, the world that Franklin Roosevelt did not live to see, is again in a state of flux. In Europe, the Western Security system is breaking up. The Russian hold upon Eastern Europe is ending. In south-eastern Europe, Yugoslavia is casting off the chains of the one-party system. In the north, the Swedish welfare state seems to have come to the end of the road. In France, General de Gaulle has resurrected a sort of *fin-de-siècle* xenophobia; and from across the Rhine come answering noises. A new exciting period lies ahead of us, but as dangerous perhaps as the 1930s.

And the Far East? I have said nothing about China. Perhaps the only thing that can be said is that the revolution is still in the stage of juvenile delinquency. And perhaps a quotation from that great visionary, Heinrich Heine, is relevant. 'I think with horror,' he wrote in 1855, 'of the time when the Communists, those gloomy iconoclasts, will come to power. Their horny hands will mercilessly smash the marble statues of beauty. My Book of Songs will be used by the grocer to make paper bags to hold coffee or snuff for the old women of the future.'

Why has France Ceased to Startle the World?

ERIK DE MAUNY   7 JANUARY 1967

A few days earlier, in a New Year broadcast to France, General de Gaulle had boasted that the country had gone through the past four years without a major crisis. Erik de Mauny, who had moved to Paris, suggested that this stability had been purchased at a price.

Where is the France that used to startle the world? It was I who was startled when the question was put to me in this form a few days ago. But the more I thought about it the more it seemed to me that it was a legitimate question and even one that needs to be asked with some urgency, since in barely two months' time the French people will be going to the polls to elect a new parliament, and this may well result in the prolongation of the present Gaullist regime for a further four years. Now, it's not my purpose here to go into the intricacies of French politics, but it is very apparent that General de Gaulle in his long reign at the Elysée has imposed a personal style on the whole country. And if one asks oneself what effect this has had on the quality of French intellectual life, then I think one is back at the question I began with: Why has France ceased to startle the world?

Now, it is possible, of course, to refute this proposition and to say that France does still startle the world. But if this is so, it is invariably in the person of General de Gaulle and through his interventions on the international scene. Internally, the country often seems to be in a state of almost somnambulistic calm. In the three years I lived in Moscow, it sometimes seemed to me that Russia had become the last repository of the great Victorian virtues. Now, after six months in Paris, I'm not sure that France is not beginning to assume the same role. It's only the traffic that is frenzied in Paris these days. In most other respects, French life seems to have attuned itself to a grave and monumental decorum. This new mood of conformity expresses itself in a variety of ways. The nearest thing Paris has seen recently to a theatrical incident occurred a few nights ago at the Olympia Music Hall when the eighty-one-year-old French novelist, François Mauriac, took violent exception to a song which he interpreted as a slur on the French

Head of State, and tried to boo the singer off the stage. Now, admittedly Mauriac is more Royalist than the King, and writing in the *Figaro Littéraire* a day or so after this episode, he expressed the fervent belief that the Gaullists would be returned to power in March out of a sheer sense of self-preservation among the electors. And actually I'm wrong in calling this the only theatrical incident in recent weeks. There was a rumpus a month or so earlier about the production at the state-subsidised Sarah Bernhardt Theatre of Peter Weiss's *Persecution and Assassination of Marat* – the play usually referred to for short as *Marat/Sade* – with the present Comte Xavier de Sade bringing an action to prevent his ancestor's name being used in the full title. But, the point I'm making here is that the Peter Weiss drama is not of French authorship, and if one looked through the Paris theatre columns when the autumn season opened, one discovered that no fewer than six houses were putting on plays by British playwrights.

It could be objected that the French theatre isn't representative of the cultural climate, but if one turns to another sphere in which Paris was for so long supreme, that of the graphic arts, then there's an even more powerful impression of being marooned at a still centre, and this is brought out most strongly by a visit to the vast retrospective Picasso exhibition which opened a month or so ago. It's rather like going on a conducted tour of all the great battlefields of modern art, but the point is that the battles are over with barely a whiff of cordite left hanging in the air. Picasso is, of course, drawing the crowds in tens of thousands as did the earlier Vermeer exhibition at the Orangerie. Both exhibitions having been sponsored by the Minister of Culture, Monsieur Malraux, whose other activities include laying bare at considerable expense the original foundations of the Louvre. One sometimes has the sensation in fact that all France is being gradually transformed into one vast museum in which the grateful inhabitants will be able to indulge in a perpetual orgy of culture watching, in much the same spirit as sports fans throng to a cup final.

Even literature seems to be in a fairly dispirited state. Total book sales have admittedly been rising by five to ten per cent a year, but the increase is accounted for mainly by encyclopedias, technical and general works; not by poetry or novels. The so-called new wave of younger novelists seems largely to have spent itself, exhausted

94

perhaps by the sheer effort of writing fiction without benefit of characters or plot. While as for the intellectual ferment stirred up by existentialism in the immediate post-war years, little trace of it remains on the present scene. Even as a centre for the expatriate writers, Paris seems to have lost its former magnetism. There is no visible evidence of a new Joyce, or Hemingway, or Gertrude Stein haunting the terraces of the Dome or the Coupole these days. Does this mean that France as an intellectual force has lost the power to startle for ever? That hardly seems likely. But we're also not likely to see a revival of it until the French have moved beyond the present narrow conception of what constitutes the national glory.

The Vietcong

DAVID WILLEY   29 APRIL 1967

David Willey was in Saigon and he reported that although the Americans had been involved in the war in Vietnam for some years, it was only now that they were getting a clear picture of their enemy, the Vietcong.

'Boxers fighting the wind.' That's how North Vietnamese Army General Nguyen Chi Thanh, the Vietcong Supreme Commander, described the Americans fighting in South Vietnam at an important war council somewhere in the jungle a year ago. We know what he said to the meeting, because the original of his speech, and notes made on it by his audience, were among the mountain of documents captured by the Americans this year during operations in the Vietcong stronghold known as War Zone D, near the Cambodian border.

The Americans are clearly surprised and delighted at the amount of Intelligence they've gained about their enemy from nearly a million pages of captured orders, operational records, letters and directives, not to mention still photographs and film. Perhaps for the first time in this war, they are fitting real faces to the elusive foe they nickname 'Charlie' and talk about in the third person singular.

First, a word about the physical circumstances the Vietcong operate in. It's an underground movement in the fullest sense of the word – thousands of yards of tunnels were found, so deep under the earth that the biggest conventional bombs would have failed to destroy them. These catacombs are ventilated by ingenious methods, such as securing a burrowing animal in a cage to the roof to build air shafts. They are well engineered and can sustain life more or less indefinitely for the guerillas. They contain hospitals, store-rooms, communications centres – even post offices. Six thousand soldiers' letters to and from home were found in one field post office.

The extent and sophistication of the Vietcong bureaucracy as revealed by the captured documents, is staggering. Written records are kept of every aspect of operational planning, and there's evidence of a considerable flow of information between Hanoi and the Southern political and military headquarters.

Communist casualty reports provided an interesting comparison with American losses and estimates. It was found that on specific battles, the Vietcong reported their own casualties fairly faithfully, but exaggerated American losses up to ten times. The Communist unit commander is under strong pressure to fulfil his norm of enemy dead, rather like a factory manager trying to keep up his production quota. There must be strong temptation to fudge the figures, which, after all, can never be really verified. On your own casualties it's more difficult to hide facts, otherwise your headquarters might draw up a plan of attack which is incapable of being carried out for lack of numbers.

It was found that few documents bore the signature of any of the publicised leaders of the Liberation Front, the political organisation of the Vietcong. The identity of the real men in command is an Intelligence coup of the first magnitude, as was the discovery of the identity of a whole series of sabotage-cell leaders in Saigon. Notebooks kept by key party workers throw an interesting light on the importance attached to political training and the time spent listening to lectures. Failures and successes are analysed in detail; shortcomings noted; targets set for next year. There is perhaps a more realistic appreciation of the situation than that portrayed in the official Communist information media, but the tone is one of continued confidence in ultimate victory.

Paper isn't all that was captured. Large rice caches were found by American troops, and laboratory analysis showed some supplies were up to three years old, which helps to explain why the cutting of rice supplies, an important part of current military strategy, appears so far to have had so little effect upon Vietcong activities. Few captured documents have so far been released to the press. Those that have are aimed at demonstrating the close links that bind the insurrection in South Vietnam to Hanoi and show Hanoi's controlling hand.

What does emerge is how little the Americans really knew about the enemy they were fighting until recently. With typical American thoroughness the facts are now all safely recorded in an intelligence computer. It may not yet come up with a solution to win the war, but at least they are not now fighting in the dark, or – as General Thanh would have it – against the wind.

Race Riots

CHARLES WHEELER   11 JUNE 1967

Again it was summer in the United States, and again the hot weather brought with it race violence. Charles Wheeler drew a picture of how race riots started.

In Tampa, Florida, rioting broke out when a white policeman shot a fugitive Negro youth in the back and killed him. In Montgomery, Alabama, it followed the arrest of a dozen civil rights leaders. In Cincinnati, the riot was touched off by the arrest of a woman carrying a placard protesting against the conviction of a Negro on a rape charge. In Cleveland, the other day, a white policeman shot and killed a Negro who was pointing a pistol at another Negro – the pistol turned out to be a toy. And similar incidents – sometimes involving police shootings of suspects, and sometimes routine arrests – touched off major riots last summer in one American city after another.

Now, in these race riots, friction between policeman and slum-dweller is usually the spark that lights the fuse. But to blame either the police or the slum-dweller for what follows is futile. It's as futile as blaming the weather. The long, hot summer of the headlines is certainly a factor. Obviously, high temperatures make crowded slum apartments additionally unbearable and so drive people on to the streets, with the result that a ready-made crowd is present whenever an incident occurs. The heat also makes slum children turn on fire-hydrants to cool themselves down; and when a police patrol turns a hydrant off again there's invariably trouble. But what follows is neither the policeman's fault nor the citizen's; the cause is the lack of an alternative to the hydrant.

Imagine a hot evening in a typical American city slum. A group of teenagers, out of work and without hope of a job, is whiling away an hour or two in an alley. They've been catching rats – probably in their homes. They've got sixteen rats altogether, so they're racing them in four heats of four rats each. After each heat the losers are killed and the winning rat goes on to the final. In the end only the champion rat survives and that's the end of the tournament and the end of the day's entertainment.

So the Negro kids slope off down the street looking for action; kicking over a couple of garbage cans, which the city collects once monthly from this part of town, passing a supermarket which charges more for food than its branches in white areas do because the turnover here is lower, and across the vacant lot where an apartment house used to be. It was torn down seven years ago in a slum clearance scheme, but nothing was built in its place. Then, just ahead, the kids see a crowd and they run up to join it.

Somebody's been arrested. He's being pushed in handcuffs into a police car which races off. The crew of a second car – they patrol in pairs in the ghetto – covers its getaway, pistols drawn. A woman, imagining beatings at the station-house, shouts out 'police brutality'. Somebody throws a stone. Police reinforcements arrive with riot-guns and a riot is made.

The teenagers rush off with the rest. They grab a brick or two from the vacant lot; they pitch it through the supermarket window, and help themselves to candy and a steak for Mum. An hour later, the heavy boys arrive, the ones with cars and petrol-bombs and guns. Three nights and many casualties later, the infantry has restored order at bayonet-point. The city fathers and the civil rights leaders debate what everybody calls the breakdown of communication; and down in the ghetto the kids are still hopping around with glee. They've had the time of their lives and they feel like men.

A month passes and City Hall makes an announcement. This has been a composite picture so far – what follows happened after last year's riots in Cleveland. The City is to construct a two million dollar playground in the heart of the riot area. It'll have a bicycle-path and an ice-skating rink, just like the Rockefeller Plaza in New

York. The announcement causes a storm. White voters accuse the Mayor of not standing up to the Negroes; Negro leaders point out that their people can't afford to buy bicycles and ice-skates and demand that the money be spent on housing. As for the slum-dwellers themselves, they register the fact that, though the City puts last things first, it at least responds to violence. Next summer, they say to each other, we'll have them raising public housing on all those vacant lots.

The chief cause of present Negro bitterness is, of course, the fact that programmes designed to help the people in the slums have been cut. Because the Vietnam War is mopping up so much Federal money, and because white taxpayers in the cities won't re-elect politicians who pay undue attention to a minority community – widely regarded as ungrateful, shiftless, riotous, immoral and generally unworthy – the drive to give the Negro a more equal chance in life has lost its steam. Here and there, private groups have moved in to fill the gaps, sponsoring temporary employment schemes and summer camps.

But sponsored fun and games, and jobs that end in September, are very often anti-riot measures and anyway are not an answer to the problem. What the Negro wants is what he's always wanted – decent schools, decent jobs, decent houses and a full share of the American good life. And the closer he gets to his desires, the more they burn him up. The fact is that the civil rights laws of the past twenty years have made little dent on the pattern of living of most of the country's twenty million coloured Americans. The laws represent promise, not necessarily performance. And the American system, being what it is, performance is something this generation of Negroes will have to wait for or fight for.

Now some Negroes have elected to wait as their parents and grandparents did. Others recognise that progress is being made and are undecided. Others jump at every chance to fight. As for the immediate future, it's totally obvious that the third group is growing at the expense of the other two.

Nigeria: The East
Threatens Secession

ANGUS McDERMID   18 MARCH 1968

*In Nigeria, 1967 had seen a wave of violence in the Northern Region
and in Lagos against the Eastern Nigerians. The Easterners, who
had occupied many key positions throughout the Federation, had
made their way back to their own region seeking refuge. Now, there
were threats that Eastern Nigeria might secede. Angus McDermid
reported from the regional capital, Enugu.*

The great ingathering of nearly two million Eastern Nigerians to
their home region after the wave of violence against them in the
North and in Lagos last year has left the region tingling with
emotion – a great upsurge of what might be called militant
regionalism, with, it must be said, a strong element of vengeance. The
return of the Easterners has placed a great strain on the region's
resources; the population has grown by about seventeen per cent.
But it's also brought a rich profusion of professional talent and
technical skills. In fact, some of the best brains in Nigeria, backed
by experts of all kinds, find themselves unexpectedly concentrated
together among their own people.

Here in Enugu you come across them all the time – the top
former Federal public servants, the parliamentary officials, the
educationists. And on a lower level, there are the newly-painted
signs showing that skilled motor mechanics from well-known firms
in Kano and Kaduna in the North are now prepared to take on
work. And in a defiant gesture, someone has called his tiny roadside
bar 'The New Refugee Hotel'.

These are the people who piled into their cars and lorries;
boarded trains and aircraft and, with what possessions they could
muster, trekked back to set up home with relatives and friends.
Most of them are being absorbed somehow into life here; but
consider the problems of rehabilitating and retraining twelve thousand spare railwaymen, two thousand postal workers, and a large
airways staff. All this has spurred the Easterners on to make plans
for a future in which – whatever happens – they intend to look after
their own interests in their own corner of West Africa.

Things will never be quite the same again. This could have a number of results. It could provide the impetus leading to rapid development of the region, a great concentration of effort. Already the East, with its oil, contributes well over a third of Nigeria's export trade and over a third, too, of its tax revenue; and it angers the Easterners that only fourteen per cent is reallocated back to the East.

There's no doubt about the calibre of the men behind the scenes in Enugu. Lieutenant Colonel Ojukwu, who as military governor is at the heart of the dispute, agrees readily that he has had for some time an alternative shadow government, a smooth-running machine ready to take over the Eastern Administration completely should the occasion arise. The talents have been mobilised.

There's considerable secrecy, of course, but much coming and going by devious routes. There's a marked sense of purpose, and a great deal of money is being spent – those full-page advertisements in London and New York papers; journalists ferried from London to Enugu; costly sets produced of long-playing records – eight hours of them – of the conference of Nigerian military leaders at Aburi in Ghana. There are four spanking-new French helicopters for top-level communication; Colonel Ojukwu uses them constantly.

He's a burly, bearded figure, usually in informal green uniform. He's thirty-three and from a wealthy Eastern family, with an Oxford and Sandhurst background. He puts his position firmly, clearly and fluently. Easterners, he contends, cannot now live and work outside their region, so how can they equitably contribute to the cost of running the rest of the country? This is his immediate argument; but he goes far deeper into what he considers to be the facts of Nigerian political life, blaming the situation on what he believes to be the Northern dream of perpetual domination of the country in which the East is seen as an obstacle. Equally, it might be said, and Colonel Ojukwu knows this well, that the Northerners fear the Ibos of the East because of their superior technical skills and literacy and their spreading influence. And there are other tribes in the East, itself, who feel the same way. The East, in fact, has its own quite serious minority problem, but, at the moment, the Enugu leaders are careful to speak of Easterners as a whole.

Colonel Ojukwu also believes firmly that preparations are being made for war against him, but the confrontation – if it comes – may be precipitated by the more prosaic workings of Government finances. He says that the East must control its own resources. Such action, whatever he may be planning, would, he feels, form a sufficiently drastic confrontation to compel the Federal authorities to act. If attacked, he says, either physically or by naval blockade – and the main Eastern port is vulnerable – the East would then – but only then – consider secession. But he's open to suggestions for outside arbitration.

If it came to force, the Easterners could probably put up a good fight, despite the warrior traditions of the North. It would certainly be a popular struggle in the Easterners' present frame of mind, because aspiring army recruits besiege the depots daily and restraint is becoming more and more of a problem. The public here is very edgy indeed. Colonel Ojukwu is said to work far into the night – a man of ability and dedication – and he leaves the impression that, whatever happens, he will not be the first to give way.

Paris: The Student Revolt

KENNETH MATTHEWS   15 JUNE 1968

The year saw violent unrest among students all over the world, but particularly in Paris. There, the rioting students, at first supported by the workers, almost succeeded in bringing down the Government, but the workers withdrew their support. The students had taken over the Sorbonne and it was there that Kenneth Matthews had been talking and listening to them.

The tourists who go to the Sorbonne to stare at the students in unorthodox residence there have certainly picked on the most extraordinary sight of modern Paris. White and black, whole and bandaged, boys like girls and girls like boys, and some so covered in tangled hair that they might be reversing the process of evolution, they seem to have only their youth in common. And when they pour out of their lair for a raid into the night streets, they're indistinguishable from hooligans, leaving a trail of burnt cars, uprooted trees and broken windows behind them.

But they're intellectuals, or should be – reasoning creatures, the élite of the society of the future. Is it possible that they're a message for the age, obscured by the smoke of their fire-raising and the police tear-gas bomb? A Paris publisher is bringing out a book of fifteen hundred slogans collected from the scrawlings on the walls of the Sorbonne, though it would be an ingenious brain which could distil a coherent philosophy from such a wild mixture of the screams of competing revolutionaries.

And yet, standing in one of their serious discussion groups, listening to these young people talking – and heavens how they talk – I've been struck by the way in which certain words crop up again and again, as if they provided the key to the whole situation. Vogue words or living ideas? It's hard to judge. There's the word – I'll give it first in French – *décloisonnement*. It's not in the dictionary. It can be translated *departitioning*, and it means breaking down the partitions in society. Pressed to illustrate it by an example, they'll tell you that in factories and offices the workers in one grade never speak to those in another. They want to open up new channels of communication between people. They've tried quite hard to make common cause with the strikers recently, but after a brief flirtation they've been snubbed. The Communists, too, have snubbed them, jealous of anyone who steals their revolutionary thunder. So the way of *departitioning* has proved rather stormy and unrewarding so far. Another favourite word is *contestation*. I've been told about six times that it won't translate into English. The nearest try seems to be *questioning*. The students distinguish between *inward* and *outward questioning*. The *inward* sort was not hard to understand and made me think of Socrates: 'The unexamined life is not worth living'. But when I asked for an example of the *outward* sort, a very earnest young woman in trousers and thick glasses told me: 'Well, we go into a theatre, interrupt a play, and invite the actors and audience to question what they're doing.' I could see that such interventions might not always be received in the spirit in which they were offered. However, the politicians have taken notice of the word. A Gaullist spokesman told us: 'Government can't be a state of perpetual questioning.'

The students, the more serious of them at any rate, accept this sort of criticism, and talk a lot about the need for *creating*. There's a vulgar English sense of this word in which one might say that the students have been *creating* more than somewhat already. But they mean by *creating* making an imaginative effort to get the social order out of its rut and helping the brave new world emerge.

More of them would probably be willing to express regret for the recent riotings, but for the unhappy proof it's provided that violence gets things done. They've seen senior professors, university administrators, leading educationalists lining up in the newspapers and on the platforms to explain how they've long been conscious of the need for university reform, and in some cases how their proposals for reform have been sidetracked and neglected. And one student is actually a candidate in the coming elections on the Government side. He says: 'It's more difficult to be a reformer than a revolutionary.'

Well, an older French revolution called for 'liberty, equality, fraternity'. I can't quite see a new one taking up the cry of 'departitioning, questioning, creating'. But at least these watchwords provide a welcome alternative to the smashing, burning, and fighting, of which we've seen so much in Paris in the last few weeks.

Czechoslovak Freedom (1)
ROBERT ELPHICK   31 AUGUST 1968

At the beginning of the year, Mr Dubček had taken over the Party leadership in Czechoslovakia and he brought to the country something approaching democracy. He carried through a series of reforms which gave liberty to the Press and Radio, and freedom of speech and movement to the people. The Russians feared that the movement might spread to the other satellites, but for a time it seemed that they did not know how to react. Then, on 20 August, together with contingents from other East European countries, Russian troops swept into Czechoslovakia, arrested her leaders, took them to Moscow, and then returned them to Czechoslovakia. Robert Elphick, in Prague, took up the story from there in the following two despatches.

As the days go by, the harsh realities of what the Russians intend for Czechoslovakia become more and more apparent. The leaders have returned from Moscow, it's true; they have survived those incredible negotiations, if one can call them that, at the point of Russian bayonets. And they are home again. But it's becoming more and more obvious that they are, nonetheless, hardly better than prisoners of the Russians, although they may speak in the name of the people from Prague Castle.

Effective rule in Czechoslovakia is coming nowadays by dictation from Moscow. And the tactics of the legally elected representatives of the people, like President Svoboda, Mr Dubček, Mr Černik and Mr Smrkovsky, are to save what can be saved of the freedom since January and bide their time for better days. But for now there seems no alternative but to accept the Kremlin's orders, backed up as they are by an army of some six hundred and fifty thousand men with modern weapons, all carefully planned and selected to outgun anything the Czechoslovak allies had.

Not that the Czechoslovaks would have had any chance at all if they had been ordered to fight. The occupation was in fact a coup, carried out in the first instance by the local manager of the Soviet airline, Aeroflot, who turned up at Prague airport just after dusk on that black Tuesday, 20 August, with forty-five plainclothes men and a Russian serving officer. They seized the control tower and the main buildings. And after that it was a relatively simple matter to guide in the huge transports, which brought in the paratroopers who were the first into Prague, while the heavier stuff was lumbering in from the frontier.

The sheer courage of the Czechoslovak people as a whole and the integrity of the leaders faced with such overwhelming force can only be admired, particularly if, like me, you happened to have been watching it all at close quarters. The disciplined defiance of the population as a whole; the activities of the secret-radio broadcasters; the journalists who went underground and turned out the free newspapers, which just made the Russians occupying their ordinary premises look ridiculous, were and are beyond praise. They enabled the voice of an entire people to be heard in what the Kremlin had hoped would have been a private piece of bullying; and, in the end, they won back the leaders they wanted and prevented the Russians from simply imposing a puppet régime.

But the question must now be put: how much power does the Dubček – Svoboda Government actually have? It's already pretty obvious that the Russians are not giving them any room for manoeuvre at all, despite the statement in the Moscow Agreement about non-interference. They are ruthlessly putting on the pressure to get them to implement the Russian demands; stop that dangerous freedom of speech; conform to Moscow's ways; reinstate the iron curtain.

The brief Prague spring and summer have already turned to deep winter. Many of the more talented Czechoslovaks that I've known are getting out of the country while the going is still good, aided and abetted by the Government itself, who evidently want to keep a nucleus of reliable people out of harm's way until better times come round.

As of now, the Russians seem determined to root out anything that they think smacks of counter-revolution. They've already as good as wrecked the premises of the Writers' Union, when their patrols went in to look, apparently, for subversive literature. They've also destroyed the million-book card index of the National Library, and nobody can quite explain that. They're still trying to stifle discussion by ordering Mr Dubček to bring the censors back, and they're importing, according to reliable accounts, some one thousand KGB men to sit in at all the ministries to make sure that everything is run Moscow's way.

The lights are going out in Czechoslovakia, but the picture is not entirely dark. If there's hope for the future, it's in the spirit of the leaders and the unity of the people against the invaders. Getting them out is now the mainspring of everyone's thoughts, even of some of the people who had thought to benefit from Russian support, but who've been appalled at the form it's taken.

Strangely enough one of Mr Dubček's strengths – perhaps the only one – is that he is, after all, a Communist, with a party at hand well-versed in conspiratorial action. The Party underground is already working well in the full knowledge that it has the support, not only of every one at home, but of pretty well every Communist Party in Western Europe. The message from the top is to call for patience, dignity, a boycott of the invader. Truth shall prevail, but until that day comes, the best the leaders can offer is to say 'we are with you; be with us'.

Czechoslovak Freedom (2)

ROBERT ELPHICK   3 SEPTEMBER 1968

The most poignant scene in Prague these days is played out daily round the big equestrian monument of the Saint King of Bohemia – our Good King Wenceslas. Since the beginning of the invasion it's been the focus for protests, hung with black flags and the Czecho-slovak national tricolour. But now it's been scrubbed clean of all the posters and slogans telling the Russians to go home, and it's become something like a national shrine – a shrine, moreover, which isn't kept up by the Government but by the efforts of the ordinary people.

Fresh flowers appear daily at the foot of the statue, and the national flag and the black flag of mourning get carried in informal relays by young people, old people, long-haired beatniks in jeans, and spruce young soldiers. They've been keeping it up for days now, sorrowing for the people who were killed in the early days of the invasion, and also for Czechoslovakia's lost independence.

By contrast, the most macabre of my experiences has been, perhaps, to watch a full-scale Soviet concert party entertaining the troops with concertinas, balalaika music and those exuberant Russ-ian dances. It was something like a celebration at a wake.

It's now a fortnight, though, since the armadas of tanks poured across the country to strangle Czechoslovakia's attempt to mix communism with democracy, and it's quite clear that the Russians grossly miscalculated the temper of the people here in believing that they had only to act decisively to destroy Mr Dubček's position. They obviously placed high hopes on the veteran President, Gen-eral Svoboda, as possibly providing a respectable head of a puppet regime. But the old President was having none of that, and it's reliably reported he threatened not only to resign, but to commit suicide, unless Mr Dubček and the other leaders were freed and restored to their positions.

Not that this – a gain though it is against the possibility of widespread bloodshed – is making much difference to the general Soviet tactics of putting Czechoslovakia back into a rigid strait-jacket. No more dreams of independence within the Communist movement; no more thoughts of holidays abroad or contacts with Western Europe, of freedom or democracy at home, or even better pay, except by leave of the masters of the Kremlin.

What's been published of the dictated Moscow settlement is already onerous enough, and nobody believes that there are not any secret clauses. It's clear, for instance, that there's no fixed date for withdrawal. It's believed they've also insisted on stopping all tour-ism, and closing the frontier with Western Germany altogether.

They've also warned the Cabinet that any signs of unrest will be taken as proof of the Government's incapacity to rule, and that any attempts to resist the invading forces will be ruthlessly suppressed.

Although the Russians are now withdrawing troops from some of the more conspicuous places in Prague and elsewhere, nothing can conceal the fact that their agents are taking over, as rapidly as possible, all the key posts in public life. The calculation is evidently that, having failed to push Mr Dubček and his colleagues out of office, they'll make them do their work for them, in the expectation that as they take the unpopular measures they're told to do, they'll lose all credibility with the public.

The Russians have already forced the Government to bring the censors back. They've also forced changes in the Ministry of the Interior, literally over the dead body of one of the deputy Ministers, who's reported to have committed suicide rather than hand his files over to the KGB.

The best that Mr Dubček and his colleagues can do now is perhaps to mitigate the consequences of Russian domination, and wait for better times. Initially, at least, they'll be helped by the massive feeling of national solidarity that the arrival of the foreign troops has engendered, and also by the natural patience of a people to whom foreign invasion is only too familiar.

Eisenhower

GERALD PRIESTLAND   29 MARCH 1969

Dwight D. Eisenhower had died on 28 March and Gerry Priestland, who had served in Washington during the Eisenhower years, looked back on them.

Looked at from the outside, the Eisenhower era might seem to have been a rather grim period: starting with the Cold War, John Foster Dulles and McCarthyism, and ending with the humiliations of the U-2 incident, the collapse of the Paris Summit, and the first Russian sputnik. Wasn't it the reaction against all this that swept John F. Kennedy to power? Yet today, many Americans look back on it all with nostalgia. Indeed, that's one of the things that brought success to Richard Nixon in 1968; the voters recalled that in the good old days of the Eisenhower/Nixon administration there had been no burning ghettos, rioting colleges or yawning generation gap, though, in fact, some visitors used to complain that the scene was rather dull.

One has to recall the context. America had had almost ten solid years of war and wartime controls. Although Eisenhower hardly solved the Korean problem, for it's with us still today, he did at least end the fighting and disperse the atmosphere of permanent mobilisation. His view of the Presidency was a somewhat old-fashioned one with a touch of constitutional monarchy about it, for wherever he went people seemed to like Ike. That government was best to him which governed least. Congress should be left to pass laws without having its arm twisted; the states should take care of their own problems; the White House should run the federal machinery and look after foreign relations. Most of the President's intimate friends were businessmen. He believed they knew better than Government what was good for them. His contribution to the economy was to balance the budget.

Abroad, it was his ambition to establish a permanent peace between the great powers, under which the smaller nations would no longer be used as pawns in a clash of ideologies. Surely his own sincerity and goodwill could achieve such a peace, if only he could meet the Communist leaders face to face.

Alas, none of it was so simple. The complexities and deviousness of the party system at home and the balance of power abroad frustrated his dreams, forcing him to use a great deal more initiative and cunning than he had expected. He was defeated in the Congress, out-manoeuvred at the Summit, and laughed at on the golf course. And yet he never lost his popularity with ordinary folk. One has only to compare his reign with that of Lyndon Johnson, a President who was far more active, yet ended up so disliked that he scarcely dared to appear in public.

Conditions, of course, have changed and they may change once more. Richard Nixon seems to believe that the public wants a President who does less but does it more effectively. Today, as in 1952, the American people are in the mood for a rest from excitement. Now, as then, people want time to think.

Throughout the Eisenhower era there was a steady undercurrent of concern about the nation's morals and goals – an undercurrent that rose clamorously to the surface when the Russians launched their Sputnik, destroying for ever the assumption that the United States was technically unbeatable, as well as morally right. And it was the President himself, the five-star general, who expressed the fear that the Pentagon and the defence industries between them – the military-industrial complex – were threatening to dominate government.

The era ended with doubt, uneasiness and impatience over the failure of the economy to expand. John F. Kennedy promised to get the country moving again. But the fact was that at the start of Eisenhower's Presidency Americans didn't want to move; they wanted to sit in front of their television with a pack of cold beer and take things easy for a bit. Yes, unemployment was high and the Negroes still down-trodden, but one could look in vain for the American Left, or for anything like Britain's 'Ban the Bomb' movement. College youth was more concerned with passing exams and winning football games. It was a curiously sterile oasis culturally, too, though for the average middle-class American an oasis furnished with a swimming pool, a second car and a deep freeze.

Perhaps America was gathering its strength for the next great leap forward; perhaps it's weary again today and remembers wistfully the President who relaxed, like his people, and didn't spend all his time at the crisis centre in the White House basement.

A French View of England

DAVID WILLEY   20 JUNE 1969

After years of frustration, there were renewed hopes that Britain might enter Europe, with the corollary of Europe's entry into Britain. How would they find it? David Willey examined the mind of a young French housewife who had recently married an Englishman.

Sophie, a French housewife, arrived in Britain for the first time in her life just over a year ago. Like most of her compatriots, she came here with a mental baggage of preconception and prejudice that perhaps does less than justice to those who believe in the possibilities of a United Europe.

Ask any Frenchman or woman, and the words will roll off the tongue: 'Britain, land of pubs, fog and freedom, home of the British arch-vice, hypocrisy, land of Marks and Spencer, free love, tepid beer, cheap cashmere sweaters, the King's Road, the pot smoker's paradise and the Changing of the Guard.'.

But, to come back to Sophie, her first impressions on arriving at Victoria were of cultural shock at the foreign-ness of a country that is geographically so close to France. Paris is, after all, nearer to London than it is to Marseilles.

The scars of the industrial revolution and modern utopia, jerry-building of the nineteenth and twentieth centuries, combined with a healthy disregard for town-planning, the jungle of the road system, make London, for all its famous views and hidden charms, a poor runner-up to Paris in aesthetic terms. The dazzling clean-up of the monuments and streets of Paris during the past ten years makes London look shabby in comparison, despite the brave start on Trafalgar Square, Whitehall and St Paul's Cathedral.

Sophie gives full marks, however, to London's open spaces and parks, where you can walk, run and lie down on the grass, without some officious attendant telling you to keep to the paths. It's all part of the radical difference in the French and English attitudes to nature and sport.

Sophie also likes playing tennis for five shillings an hour, instead of three pounds ten, which is what it costs in Paris where, incredibly, tennis is still a snob pastime.

If you come to Britain to live, instead of just visiting the country like the hordes of European students who now cross the Channel every year to learn English, or like the astonishing numbers of French housewives who found it cheaper to come and do their shopping over here, until the currency clamp down, you become aware, Sophie's found, of enormous variations in the quality and style of life in France and in Britain. Of course food is the obvious one. The pleasures of French cooking are too well known for me to dwell on, but Sophie got quite a kick out of reading that a senior inspector of a well-known French hotel and restaurant guide that also covers several foreign countries has come incognito to Britain to see if we're now worthy of having a guide of our own.

If you tell Sophie that eating out in England has improved out of all recognition in the past ten years, she'll tell you wryly that she's glad not to have visited us at that time. Sophie does find food prices in Britain remarkably low, but points out that we probably lose some of this advantage by higher taxation of wages and salaries than in France. In quality and variety, she finds food standards also generally low in comparison. Of course, the taste-buds suffer in the country that's the world's biggest food importer. France is practically self-sufficient in food production, and the joy of shopping in a French market is one that cannot just be reproduced here, Sophie says, and she wonders why those markets we do have don't open on Sunday mornings. She finds the Sunday opening laws in Britain defy common sense. Why does a nation of shopkeepers not arrange opening hours to coincide with the times when people are free to shop; and that means after five-thirty at night as well?

Sophie finds most women's clothes in Britain an odd mixture of the Carnaby Street way-out and the provincial department-store style; this is a matter of very personal taste which I can't comment on, apart from remarking that French women's clothes do tend to be chic. But Sophie does like English woollens and tweeds and their prices.

She found looking for somewhere pleasant to live in London a difficult experience. Although rents and property prices tend to be lower than in Paris, at least in the central areas, she was shocked at finding rooms fit for dwarfs; the lack of efficient central heating systems, and the poverty of the average English bathroom fittings – few bidets or mixer taps. It's nice to know that the French also have their English plumbing jokes.

So, having settled in and absorbed the immediate strangeness of Britain, what does Sophie feel about the people who aspire to become part of the continent to which they geographically belong, but historically have remained aloof from. She's pleasantly surprised in her everyday contacts with officialdom, at the courtesy shown to a foreigner, and the time people take to explain things to her. On the whole, British bureaucracy seems slightly less weighted down with paper than the French variety. And the only impatience she's experienced was with a testy immigration officer at London Airport. She has nothing but praise for the British police – their politeness and lack of sinister overtones in comparison with the French Gendarmerie and CRS.

The British Welfare State in its present form, Sophie feels, is cheapening the quality of life, not enhancing it. French social security costs more, both to the employer and to the worker, than in Britain, and the benefits do not try to be all-embracing. You recover eighty or ninety per cent of basic medical costs in France from the State. But the doctor/patient relationship is still that of the fee-payer, which prevents the medical mass-production line as in most hard-pressed British doctor's practices. And there's still provision for those who cannot afford even a modest personal contribution for their doctor's services.

Sophie believes also that the British personal taxation system discourages hard work and initiative and is partly responsible for Britain's current economic troubles. Personal taxation is lower in the Common Market countries, while a general value added sales tax is being standardised throughout the European Community to tax consumption rather than wages. She finds in general that people in Britain work less hard, for shorter hours, for less pay and shorter holidays than in France.

How well do we understand our continental neighbours? Sophie is surprised at the renewed interest in the press and the general knowledge about what goes on in Europe, but she feels that the British press and television coverage of last year's dramatic student troubles and workers' strikes in France bordered on the hysterical. It was not exactly 'The French Revolution 1968,' as one television programme described it. And she feels that it's not understood enough that the French Government's main preoccupation at the moment is with the future of France, not whether or not Britain should join the Common Market.

In brief, Sophie is convinced of our need for closer relations with the Continent to which we are almost attached. But she fears that British people must accomplish an important psychological change in order to make anything meaningful out of the European idea. Traditionally, historically, geographically, linguistically, we are the odd-man-out in Europe, and it'll require more than a channel tunnel to change the present state of relations.

The story is told of a visit by Montesquieu to the Duke of Marlborough at Blenheim. The French writer, after going on for an hour in English about the British political system, was stopped by the Duke, who said he regretted he could not understand his French. It's to be hoped that the next Common Market dialogue with Paris is going to be more fruitful.

The Battlefields of Vietnam
ANTHONY LAWRENCE 23 MAY 1970

*The first American soldiers had arrived in South Vietnam in 1954
and in 1970 they were still fighting there. Tony Lawrence, Far East
Correspondent, had covered the war almost from the beginning,
frequently visiting the battlefield, from where he sent this report.*

From time to time, reports come out of South Vietnam suggesting
that the morale of the American troops there is sinking. And
discussion of this will grow as the American Army takes in more
young men from the age-groups that have been demonstrating on
University campuses, smoking pot and rejecting today's American
society.

Soldiers' morale is difficult to analyse, especially here in Vietnam. Wars are different now. The old vocabulary: words like
bravery, discipline, morale, doesn't meet the problem. In the Vietnam war you mostly don't need brave men; you need efficient ones
able to handle highly-sophisticated instruments of transport and
death. And the standard length of service in Vietnam is one year. For
most of the four hundred thousand Americans still out here, the
best morale builder of all is that you can actually count the days to
going home.

But there are tremendous contrasts. Many of the soldiers have an
easy time, with their nightly cinemas, good food and modern
plumbing. Many are better off than they would be in the States.

But when you leave the big bases and maintenance areas and get
out into the wilds, then it's different. There you meet the real
soldiers: the men of the infantry, and the air cavalry units. There are
about eighty thousand men – less than a fifth of the total US army in
Vietnam – who really meet the enemy close up: killing and getting
killed. They're young, mostly drafted men, graduates, college drop-
outs, a large proportion of Negroes. Their nickname is 'grunts',
from the way the soldier grunts as he shoulders his heavy pack.
They spend most of their time out in the wild forest near the
frontiers, where the enemy is always infiltrating. They may be out
for as long as a whole month at a time. And when they return it's not
to a camp with cinema shows and hot showers, but to a so-called
fire-base with gun-pits and holes in the ground to sleep in. And
their chance of getting killed or wounded is very high.

That's the sector where morale is under pressure. It's such a chancy business this patrolling. You can go for months and meet nothing, and then three times in one week you meet some awful ambush or firefight. The man next to you goes down yelling with a leg blown off; the platoon commander is bleeding to death against a tree. It's over in fifteen minutes, but it's sheer nightmare; and it may come again tomorrow night.

When you get back from all that, the re-enlistment sergeant is waiting for a little chat. He can get you out of all that, he says, if you're ready to sign on for a longer spell in the army: get you a cushier job.

In this infantryman's life, the great thing is to come safe home – to keep your arse covered, as the soldiers call it. There's a vast gap between, on the one side, the junior officers, NCOs and men, and on the other, the higher ranks, the career officers, the so-called 'lifers'. It's the 'lifers' who believe in conventional discipline. But the men who stay out in the forests – beating the bush, as they call it – they're all, including lieutenants, on Christian name terms and no formality, except that everyone does what he has to do.

'I never thought about morale,' said one young lieutenant. 'The life certainly changes you a lot. Luxury, to me, is staying in a forest clearing for one whole afternoon without having to move on. A drink from a cold stream's a gift from heaven. A bed to sleep on – unimaginable.'

What about pot-smoking? Platoon commanders confirmed to me that a lot goes on. But there'd be big trouble if some idiot smoked just before going on patrol. It brings on enormous thirst and for a while dulls perception, which is fatal.

Most of the young men I spoke to thought the army was badly run and the war a great mess. But that's not bad morale; they wouldn't run away. It's the case of old soldiers doing what can't be got out of, doing their duty.

And again, in the old tradition, their main contempt is for the overweight sergeants back at the base, the generals' talk of kill ratios. Their only respect is for each other and for the enemy who kills and dies like they do, along the forest trails. And they know, too, that when they get back to the States, there's no one to talk to about what they've been through; no one who wants to listen.

Cats and Ruins

DANIEL COUNIHAN   27 JUNE 1970

Not all contributions to the programme were directly linked with the news – certainly not this one from Dan Counihan, a member of the BBC's diplomatic staff based in London.

When I used to live in Rome rather a long time ago, one of the things that gave me pleasure was an enormous antique marble foot, which for several centuries has half blocked one of the narrower streets. I looked for it when I went back earlier this year, but vainly, because memory was dim, until I was led to it by a cat and five kittens. The black-and-white mother cat at the head of her prim procession reminded me of a nun conducting a crocodile of school-children, and the image was sustained when I caught up with them in a dark side-turning. They were sitting on the stone foot – the cat on top, and the kittens squatting facing her, one on each toe, trying to look attentive, as if in class. Now, in case any stomachs are starting to heave at the possible prospect of a meal of cat whimsy, let me say at once that though I like cats, I can take them or leave them alone, and I wasn't seeing this as some kind of Beatrix Potter situation. I did let my imagination run a bit in that very gloomy alley, but what I fancied was that if those kittens were being taught anything, it was probably something pretty sinister. 'Witchcraft' was the word that crossed my mind.

However, to be quite fair, I found out afterwards that it might have been a religious lesson; for it seems the marble foot is believed by some to be all that remains of a colossal statue of the Egyptian goddess, Isis, whose cult was quite popular among the Romans, and, of course, cats were a good deal mixed up with it. In fact, the temple of Isis in Rome was somewhere in the general area in which the foot still stands, and the only other remnant of it that I know about – though there may be others – is a stone cat – a rather weather-worn tabby – who at some time over the years has succeeded in getting herself built into the wall of the Grazioli Palace.

Or perhaps the lesson was just plain classical studies. I started to pay rather more attention to the cats of Rome after I'd seen it, and I did notice that they are crazy about classical sites. For instance, not very far from the stone foot is the celebrated Pantheon; and clearly, the cats who swarm around it think it was built specially for them.

I've seen them there under arches, on steps, sleeping, taking the sun, brooding with dignity, making love, or simply lurking. I and a friend once counted fifty of them there between us – no duplicates and kittens included – in under an hour.

Now it could be that it isn't love of classical sites that sends the cats swarming to the Pantheon. I've heard it snidely suggested that they go there because people give them food and because there are lots of pigeons around. People *do* give them food, of course. There are a number of ladies – Italians and some resident foreigners – who bring regular daily supplies, and a butcher's shop just over the way does very well out of it. They get fish, too, though there isn't a fish shop anywhere very near there, so far as I know. But there must have been cats at the Pantheon before people started taking them food; one hardly imagines that the food was taken first in the hope of attracting cats. And as for pigeons, there are plenty of those at St Peter's, but I've hardly ever seen a cat there. I have heard an Italian woman muttering 'Poor Christians!', as she fed the Pantheon cats, but the evidence is that the Roman cat is determinedly pagan. Hardly a cat at Santa Maria Maggiore, but cats behind every broken column in the Forum and in the ruins of the temples and palaces. One of their favourite places is Trajan's Market, especially the part where, according to tradition, fish used to be kept for sale alive in huge tanks – which, if one continues to be fanciful, might be seen as a striking instance of feline folk memory.

Perhaps the biggest classical cattery of all in Rome is the tomb of Augustus which, if you know the city, you may remember as the big, round, dingy brick affair that looks as if it might have been an Imperial gasometer. It's a gloomy, secret place, its vaults shut off by a rusting iron gate, and made uninviting by the muddy path which surrounds it. The ashes of the emperors and their relations have gone long since, though an urn which held some of them turned up many years ago in a house where it had been used for generations to soak dirty washing. Few tourists spend long there, and the only ardent visitors are the ladies with food for the cats. It was one of these ladies, kind but fey, who told me she thought the souls of the emperors had entered into the cats, who were now in complete command. 'Wait a minute,' she said, 'and I'll show you the Emperor Augustus himself.' Presently a very large, grey Tom made a stately progress from the dark interior, escorted – at least, that's how it looked – by four or five other tough males like a praetorian guard. Lesser cats gave him uninterrupted first sniff at the food that had been laid out. I don't think he was Augustus. He might have been Nero.

The Funny Side of Espionage: Stealing a Missile

IAN McDOUGALL   26 SEPTEMBER 1970

In West Germany the more hilarious side of espionage and the international arms race was illustrated at a trial in Düsseldorf, where the presiding judge had difficulty in getting spectators to control their mirth. Ian McDougall was there.

Those on trial were three men in early middle-age: an architect, a locksmith and a former German Air Force Staff Sergeant, who had piloted American-built *Starfighters*, the main West German combat plane. They were charged with attempted high treason, theft, and breach of confidence. Behind these accusations, on which the court has not yet passed judgement, lies a story that might not only have supplied the script for one of the old Ealing Studio comedies, but also throws a disturbing light on NATO security. The allegation is that these three men stole a *Sidewinder* rocket missile from a NATO air base in southern Germany, and shipped it to Moscow, together with secret aircraft navigation instruments. They're also said to have planned to steal a *Starfighter*.

According to the evidence produced in court, the accused were recruited by Soviet agents in Cologne, and were paid altogether the equivalent of some thirteen thousand pounds for their services. It should perhaps be pointed out that this took place three years ago, at a time when the Russians were presumably more interested in *Sidewinders* and *Starfighters* than they would be today. From then onwards the episode slides rapidly into farce. The three men began their exploit by hiring two professional underworld cracksmen to break into the NATO air base. These two promptly disappeared, and later blabbed out their part of the story in their cups. Then the locksmith concealed himself in the boot of the staff sergeant's car, and having been driven thus into the air base, broke open various

118

doors and removed the secret navigational equipment. This was taken by the third man, the architect, to Moscow by air in his personal luggage. He says that in Moscow he was asked to get hold of a *Hawk*, a *Nike*, or a *Hercules* rocket, if possible all three. At first he refused, but under pressure agreed to steal something 'a little smaller', to wit a *Sidewinder*. So, back to the air base in southern Germany, where his two comrades this time got in by the simple expedient of climbing the outer fence.

Two hours later they duly returned, staggering under the weight of a genuine *Sidewinder*, which is nine feet long and weighs one-and-a-half hundredweight. It was too long to fit into their car, so they broke the rear window and let the pointed end of the rocket stick out behind. They then travelled several hundred miles across country to Krefeld in north-west Germany. Nobody on their route took the slightest notice of the *Sidewinder*, a fact which the defence attributed to their precaution of attaching a red flag to the protruding end of the rocket so as to comply conscientiously with traffic regulations. Throughout the long journey, as it later emerged, the *Sidewinder* had been fully primed, ready for instant detonation. It was later taken to pieces in a garage and packed in a cabin trunk and in a wooden case specially commissioned from a carpenter. At the airport, the architect and the locksmith were courteously advised by an official of the national airline, *Lufthansa*, that it would be cheaper to send their excess luggage to Moscow by air freight. Before agreeing to this the two travellers asked if this meant they'd have to open the cases? 'No,' replied the helpful official, and I quote from the trial evidence, 'No, we are interested only in what comes into the country, not in what goes out. Any customs duty will have to be paid in Moscow.'

It appears that even the Soviet intelligence services at the other end were flabbergasted by these proceedings, being astonished, as one of the accused put it, not only that the *Sidewinder* had actually arrived, but that it had arrived in quite this fashion. Still, the Russians paid up as promised.

As the trial continued, and as it became clear that the gravity due to the process of law was being somewhat impaired by the spectators' hilarity, the presiding judge was moved to observe that there must be something seriously amiss with the supervision of West German defence establishments. It seemed a fair comment.

Visit to Haiti

CHARLES WHEELER   24 APRIL 1971

Reports that the sinister and ruthless President Duvalier, the Haitian dictator known to his people as 'Papa Doc', was gravely ill sent a flood of correspondents to the capital, Port-au-Prince. Charles Wheeler, based in Washington, was one of them.

Monsieur Aubelin Jolicoeur is a lithe little man in a blindingly white suit and pointed black shoes, who welcomes lady tourists to Haiti's International Airport and promises to dance with them later that evening. He's employed by the Government Tourist Office; writes a column called 'Twenty-four Hours' in the Government newspaper; takes pride in his resemblance to a character in Graham Greene's *The Comedians*; and for years has supplied foreign reporters with the Duvalier view of Haitian affairs.

Monsieur Jolicoeur has had a busy week. Not only has there been a revival of tourism, but the place has swarmed with foreign reporters, attracted to Haiti by the preposterous notion that the disappearance from public view of the leader of the nation signified something more than, in Monsieur Jolicoeur's words, 'a very minor indisposition brought on by overwork in selfless devotion to the welfare of the people'.

Fifteen minutes after that assurance – or thereabouts – the President was dead and we sought out Monsieur Jolicoeur next morning with some curiosity, knowing him to be close to the Duvalier family and expecting to find him in a state of shock, or at least depression. But not at all. Every reporter's friend was as sprightly as ever. 'As I told you last night,' he said, 'our leader has sacrificed himself.' And with a wave of his mahogany walking stick, Monsieur Jolicoeur danced off to a previous engagement.

In the immediate aftermath of Haiti's loss, Monsieur Jolicoeur is not alone in his resilience. As far as a foreigner can tell, the disappearance from the scene of the dictator who, in fourteen years of power, is said to have ordered the execution of thousands of real or supposed opponents, to have wiped out whole families – in some cases, so it's whispered, by crucifixion – as far as one can tell, his death has brought his people neither joy, nor a feeling of release, nor sorrow, nor even visible curiosity. Apart from one brief demonstration of support for the son and heir, crudely stage-managed by the secret police and attended by perhaps a hundred and fifty people, there has been no public reaction whatever. On the day of the announcement it might have been the President of Outer Mongolia who had died.

One of the few Haitians I've met who has shown interest in the subject has suggested a reason for the general calm. Most people, he asserts, disbelieve the regime on principle, and are waiting until they themselves, or trusted friends, have identified the body. It just might be, he says, an elaborate plot intended to encourage dissidents to reveal themselves – with a climactic ending, a national miracle in which the Doctor will rise from his bed to rule with redoubled ferocity.

Taken literally, the suggestion is completely far-fetched of course, but Haitians do have every reason to be prudent. At the Palace, nothing much has changed. A reshuffle of posts and people has left all the Doctor's principal henchmen in high positions, and their instruments of power, the police, the army, the secret police and the courts, are intact. Indeed, as if to underline the point that the young Jean-Claude will continue his father's life work, the secret police is displaying itself and playing a major part in all the celebrations. The appearance in public of a few hundred members of Duvalier's army of killers, the Tontons Macoutes, is intriguing, at least to a foreigner who has never been able to identify a Tonton Macoute before. They come in every imaginable shape and size, from near midgets to giants, and collectively they lounge about in clusters at the West Gate of the Palace. They look such thugs that it's impossible to believe that this force has been able all these years to mingle unrecognised with the general public. Or could it be that the Commander of this dreadful band, said to number from fifteen to twenty thousand men, has chosen to expose his paramount uglies as a living warning. It could.

So far we have caught only a glimpse of Duvalier Junior – Jean-Claude – the newly proclaimed President for life. He is said to be twenty, but nobody seems to know. From a distance of five hundred yards, or from the Palace pavement gutter – the pavement itself is out of bounds – to the Palace steps, he looks discomfitingly artificial, like an overinflated disposable toy. He is said to lack not only the usual qualifications for office, like experience and a reasonable education, but also to lack certain essential characteristics, like cunning and inborn viciousness. It might be supposed that Jean-Claude will develop in the direction which his father would have wished, but Papa Doc to the end detested the idea of sharing his power and he neglected to train the boy.

One has to pity Jean-Claude, for he has inherited not a palace, but a great gleaming cesspool. Surrounded, as he is, by his father's old associates, he will be powerless to change this country and yet change is bound to come. Haiti's new, and probably reluctant, young dictator will be lucky to survive.

Soviet Jews in Israel
MICHAEL ELKINS   14 DECEMBER 1971

One of the recurrent themes over the past twenty-five years has been that of Soviet Jews wishing to emigrate to Israel. From Jerusalem, Mike Elkins described how they got there.

On a wind-swept plateau among the Judaean hills, about two miles north of Jerusalem, there is a cluster of small houses – box-like, simple, their austerity relieved only by the exotic rose-veined Jerusalem stone of which they are built. This is the immigrant absorption centre called *Mevaseret Zion* – the 'Harbingers of Zion'.

The place is aptly named, for among the newcomers living there are some of those who came forward as 'Harbingers of Zion' in Moscow, in Riga, in Leningrad, and in the distant villages of Soviet Georgia, declaring the primacy of their Jewish identity and demanding of the rulers in the Kremlin that they be allowed, as Jews, to go home – *home* being Israel.

This rising of Russian Jewry began for most of them with the outbreak of the Arab–Israeli war of June, 1967. One of the immigrants at Mevaseret Zion is Yefim Sevela, who was one of Russia's most successful film writers until he came to Israel three months ago, with his actress wife and their young daughter. Mr Sevela's English is fragmented and hesitant and, withal, marvellously articulate. And when I asked him why he had come and why now, his answer encapsulated the mystique that moves the Jews of Russia. What Mr Sevela said was so illuminating and so crucial to an understanding of the Russian Jews, that I give it to you now exactly as I noted it down. 'When the Six Day War start,' Mr Sevela said, 'the Russians tell us on radio, in newspaper: "Israel is beaten on first day, is ended". This is tragedy, and in this tragedy every Russian Jew is only Jew. Then in afternoon, by BBC, we learn of victory. Half day black tragedy, other half day – greatest joy. From this day, all Jewry in Russia stands Jewish; so I also. I can no more in Russia. I am Jew.' Thus Mr Sevela.

Out of this discovery, thousands of Russian Jews have come to the Jewish State. One may not report accurate statistics from Israel, but foreign sources have put the figure this year alone at ten to twelve thousand, and this estimate is low. For in November and thus far in December, the number of Russian Jews brought in the planes from Vienna is far greater than any previous monthly averages.

Well, so they arrive – Jews in the Jewish State. What happens to them? Most of them go to apartments prepared for them by the Israeli authorities in the smaller cities and in new development towns, where there is a need for workers. Some – intellectuals, professionals, highly-skilled craftsmen – who need Hebrew in their work are sent to absorption centres, where their expenses are covered while they are taught the language six to ten hours a day.

There is no doubt that this reception of the Russian Jews is better, smoother than Israel has been able to arrange for any of the previous waves of immigration that have brought in a million and a quarter people since the State was established. In any kind of social planning, the Russian Jews – all of them seen as heroes of the Jewish affirmation – come first. Many thousands of Israelis, native-born or long resident in Israel, live in sub-standard housing and can afford no better; thousands are desperately poor, even their children ill-clothed, ill-fed. There just isn't money enough in the State's coffers. But for the Russian Jews, the money is found. 'It must be found,' one official told me, 'for the Russian Jews cannot wait. Who knows when the Kremlin may close the gates again?' Even so, with all the effort and all the money spent, the absorption process is far from painless. Jews out of Georgia, deeply religious, are offended by the – to them – unexpected, largely secular nature of Israeli society. Men who were merchants in Russia, or teachers, find factory work hard; and despite their own determined effort that brought them to Israel, there remains the tug of remembered things – the familiar language, the familiar places, the accustomed ways.

But the Russian Jews will find their place and ultimately the impact of their numbers will be felt throughout Israeli society. What that impact will be, especially in politics, time alone will tell.

Strange Customs

ERIK DE MAUNY   8 JANUARY 1972

When the Common Market was launched, one of its objectives was the progressive dismantling of customs barriers, conjuring up the agreeable vision of their eventually withering away altogether. It hasn't happened yet; and it certainly hadn't happened when Erik de Mauny sent this contribution from Paris.

A few weeks ago, some friends of ours in England sent us a present for our small son; a brass rubbing from a fifteenth-century tomb in a Hertfordshire village depicting the eighteen children of a local landed family. In their stiff, prayerful attitudes, they seem to have been an ill-fated lot. But their final memorial has great charm. The charm, however, was plainly lost on the central customs in Paris, who deluged me with mimeographed questionnaires demanding to know the exact nature, fabrication and value of the said object.

Brass rubbings have never had much currency in France. So I hoped they were mollified on being told that it was '*Un frottis d'inscription monumentale anglais du 15ème siècle*'. Anyway, they released the packet without further argument. This was not the case a few weeks earlier when my wife and I returned to France on an overnight boat from Southampton and landed at Le Havre at seven in the morning in a steady drizzle. On that occasion there was argument aplenty. In fact it went on for most of the day with a leisurely pause for lunch.

It's true that the car was heavily laden. And it's true that we were carrying a Spanish rug wrapped in brown paper on the roof rack. But in our view, the entire load had an innocent homely quality, consisting as it did mainly of children's cots, playpens, pushchairs, and tins of black treacle for making Christmas pudding. The Spanish rug was our undoing. There was nothing on paper to prove that it wasn't a priceless example of the finest work of Bokhara or Kermanshah, and only an agonisingly prolonged exchange of telex messages with the London store where it had been purchased convinced the customs that it was not actually worth about a million old francs. In the meantime, my son had his nappies changed at least three times on various customs officers' desks while this dispute continued.

There then followed an interesting discussion about the origins of the car radio – in fact installed in Paris a few months earlier. But this was tame stuff and our spirits were beginning to rise when the indefatigable customs officer spotted the one remaining unexamined parcel. 'And what,' he said, 'is that?' 'That,' we said, 'is a bust of Chopin.' We were asked to repeat this assertion several times, which we did, while I stripped away the wrappings under a steadily increasing downpour, explaining as affably as I could, that my sister-in-law was a promising sculptress who had merely asked us to enter this particular bust in a competition at the Beaux Arts in Paris. 'In other words,' said the customs man sombrely, 'illegally importing works of art in contravention of Articles X, Y and Z, to say nothing of the cultural convention of so-and-so'; and at which point I began seriously wondering about the amenities of the local lock-up and whether there were married quarters for prisoners on a life sentence.

But God tempers the wind to the shorn lamb. Another customs officer was consulted, who summoned a local transport agent, who in turn, upon our depositing a cheque as guarantee, provided papers allowing Chopin to enter France for a temporary stay of three months. I am not saying this in any carping spirit, since some of my colleagues have had even more unnerving experiences. One of them, ten or eleven years ago at the height of the Algerian war, flew in to Le Touquet one festive season with a gross of Christmas crackers. They were intended for a children's party in Paris. But Christmas crackers are even rarer in France than brass rubbings. Several customs officers gathered around and began dubiously examining a specimen cracker. 'What is it?' they asked. My friend sought in vain for an adequate French translation and then said in desperation: 'It's a sort of children's game. You pull both ends and it goes Bang! – like this.' Whereupon everyone dived for cover.

The word customs has, of course, a double meaning. And the French obviously think some of ours pretty odd. I remember driving back to France one summer with my wife and some cousins, one of them being a small girl. So the car on that occasion, too, was well laden with domestic trivia, like disposable nappies, rose-hip syrup and, of course, black treacle, on all of which the customs officer turned a benevolent eye. But we were also carrying a large cardboard box on the roof, its contents destined to relieve the calls of nature in our rather primitive farmhouse in Normandy. At the last moment, the customs man gave the box a cursory tap and asked 'What's that?' 'It's a chemical lavatory – "*water chimique*",' I explained. If I've ever seen a Gallic shudder I saw it then as he rolled his eyes heavenwards and waved us through. I imagine he's still dining out on the story of the English Milords who were so fastidious they took their own lavatory everywhere with them like a camel with its hump. Anyway, I hope so.

Summer in New York
BRIAN SAXTON   22 JULY 1972

Summer in New York – temperatures in the upper nineties and the city blanketed in a hot smog. Brian Saxton told how he learned to live with it.

Summer in New York: and over the placid waters of the East River beneath my office window a small white sailboat glides gently out of Manhattan towards the cooler reaches of Long Island. The sight of such a free spirit on such a day as this, with temperatures in the high nineties and no sign of a break in the torrid weather, is nothing short of pernicious. For here in the nation's largest city, where the airless streets shimmer in the hot and humid stillness of summer, the major occupation every year is trying to escape from, or learning to live with, the relentless heat.

How one does this, of course, depends very much on one's pocket. But whether one rents a summer house overlooking the sea or sits in the shade of the dusty trees in Central Park, the same motivation is there – escape. The rich and the determined not-so-rich, of course, have less of a problem. The rich either own or rent houses in the expensive residential beach areas of Long Island, about seventy or eighty miles out of the city, or they go to Cape Cod in Massachusetts, up-state New York or Connecticut. Many wives and their families, in fact, leave the city when the summer season begins at the end of May and stay at their beach and country homes until the early part of September, when the season ends, leaving father to look after himself during the week in the city and expecting him to struggle out of Wall Street to join them on the weekends.

The not-so-rich – the young, single, career people – for instance, take summer homes nearer the city, often sharing a house between as many as six or eight. The homes are expensive, the rent on some houses costs as much as two thousand pounds for two months without gas, electricity, food, drinks and so on. But when temperatures in New York start reaching the giddy nineties and people appear to be melting in their shoes, the price of being able to exchange this sultry nightmare for a long, flat beach and clean sea air never seems high.

But what of those who can't afford this expensive form of escapism? Where do they go when the atmosphere turns to syrup?

A great many New Yorkers pour into Coney Island, a resort area thirty miles or so from Manhattan, which many Europeans visiting here think is rather like Blackpool. In many ways they're right. Coney Island has candy floss, roller coasters, amusement arcades and aquariums, skating rinks and a zoo, and it's also got a beach. The beach is public, although there are private locker rooms for changing, but no one expects much privacy. Last year on 4 July, America's big annual national holiday celebrating her independence, over a million people squeezed on to the sand.

There are other local beach resorts, too. In a nation like America where distance is never much of an obstacle, people will take anything from commuter airlines to cars, seaplanes to speedboats, yachts to motor launches, to get away from the city to that blissful Utopia of which they dream throughout the long perspiring week.

Utopia, of course, needn't always be a summer house. There are many other ways in which New Yorkers escape to relax during the seemingly endless summers. Some, for instance, go ballooning. There's an airline company not far out of the city which runs two-hour flights for thirty pounds or so; and if you tire of being a passenger you can even learn to fly yourself. Or you might go canoeing for the weekend, paddling thirty miles of the Delaware River from Port Jervis, New Jersey, to Bushkill, Pennsylvania. Still on the water, you might even like to take a berth aboard a twenty-nine-passenger square-rigged schooner called the *Shenandoah*, which sails out of Martha's Vineyard near Cape Cod on weekly cruises. Of course if you're really stuck in New York all day and every day during the sort of heatwave we've been having this month, life can be depressing, for as well as the heat there's always the smog, caused chiefly by what the weathermen call 'hot air inversion', which smothers Manhattan like some great stagnant blanket and keeps the heat and pollution trapped among the sky-scrapers. It happens every summer, and it's happening now as I write.

One of the few oases in this concrete desert is the air-conditioner, which is essential to keeping one's sanity. Having come to regard the machine as their close ally during the summer months, New Yorkers tend to base all their movements on being able to hop from one air-conditioned venue to the next. Those who don't have air conditioning, and there are many, especially in the older houses and apartment buildings and who have little more than a fan with which to churn up the buttery atmosphere, have to seek sanctuary either with friends and neighbours, or in museums, art galleries, theatres, cinemas and restaurants. Perhaps some of the bravest people in New York during the summer are the tourists, whose indefatigable zest for seeing all the sights seems to overcome everything, and who, despite the weather, drag themselves dutifully from one high spot to the next. As for me, especially after seeing my little sailboat heading for the open sea, it will be a journey in itself after this broadcast to get home to my air-conditioned apartment, which is not more than ten minutes away. After all this is summer, in New York.

Brussels Waits for the British
IAN McDOUGALL   14 NOVEMBER 1972

In Brussels, the Common Market Commission announced plans to get rid of more than two hundred of its senior officials to make room for others from Britain, Ireland and Denmark, the three new members of the Market as from 1 January. Most of them would be British, and Ian McDougall described what would be waiting for them.

The British officials will be moving into offices vacated by the men thus drastically removed. Many of these – as has been publicly admitted – were among the Commission's most competent servants. One aim was to economise, since salaries in the top three grades range between seven and twelve thousand pounds a year. Another was to keep the high command compact in the interests of planning efficiency.

Brussels has not, however, been bracing itself for the advance of a bowler-hatted army straight out of Whitehall, because the recruiting net – by means of competitive examinations – has been stretched wide to catch also men and women from business, the trades unions and universities. One sometimes hears the Commission described as the European Community's *civil service*. But this is not quite accurate because it actually plans all policy as well as implementing it. The Ministers themselves have the power to approve or reject, but not to plan.

Thus the initiative and imagination of the men who will cross the Channel to occupy the curiously-shaped glass-walled building that has arisen out of the surrounding shabby streets will be as important as their qualifications to be a faceless Eurocrat. Furthermore, they will cease to represent Britain as such, however often they turn out for the Brussels British Rugby team – which has been having a particularly good season – or however much time they may spend in the saloon bar of the Queen Victoria just across the square from the Commission, or however enthusiastically they take part in the productions of the English Comedy Club, which will be putting on *The Lady's Not For Burning* just about the time Britain joins the Market.

Once inside the Commission, the British officials will become European officials and may neither seek nor accept instructions from any government at all. This means that it is perfectly possible for a British-born official in the Commission to be advocating a policy which another British-born official – in the British Government delegation just along the street – is determined to undermine. The Commission incidentally has one spokesman who, although an American citizen born and bred, thinks nothing of starting a sentence: 'Our European point of view is –' et cetera.

English will now, of course, become an official language and since the Irish – and, for that matter, the Danish – newcomers speak it too, it is likely in the long run to rival or even usurp the place of French as the main working language in the lobbies.

As to housing, the new arrivals will have little trouble finding accommodation in the higher rent brackets, but an agent told me that he has three hundred requests for houses at around £150 a month, and had great difficulty at that price in providing anything his clients would enjoy living in. Schools are abundant: there's an American school, an international school which basically is also American, a German school, a French lycée, a British school which has expanded by leaps and bounds since it was opened only two years ago and now has over seven hundred pupils, and a European school which is mainly for children of the Common Market officials. For the first time, an English-language section was added this term.

One side-effect of imminent British entry is that British property companies are also moving into Brussels in a biggish way, apparently in the expectation that it will increase in importance as an international centre. Belgian newspapers have recently reported that of forty new office blocks due to rise up against the skyline within the next three years, more than half are being built for British companies. There have been complaints that the prices paid for buildings already constructed are well above the actual going rate, and that therefore rents will rise proportionately.

These irritations apart, the Belgians are basically sympathetic to the idea of Britain's arrival. They enthusiastically share a number of British tastes such as pubs, chips with almost everything, and horses. Belgium must be one of the very few countries in the world where you can buy riding crops and spurs in self-service supermarkets; and being on the same side at Waterloo and in two world wars counts for something, too.

The British certainly make themselves at home here. A bright young ladies' group, called 'The British Birds', regularly inserts notices in the Press inviting what are described as 'single men at a loose end' to drinks parties. One 'British Bird' recently complained that the same old faces turn up again and again. And a sizeable section of the British population has recently been trying by every legal means, including demonstrations, to get traffic banned from the city's main square because they think it spoils the view. This is the equivalent, I suppose, of Belgians in London running a campaign to change the layout of Piccadilly Circus. But the Belgians don't seem to mind.

They're still a bit puzzled, though, as to why British officials have taken so long to arrive in Brussels. It will depend a good deal on the performance of those officials inside and outside the Commission as to whether the puzzlement survives or not.

Liquor Laws
JOHN HUMPHRYS   9 DECEMBER 1972

In Britain, Lord Errol had been heading an enquiry into the possibility of changing the licensing laws. In the United States, various aspects of the liquor regulations were also under review, as John Humphrys reported from New York.

In New York, assuming you have the time, energy, financial resources and, not least, the inclination, there's nothing to stop you sitting in a bar drinking non-stop from eight in the morning until four the following morning. For entertainment, you can watch a row of under-dressed ladies performing highly improbable movements on a table not two feet away. On the other hand, try ordering a beer with your lunch in any number of less sophisticated towns and cities throughout the country and you may well fall foul of the law. Such are the strange anomalies in the licensing regulations in the United States.

Liberal as the rules may be in cities like New York, they are still too stringent for some, including, of all people, the police. They want the bars here to be open around the clock. So many people feel the need to drink beyond the permitted hour that a whole string of so-called 'bottle clubs' are operating illegally and the police say they are spawning grounds for gambling, prostitution and narcotics crimes. Mayor Lindsay and his men at City Hall approve the change, partly because they are losing tax revenue to the illegal clubs, but also to seal off one more source of police corruption in the shape of handsome bribes being offered to and accepted by detectives who are supposed to bring the owners to court. For owners of bottle clubs in New York then, the future is less than rosy. So it is over on the West Coast for the men who run the 'sexy bars' where the sight of totally naked dancers and the most explicit sex scenes imaginable have been readily available for the price of a beer.

The Supreme Court, no less, is responsible for the threat to their existence, because of its ruling a few days ago which has given individual states the power of censorship. In the words of a spokesman, 'for six nude bars on San Francisco's Broadway, the Department of Alcoholic and Beverage Control is going to end up being a censorship board in every topless and bottomless club in California'. The Board won't be able to shut the places down, but if they decide the bars are allowing conduct contrary to public welfare or morals, they can revoke their liquor licences, and since that's where much of the money is made, many will go out of business. In those which remain, the voyeur will have to take orange juice with his sex.

For all that the Supreme Court is safeguarding public morals by its firm stand on not mixing sex and liquor, the honourable justices are left well behind in the morality stakes by some of the individual states themselves. I well remember a bakingly hot summer afternoon in North Carolina, when I was accused for the first and, I sincerely hope, the last time of corrupting young children. My offence? Well, I was sitting with a BBC colleague in a park, drinking a can of cold beer. Hardly a heinous crime in itself, perhaps, but a couple of hundred yards away a group of children were playing on the swings, and it was made perfectly clear to us by an outraged citizen that ours was simply not an acceptable example to present. The fact is, in North Carolina, it's not easy to get a drink of any sort; but if you actually want to drink spirits anywhere other than at home, you must indulge in what's still referred to as 'brown bagging'. I should explain that. You buy a bottle of whisky, say, in one of the state-controlled liquor stores, and take it, still in the brown bag in which it was sold to you, to the licensed restaurant of your choice. There you can pour yourself a drink so long as you do not put the bag on the table, or take the bottle out of the bag. Of course, if you know your way around or meet a friendly taxi driver, you can get yourself an invitation to somebody's front parlour where you drink furtively at inflated prices, and at the risk of being raided by the police.

It's typical of the puritanical double think that while the State may maintain such censorious laws against drinking, at the same time it makes a handsome profit out of its own liquor stores.

To the dedicated drinking man travelling across the country, the rules and regulations are a confusing maze. In Pennsylvania, the State Code on Alcohol is a book two inches thick, and woe betide you in Virginia if you're not aware of the law which says you can't have another drink until you've finished the one in front of you. To think that here, in America, they say Britain's drinking laws are quaint.

News Patterns

CHRISTOPHER SERPELL   30 DECEMBER 1972

A sad occasion when the BBC's Diplomatic Correspondent, Christopher Serpell, on his retirement broadcast his farewell to From Our Own Correspondent *and described the patterns of news as he'd observed them over his years as a correspondent.*

When you are a correspondent – and above all when you are a *foreign* correspondent – you positively need an outlet of this kind. Obviously your main activity must be to report the news from your post with as much accuracy and objectivity as you can manage. But inevitably, while you are doing that, you begin to see patterns in the events you record; you perceive links between this or that aspect of the local situation and the rest of the world; and you also feel an increasing need to explain to your home audience the ordinary, non-topical facts of the life around you. All this is a valuable part of a foreign news service, even though there's neither time nor space for this sort of material in the daily news bulletin, or in the current affairs programmes in their present form. There is, indeed, only 'From Our Own Correspondent' which, through the years I have worked for BBC News, has provided a regular channel through which we could communicate our feelings and our more general ideas to people who were prepared to listen sympathetically.

There are, I think, three different types of pattern, or configuration, to be detected, at any given moment, in the great confused tapestry of world affairs. The first is geographical: there is always some area of the earth's surface – anything from a country to a continent – which seems to capture the public imagination and therefore to acquire an automatic importance for the news media; even when important events are happening elsewhere, they tend to be seen in relation to this geographical focus of attention. The second type of pattern is one of conflict – a clash of ideologies or power or both, which makes a double claim on our attention. As a situation which can result in war and possibly world war, it has a direct bearing on our lives and safety. As a drama, it provides a spectacle in which we feel obliged to take sides and thus become personally involved. The third pattern is more elusive; for want of a better word I might call it *spiritual*. It's concerned with the human race's persistent, if frustrated, efforts to better itself and its opinion of itself; at almost any moment there is some general ideal, not always expressed in religious terms, which is in vogue among thinking people. It is pursued, often in a somewhat haphazard manner, until it is felt to be unattainable; and then, as disillusionment sets in, somebody somewhere begins to formulate a new ideal, a new objective, for the reformers to aim at.

But if those are the three news patterns, the contents through which they are manifested keep changing. For instance, when I began as a broadcasting journalist at the end of World War II, the dominant geographical factor was the United States. It was not only the leading power in the free world – the nation that had made the biggest material contribution to victory. It was also a gigantic benefactor, capable of so generous and far-reaching an act of statesmanship as the Marshall Plan which restored economic stability to Western Europe. At the same time, it offered to the exhausted and war-worn peoples of the West a rich and invigorating spectacle of prosperity and vitality, of inventiveness and willingness to experiment, which made it a continuous and compelling news story. There were some, like General de Gaulle, who rebelled against its dominance; and there was our own government, clucking away in a possessive manner about our 'special relationship' – rather like a hen that has fostered an eagle-chick. But nobody could remain indifferent. Today they can: the American image has been eroded by internal discontent and the failure of its pose as world policeman. Of course the United States remains a super-power, and its junketings on the moon still proclaim its technological pre-eminence. But the rest of the world no longer believes in the American dream, and the affairs of the United States no longer have an automatic claim on our attention. The spotlight has wandered away across the world, and at this particular moment I shouldn't be surprised if the new Europe we are joining didn't regain the geographical importance which the old Europe enjoyed during the nineteenth century.

The conflict dominating the news when I started was, of course, the Cold War confrontation between the United States and the

134

Soviet Union. No one could afford to ignore it, and it was perhaps only the conspicuous barbarity of Communist leadership which saved Western Europe from being deeply divided by Cold War tensions. But now the whole trend of that confrontation is towards compromise and co-existence; instead we are faced with a new and more generalised type of conflict, manifesting itself with various symptoms all over the world. Fundamentally it appears to be a revolutionary situation – a battle of subversive violence against the rigidity of established authority. In one place it may manifest itself as youth rebelling against an elderly establishment; in another, as a racial or religious group trying to assert itself by the use of force against the vested interests of a political regime; in yet another, it is a creed of anarchy challenging the forces of law and order. Once again we are all involved – not only because it could break out anywhere, but because each side in the conflict will claim that vital principles are at stake. And yet, for the first time in modern history, we see innocent bystanders being used as hostages and instruments of blackmail; for the first time, in so-called civilised countries, we see established authority defending itself with torture and brutality.

We can only look away to the third pattern, expressed in human aspirations; and here again the picture has changed completely in my working lifetime. Just after the war, this pattern was embodied in the United Nations Charter – that wistful testimony to the principles of civilised life. The United Nations got attention from the news media not so much for what it was managing to do, as for what it stood for – the prospect of peace and good order achieved by democratic machinery. But when that machinery failed to work – when the United Nations became an arena for nationalism and the manoeuvres of the Cold War – public disillusionment was so strong that it still obscures the limited but useful successes of the UN organisation. Instead we have seen the gradual development over the past few years of a totally new effort at human self-improvement, the effort to save the physical world from the pollution that results from overcrowding and from a careless pursuit of industrial profits. Like all ideals, this one too is slightly fuzzy round the edges: it is not clear which world we are trying to save – the world as it might be if there were no people to spoil it, or a world that will permit healthy human life. But at least mankind is once again trying to save itself from its own shortcomings, and doing so in a practical way that offers perhaps the best outlet for enthusiasm in a non-religious age. One of your own correspondents feels he can say goodbye now with undiminished faith in humanity's instinct for self-preservation.

Peace in Vietnam
CHARLES WHEELER   30 JANUARY 1973

After more than eighteen years, America's war in Vietnam had ended and, from Washington, Charles Wheeler described the impact of the peace.

On Thanksgiving Day in November 1954, seventeen American officers were handed sealed travel orders by the Eisenhower Administration. Their destination was Saigon. The seventeen were the first American advisers to be attached to the Army of South Vietnam. That was eighteen years ago. The war in Korea had ended only a year before and nearly three thousand six hundred American prisoners were only now settling down to life with their families. Eventually that tiny contingent of seventeen men became an expeditionary force of over half a million. But to reach that peak took fourteen years. No sooner had America reached it than the Commander-in-Chief was attacked by anguished doubts about the extent of the national commitment and began earnestly to sue for peace.

It took his successor four more years to secure that peace and even now the commitment hasn't been laid to rest entirely. America's involvement in Vietnam began so gradually that Americans have to go to the reference books to find out when the longest war in their history started. It has ended almost as gradually and quite as untidily. For some, the young men who expected to be conscripted and were reprieved, it ended last summer. For others, the families of the prisoners and the missing, it will end in sixty days, when the last of the captives are back from the camps and when the missing who can't be found are pronounced dead. There has been no celebration here of the end of the war, only relief – relief tempered by several other emotions, mostly uncomfortable ones. The Christmas bombing left deep scars in this country too and not all Dr Kissinger's listeners on Wednesday were comforted by his claim that that final surge of American military power hastened the peace. So did the Atom Bomb in 1945. Also, the Americans are not blind to the fact that if the war is over for them, it is unlikely to be over for the people who've felt its impact most.

Americans have pored over the peace settlement with mixed feelings, admiring the ingenuity of its authors, but uneasily aware as well that to accept the simplistic assurance of the White House that this is in every respect a peace with honour requires a good measure of wishful thinking, if not self deception. Most of them, I think, would rather it were called the best settlement we could get. After all, the election campaign is over, and there has been too much officially inspired self-delusion in recent years. But people who are finding the word *honour* embarrassing aren't conjuring with words like *surrender* and *sell-out*, as a few did last October. If there hasn't been an outburst of joy here, neither has there been any bitterness. Americans who suspect that their government might have been able to end the fighting sooner see no merit in a vicious public argument. Not only has there been more recrimination already than a healthy society can stand but it's obvious that many of the lessons of Vietnam were well and truly learned long ago. In other words, the process of readjustment to peace is well under way. It began somewhere about the middle of President Nixon's first term, say two years ago.

The war did divide American society and in some respects the damage is probably permanent. But the process of healing is already far advanced. To a lesser extent the same is true of America's economy. The war and President Johnson's policy of *guns and butter* caused in turn inflation, reduced profits and unemployment. It wrecked America's payments balance and weakened the dollar, creating a crisis in which America's relations with some of her allies were subjected to painful strains. But the war has never absorbed this country's energy totally, as two world wars did Britain's. And the experts would probably say that words like *post-war recovery* don't apply. Unless, that is, you take the broader view and assert that the real tragedy of those wartime years has been the dismemberment of America's infant welfare state. The war stopped social reform in its tracks and today, with the budget deficit huge and growing, there is no prospect that a windfall of money released by the war can suddenly be applied to the needs of the poor in the cities. According to the experts, the so-called peace dividend is effectively a myth. The country spent it long ago. So life goes on here much as before. If there are changes ahead they're scarcely perceptible. Here in Washington, for example, there are stirrings in the Congress. Senators and others, who've been divided by Vietnam for many years, are beginning to find themselves in agreement on the need to provide checks on an executive branch that is able to take the country largely by stealth into an undeclared war, and keep it locked in conflict for years after everybody has agreed that the whole enterprise was a ghastly mistake. Now whether anything will come of this realisation that the war has revealed a grave weakness in America's system of government, nobody can say. Presidential accountability can't be created by the passage of a new law. Public opinion must first perceive its absence. This hasn't happened yet. Though the debate about power promises to occupy Washington for many months, there is no sign that the country is so far deeply concerned.

POWs Return

CHARLES WHEELER   10 FEBRUARY 1973

After that last despatch, Charles Wheeler flew off to the Philippines to report on the preparations being made to greet the American prisoners of war being released by the North Vietnamese.

Lieutenant-Commander Everet Alvarez was shot down and captured by the North Vietnamese on 5 August 1964. He's been a prisoner of war for eight and a half years.

The Commander is one of five hundred and sixty-two American servicemen whose names are on lists provided by the North Vietnamese and the Vietcong, and are due to be released in the next fifty days or so. Under the Paris agreements a first batch should be freed by Monday. They'll be collected from Hanoi and, in the case of prisoners of the Vietcong, from South Vietnam, in American hospital aircraft. Nobody knows who'll be in the first party or what state the men'll be in, so the planes are equipped for emergencies. The crews include doctors and flight nurses. There is an intensive-care unit in each plane and men can either sit up or travel on stretchers. The flight from Hanoi to Clark Air Force Base in the Philippines will take three or four hours.

The plans for their arrival at Clark Base, the first stop on the long journey home, are elaborate and sensible. There will be no bands, no ceremonial at all. Because this first appearance of the prisoners is a major national event, it will be covered on television by satellite, but the cameras are being kept at a distance and reporters will not be allowed to talk to the prisoners or even get close to them. And for once the press isn't quarrelling with the authorities about the arrangements. When the planes have landed, the first men to disembark will be the stretcher cases. Deliberately they'll be unloaded out of sight of the cameras. The idea is to spare relations at home unnecessary distress. Then the walking prisoners will come down the aircraft steps, and these we shall see. They'll board special buses fitted out as ambulances, and these'll take them straight to the Base Hospital two and a half miles away. There they'll wait, two to four men to a room, until the doctors arrive. A team of sixty doctors and dentists is standing by and the medical examinations will be thorough. The doctors will decide who is fit to fly home forty-eight or seventy-two hours later – the flight to the west coast of America takes fifteen hours – and who, if anyone, will have to be kept in hospital here in the Philippines. In that event a man's family will be flown out here to join him.

As soon as the medical exam is over, each ex-prisoner will meet his personal escort. This is a serviceman of equivalent rank and in a few cases a personal friend, whose job it is to ease his return to normal life. For example, he has been carefully briefed about his charge's personal circumstances. He'll hand over letters and photographs of wife and children, and if there's bad news to be broken the escort is the one who'll have to break it. He then takes his ex-prisoner off to a private room, puts through a call to his family in the United States, and leaves him alone. This done, the escort produces a uniform complete with the right medal ribbons and badges of rank – many of the men have been promoted while behind bars – and a tailor appears to make adjustments. Fitting the ex-prisoners with proper clothes is regarded here as an important morale raiser and one can see why. Many of them have spent years in the same depressing prison overalls. The escort flies home with his charge and he stays with him until he's reunited with his family.

Each man will also get two hundred and fifty dollars for his immediate needs, a statement showing him how much back pay he's entitled to – in some cases the amounts are considerable – and a copy of a special edition of the Army's tabloid newspaper *The Stars and Stripes*. Now this is something of a collector's piece. It's a fifty-six-page round-up in words and pictures of the principal news stories from 1965 to the end of 1972. The front page lead, chosen in a poll of the paper's staff, is the first landing on the moon in 1969. It's all there in striking detail: the big city riots in America from 1965 to 1968; the assassinations of Robert Kennedy and Martin Luther King; the civil wars in Nigeria and Bangladesh; the re-marriage of Jacqueline Kennedy; the deaths of Churchill, Nasser, Schweitzer, Khrushchev, de Gaulle and Harry Truman. And there's a blow by blow account of the war in Vietnam and of the making of the peace.

At some point in the homecoming routine, the ex-prisoners will have to eat and drink. Any man who announces on boarding the hospital plane at Hanoi that he's spent the past seven years dreaming about his first whisky and soda and wants one now will have to wait at least until the doctors have finished their blood tests. As for the food he gets, it all depends on his condition. The dieticians have made up nine sets of menus, anticipating every imaginable condition of the human stomach, and the most exciting dish is described as 'bland burgundy stew with curled carrots and noodles'.

There is also to be a prolonged debriefing session here at Clark Air Force Base. Hundreds of American servicemen are still missing and not accounted for, and the men who do return may have valuable information. This has to be done early before a man's memory becomes confused by a mass of fresh impressions.

One thing the ex-prisoners will not be subjected to is an automatic session with a psychiatrist. There was a battle about this behind the scenes and the general practitioners won the right to decide whether a man needs psychiatric help or not. The view that prevailed was a simple one – that the best treatment is to make the men comfortable; make them feel cherished, and get them back to their families as quickly as possible.

Israel: the Archaeologist's Paradise

MICHAEL ELKINS   27 MARCH 1973

Mike Elkins on Israel's national mania.

There's a lady who comes in once a week to clean the house in which my son and I live in Jerusalem. She is, I should judge, in her late thirties. She was born and lived for much of her life in a tiny village somewhere in Morocco. She's married and has four children. I know little else about her . . . she comes, we exchange routine pleasantries, she does her work, and goes. She's not all that comfortable, you see, alone for some hours in a place with two men (my son, Jonathan, just over sixteen, is already a man within her culture pattern).

Not long ago, she – I dare not mention her name for fear it would offend her – she hovered at the doorway of my study, and when I turned toward her, she held out a tiny clay figurine – female, rather like an old-fashioned dressmaker's dummy, perhaps an inch and a half high. 'Was the thing old?' she wanted to know . . . 'And was it valuable?'

I sent her to a friend who has expertise in such matters, and asked her about it the following week. 'It was', she said, 'old Byzantine, and quite valuable.' 'How had she comes by it?' I asked . . . Well, on most weekends when the weather is fair, she and her husband visit relatives living in Ashkelon along the Mediterranean coast, and they all picnic on the beach and search for artefacts. And would she sell the figurine, since it was valuable? 'Why no! of course not! It's a treasure,' and she would give it to her first-born grandchild (whenever he arrives), who would keep it for his first-born son, and so on . . .

I tell you this story precisely because it is not unusual – it is an illustration of the national mania. Comes the Sabbath – and given fair weather, and except for Orthodox Jews who are at home or at synagogue, it seems that nearly everyone in Israel is either at the football games or scrabbling away, digging up the ground for relics of the past. The law requires them to report their finds, but no one troubles the amateurs.

Perhaps pre-eminent among the amateur archaeologists – and some would dispute the qualifying term 'amateur' – is the Defence Minister, Mr Moshe Dayan. Mr Dayan's collection of antiques is so vast, and his own digging was so incessant, until the wall of a trench he had dug collapsed on him a few years ago and nearly killed him, that he has been frequently charged with exploiting his position for his personal profit – charges, one must report, which have never been upheld by official bodies.

Israel's most renowned archaeologist is Professor Yigael Yadin, of the Hebrew University, who discovered some of the famed Dead Sea Scrolls, and acquired others, and who directed the tremendous excavations at Masada – the Herodian fortress above the Dead Sea, where the Jewish Zealots of biblical times made their final fierce resistance against the Roman Legions. Professor Yadin, like Mr Dayan, is a former Chief of Staff of the Israeli army.

Archaeology seems to be the traditional hobby of Israeli soldiers. In the days of the British Mandate in Palestine, the hobby was encouraged within the Jewish underground army, Haganah. Archaeological field trips were a splendid cover for field reconnaissance and for mapping terrain. However it began, it stuck. It seems to me that every army officer of my acquaintance has a little shelf of antique goodies in his home.

At the professional level, the archaeological activity here in Israel is enormous. There are sixty official digs going on right now: Israeli, French, German, American. More than a thousand foreign volunteers come each year to join Israeli archaeological projects – some of them pay for the privilege.

The largest of these and the longest lasting is that of Professor Benjamin Mazar, of the Hebrew University. Begun a few months after Israel conquered the old, Holy City of Jerusalem, Professor Mazar's dig is designed to expose the entire length of the great retaining wall that encircles the Temple Mount – the biblical Mount Moriah – where stood the First Temple of the Jews, destroyed by the Babylonians, and the Second Temple, levelled by the Roman legions under Titus. Nearly six years' work have brought to light two thousand years of history in Jerusalem. Each new find is reported on the front pages of the Israeli newspapers, discussed on radio and television, and in the coffee houses of Tel Aviv . . .

And I . . . a not-too-interested observer . . . well, I have a stone head of Roman times . . . and what am I bid?

Are Britons Europeans?

IAN McDOUGALL   17 APRIL 1973

Britain had now been a full member of the Common Market for more than three months and, said Ian McDougall from Brussels, the honeymoon was over. What had taken its place?

The blunt fact is that the neighbours are starting to gossip. A fairly typical example of this was contained in a recent newspaper article quoting rumours that the resignation of the Secretary-General of the Community Council, a Luxembourger with a high reputation, had been forced by Britain as a condition for its not vetoing Luxembourg as the site of the proposed Monetary Cooperation Fund. The article went on to admit that the rumours seemed rather improbable, but should be formally refuted. In fact the rumours are thought by the British to be such rubbish that they don't deserve formal refutation at all. And this is also the case with recent allegations by certain African leaders that Britain has been trying to stop Commonwealth developing countries from joining African nations which already have association links with the Common Market.

But even when the gossip has been dubbed as 'rubbish', out comes the old wives' comeback that there's never smoke without fire. What seems to be happening now is that a certain amount of smoke has been observed rising from the British outposts on the Continent and has been interpreted as coming from fire-eaters rather than from pipes of peace.

It is true that the British – or the 'Brits' as they are generally referred to by those who can't stand them – have seemed on a number of occasions to be the odd-man-out. They want the Monetary Fund in Brussels, while others want it in Luxembourg; they won't come in on the joint float of Community currencies, which is regarded as a grave blow to the proposed economic and monetary union; they've been holding out against farm price increases, which most others support; and they're refusing to conform with decisions about lorry weights taken by the Six before the Market was expanded. They're accused of grabbing as many of the best jobs for 'Brits' in the Commission as they possibly can; and the behaviour of a few of their representatives has been described as that of 'men discovering with delight that Britain's Indian Empire never really died'.

In the final analysis – or so it seems when looked at from the perspective of only three months' membership – the British are now having an awkward time finding their feet in a grouping which they feel they should be able to lead, but in which they are still regarded as rather unusual strangers. And since there's an enormous gap between these two conceptions, there is a corresponding gap in mutual confidence.

One might have expected Community membership to bury phrases like 'perfidious Albion' for ever. But in fact, after not hearing it for years, I've heard it and read it three or four times in the past three months. This is unfair for several reasons: the Monetary Fund, looked at from a purely European point of view, would probably be better sited in Brussels; the reduction of lorry weights would be in the European environmental interest; the prevention of farm price increases would benefit European consumers; and the staffing of the Commission with as many top-level British Civil Servants as possible is better than staffing it with mediocrities simply for the sake of being nice to smaller and weaker nations.

Having said that, I am at once aware that I've spoken like one of the 'Brits' that all the trouble is about. In other words, it may at this early stage in the development of the Community be a wise thing to be nice rather than right. And an even wiser thing is to remember that the British way of life and politics really is very different from that on the Continent.

The fact is that there's no known standard or precedent for the development of a community of this kind. Between those who believe with starry eyes that European union is the golden answer to all our woes, and those who believe that if God had wanted a united Europe he would never have started us off speaking twenty different languages, there's endless ground for compromise. At the moment, there's a great deal of scurrying around in that compromise area by all nations concerned. And the fact that the British have made themselves conspicuous will not prevent some of the others doing exactly the same in the months and years to come, just as the French have done in the past.

In the meantime, Britain, having at last chosen Europe rather than the open sea, is in for a long period of adjustment to the ways of foreigners who, as Mr George Thomson recently pointed out, now have a higher average income than almost the whole of Britain except the south-east region.

They will, therefore, look for deeds rather than words if they are to be convinced that British really is best.

Black Power

ANGUS McDERMID   8 SEPTEMBER 1973

Ten years before, a quarter of a million Americans, mainly black, led by Martin Luther King, had marched through Washington to draw attention to the Civil Rights Movement. Angus McDermid examined how the lot of the black Americans had changed since then.

Recollections of that great gathering on the green slopes around the Washington Monument are still vivid; those who were there speak of it as though they had been in the presence of a miracle. It was, they say, a moment of magic, when sordid frustrations became transmuted briefly into a pure, golden vision of fulfilment, and when, with the past forgotten, black and white, young and old, joined in 'We shall overcome', and, transported with tears and joy, heard Martin Luther King declare: 'I have a dream . . .' 'It all seemed possible then,' as one black journalist wrote recently, 'for they were innocent, with an innocence that would never return.'

He meant the disillusion, the violence, the viciousness that were to follow – the riots, the assassinations and, finally, the decline of the Black Power movement. At the time, the march was hailed as the triumphant symbol of victory over racial injustice, poverty and inequality; yet its tenth birthday was marked mainly by cautious reappraisals of its value and meaning by black activists, more mature now and wondering where the generation of militants who should have followed them has gone. They claim that there has been no real progress in the elimination of racism and prejudice; that the Nixon administration is essentially hostile to their interests; that a third of America's twenty-two million blacks are still as poor as ever; and they warn that the real reckoning has yet to come.

Their cause is at a low ebb now; the vast changes in the Southern States – rather as if apartheid were to be abolished in South Africa – mean that the rallying cry of 'Civil Rights' no longer has the same impact there. The Southern Christian Leadership Council, the team which Martin Luther King hoped so fervently would carry on his work, lies almost defeated by debt and lack of interest; more militant bodies have completely gone from sight.

Much white sympathy was lost in the backlash against violence. The weight of liberal discontent turned against the Vietnam War, rather than racial prejudice, and an average white viewpoint today might be: 'Well, they've got their equal privileges – let them get on with it.' And it may well be that much of the energy that went into the Black Power Movement is now channelled into the reasonably satisfying alternative of 'Black is Beautiful', the Afro haircuts, the distinctive clothing, the departments of African studies at the universities. It fosters an identity, a pride in race, that has often been sadly lacking, and helps provide the self-confidence so necessary for progress. Black students can learn Yoruba, wear the Nigerian *dashiki* and study the culture of their own distant forefathers.

To hold one's own in a larger society and move upwards on the socio-economic scale, it's psychologically useful to have an identity of this kind. Certainly black Americans are moving up, but as a group, now, segregated in some ways, with their own educational and commercial institutions, radio stations and television programmes. And while militants may despise what's called 'tokenism', it has helped many blacks along the upward path. And, after all, to move up is essentially what it's all about. 'Tokenism' means the desire to employ blacks at higher levels so as to avoid being accused of prejudice. Thus, in many professional and managerial areas, qualified blacks are urgently needed. Big concerns like General Electric deliberately set out to train black engineers, since only one per cent of America's engineers are black.

It's easy for the blacks to speak of late-blooming white consciences, prompted by the profit motive; to argue that 'tokenism' stems from fear rather than from shame, and that there is in reality no easy relationship, nor significant desire for it. And it's true that there can be no legislation for goodwill, but today's black leaders do argue that under President Nixon, the national leadership, which could make a difference, is no longer there; that the attitude of the present Administration is inherently negative towards black problems.

Yet in real terms of equal opportunity, material success is now more nearly within the black American's grasp than is often the case elsewhere in the black world. Thousands of Nigerians and Ghanaians have seen America as a land of opportunity and have settled, in Washington for instance, very comfortably, secure, by virtue of their origins, in the Afro-American society.

The Civil Rights Commission may report that legislation for equality is inadequate, and there may be headshaking that America is polarising into separate and unequal societies. Yet black achievement is there on all sides. And as every black family moves up the social scale, there's a shade less discontent, a little more to work for and less to protest about.

The Left Bank

IAN McDOUGALL   24 NOVEMBER 1973

The Paris City Council had finally approved plans to build a motorway along the city's Left Bank, an area of bookstalls, art galleries and student life. Ian McDougall had known the Left Bank for many years and recalled some other changes there.

When I first lived on the Left Bank in the thirties, I was a schoolboy doing a course at the Sorbonne and I stayed in the Rue de Vaugirard, which is the longest street in the city, but otherwise rather undistinguished.

The French family I was with had a sixteen-year-old maid who looked out of the window all the time and cried. She even cried when she was serving at table and this puzzled me for a bit until I found out that she was passionately in love with the policeman on point duty at the corner, but was getting nowhere. This was perfectly normal of course, but my point is that it would be abnormal today to find a maid in the home of a rather poorly-off Left Bank family like that. It was a status symbol, I suppose, which set them apart from the writers and artists and other riff-raff, who themselves harboured different snobberies such as the belief that they were free-thinkers to end all free-thinkers.

The Left Bank's old streets, cultured cafés and strongly student flavour still exert a powerful influence on foreigners determined to go native at any cost. *At any cost* is the crucial phrase here, since life on the Left Bank is no longer cheap. Tourists have seen to that.

When I lived there after the war in the Rue de Seine, which runs off the riverside quays and up towards Saint Germain, I paid the equivalent of fifteen new pence a day for my room. It was equipped with *tout confort*, a widespread but totally misleading French phrase which merely meant there was running water in the taps. Students in the area were paying even less, but it was scarcely worth it because as from about five in the morning, the taxis turned the narrow street into an inferno of sound with their klaxons. I used to work a shift at the Agence France Presse, which got me back home just an hour before that – that's the sort of shift young journalists tend to get stuck with – and so I have good reason for thinking that one of the great improvements in Parisian life over the past few years has been the ban on the use of car horns.

The restructuring of the city which has gone on recently has seemed to many to have been a sell-out to the motorist. The existing motorway along the Right Bank is criticised on the grounds that, instead of thinning out the traffic, it has attracted more cars into the centre of the city. Almost nothing has been done to set aside streets for pedestrians, now commonplace elsewhere in Europe. The fast road along the Left Bank will, as a concession, be subjected to all sorts of cultural coyness, such as putting it into tunnels where it runs past Notre Dame and other noted monuments, and it seems that it won't, after all, force the total disappearance of the bookstalls that line the banks of the river and provide hours of pleasure to one and all. But the old Pont des Arts will go, a charming bridge that has always been a must for painters, and some of the spots where I used to fish for small and bony fish will disappear for ever. Not that I think the Left Bank can't do with a bit of modernisation. I'm glad, for example, they've stopped charging people a franc to use those rusty old iron chairs you find in parks, the cash being collected in those days by elderly women of terrifying toughness. One such character near the Luxembourg Gardens was widely rumoured to perch in a tree so as to achieve a better supervision of her chairs, and I wasn't a bit surprised to see in a quite recent newspaper item that there is still rumoured to be an old woman perched in a tree there.

On the other hand, there has been a great deterioration in the general quality of life and I don't think I'm suffering from over-rosy memories. The Left Bank streets in the 1940s were shabby and grimy, but they were not completely jammed with motorcars and they were not disgustingly fouled every few yards by dogs. One odd thing about modern Paris is that prosperous streets are much filthier than poorer streets. It's considered smart to own a pedigree dog, even if you haven't got the slightest chance of taking it for a proper walk in a park or the open country. Such legislation as exists against this curious example of simultaneous cruelty to animals and to human beings is virtually ignored. One gets the impression in other environmental matters, too, that the French are perplexed as to where the line can be drawn between the rights of the individual and the rights of society. The history of the construction of the high-rise buildings to the south of the Eiffel Tower on the Left Bank and at La Défense on the western approaches to the city appears to have been one big muddle from start to finish; and all anyone can actually do at this stage is to grumble about how hideous they are. This apparent failure to blend the architecturally new successfully with the old, to clamp down on pollution in all its forms, and to keep the motorcar under control have all contributed to the fact that the Left Bank road had a particularly difficult time getting approved. But now it will definitely be built and then the grumbling can start all over again.

Across the Sahara

DONALD MILNER   1 JUNE 1974

The Sahelian Zone in West Africa had been stricken by drought and Britain had given some fifty lorries to help in food distribution there. Twenty of them were driven by the Army right across the Sahara to Niger, and with them went Donald Milner.

Travel is not what it was. Even the Antarctic, which still had a certain cachet when I went there in 1957, has become altogether too accessible. The Sahara is no exception. It's not yet quite on the hippy trail, but it's only a matter of time.

There are two roads across the Sahara, or at least two routes marked on the Michelin map. The one we took lay to the east. The Algerian Army seconded a captain as our guide, and we needed him. There is indeed a metalled road of sorts for the first seven or eight hundred miles, but thereafter we hit the sand with a vengeance. One moment you're bowling along at fifty or sixty miles an hour: the next you're up to your axles, digging in deeper with every effort to coax the vehicle out. In theory we were supposed to maintain line-ahead to stay in our sections, and keep our distance. In practice, for much of the time, there was no recognisable track at all; only a line of more-or-less visible markers – cairns of stones, or iron bars, or the burnt-out wrecks of the many cars that didn't make it across the desert – and the lorries fanned out anyhow, picking their way as best they could.

The going varied from the extraordinary Plateau of Tidemait, which for a hundred miles or so presents the appearance of a vast airfield, perfectly level, and covered with an even surface of small black basalt stones, to something akin to mountain passes; and the motion of the truck varied accordingly. But it was the smaller bumps and sudden hollows which were the bane of the whole business, catapulting you without warning to crack your head on the roof of the cab or throwing you all over the place as the drivers struggled to regain control. Somehow I found the Sahara concentrated the mind in a way that one could not have expected from such chaotic movement.

Again and again, I was reminded of Antarctica, and the diary of my impressions – jotted down in a crabbed, arthritic hand I can hardly decipher, as we leapt from bump to bump – contains many maritime analogies: 'vistas of flat-topped mountains, like tabular icebergs; a vast, shallow basin of sand, lined by low hills, like the dried-up bed of an inland sea.' Sometimes the prospect was so totally featureless, so utterly unrelieved in its flatness, that one fancied one could see the curvature of the earth. Nothing moved except the occasional dust-devil swirling inconsequentially away across the desert. 'Tricks played by mirages,' runs my notebook, '– lakes and islands; a distant mound of earth becomes a house; stray stones on the skyline are men or goats or palm trees; and the lorries at the head of the convoy like big black boulders, floating above the horizon.'

Hour after hour, mile after juddering mile, the vicious vibro-massage of the corrugated sand continued. Rising at four-thirty, we drove all days; arms, legs and nerves tense to absorb the next shock. Luckily, as we moved south, the noon-day heat was filtered through a dust fog which shielded us from the sun. As darkness fell, we camped in a square laager of lorries. Then up again next morning for another five hundred kilometres of dust and thirst, slaked by warm salted water in mud-caked canvas bottles slung on the bumpers to cool.

Sometimes the sand-castles in the air were solid enough. 'At the entrance to Arak Gorge,' runs another entry, 'a truly beetling crag in the form of a magnificent ruined Norman castle.' A few miles on, a man holding up an empty goatskin. His camel has died under him and around them both lie the scattered trusses of his load. We stop and pick him up. It is two hundred kilometres to the next oasis. How long would he have survived without us? The desert is like the sea in another way, I reflected; distress signals are imperatives.

I note that a camel-train in silhouette looks like a single creature – like some slow-moving, long-legged centipede. 'In such conditions,' I remark sententiously, 'one looks upon the very humblest plant with a fresh respect for the phenomenon of life. How can that tree be here, serene and green, and not a single blade of grass in sight?'

But as we passed at last through the Sahara proper and into the equally barren plains of northern Niger, it was painfully clear that all the trees had died. We were entering the so-called Sahelian Zone – the southern fringe of the desert – where, for the past seven years, a relentless drought has stripped the landscape and robbed the people of their livelihood. And, as we moved on into the dusty, dead savannah – the heartland of hunger – I marvelled at the tenacity of man in his determination to inhabit the uninhabitable, and reflected that, if the world's population goes on rising as it is, he will either have to make the desert bloom or die.

No Wagner for Israel

MICHAEL ELKINS   11 JULY 1974

Because of his association with Hitler's idea of Aryan supremacy, Richard Wagner's music had been banned in Israel. The Israel Philharmonic Orchestra voted to end the ban and scheduled a performance of his works. The result was a heated public discussion, threats of violence, and the scheduled performance was dropped. From Jerusalem, Mike Elkins discussed the impact of the Nazi holocaust upon modern Israel.

It seems evident that only a very small minority of present-day

Israelis were outraged at the prospect of Wagner's music being played by a Jewish orchestra in a Jewish state, but that was enough. 'Rightly or wrongly,' a spokesman for the Philharmonic said, 'these people associate Wagner with the gas chambers, and we don't want to create a war of the Jews over Wagner's music.'

The issue reflects the agony of ambivalence that still occasionally surfaces here in Israel around all things German. There was a time in Israel, and that time long-lasting, when the memory of the Nazi slaughter of European Jewry fuelled a searing hatred of Germany and Germans. There were massive riots in the streets in 1951, when the Israeli Parliament was deciding whether to ratify the agreement whereby West Germany would pay reparations and restitution to the State of Israel and to the Jewish people.

Many, many thousands of Israelis saw the issue as money for blood, the acceptance of such money a betrayal of the Jewish dead, signifying Israel's concurrence in the Germans' return to respectability within the world community. It was all valid enough, but there were weighty arguments on the other side also. West Germany was too great a power to be kept out of the community of nations no matter what the Israelis might do or wish done. A new generation of Germans was arising, untainted by Nazism. The money was desperately needed in Israel, a great part of it needed to absorb the hundreds of thousands of refugees from the Nazi concentration camps. And why shouldn't the Germans pay for the redemption of their victims?

Parliament ratified the agreement; the riots were suppressed, to flare again at the next stop of the, by then, inevitable progression when Israel and West Germany established diplomatic relations in 1965.

The Reparations Agreement brought heavy German industrial equipment to Israel – steel mills, factories, raw materials, ships. The restitution payments were made in German marks and the Israeli recipients used them to buy German goods: Volkswagen automobiles, television sets, record players, typewriters, electric shavers. Economic and diplomatic relations inevitably led to social intercourse. With money awaiting them in West Germany, increasing numbers of Israelis went there for holidays and on business trips.

Some Israelis, some of these with the concentration camp numbers indelibly tattooed on their arms, returned to the land of their persecution to live. The pull of familiar places, the familiar language instead of the difficult Hebrew; the familiar culture that they knew before the Nazi aberration, all this proving too strong to resist; and besides, was this not a new Germany? They went back – not very many, and often ashamed; but they went back. Others, the great majority, were appalled by all this. They could never again set foot in the country that had made of all Europe a graveyard for the Jews. But many, perhaps most of these Israelis, would not boycott German products and saw no reason to boycott the German cultural evenings programmed by the German Embassy in Tel Aviv. Others spat on all things German. The years passed; time and the exigencies of 'realpolitik', Israel's need for every possible friend in the world – these combined to erode, but not entirely to dissolve, the corrosive issue in Israel of Germany and the Germans.

It all flared up in 1960 when Israeli agents snatched the one-time gestapo colonel, Adolf Eichmann, from Argentina, and the Israelis put him on trial in Jerusalem and hanged him – the only man ever to suffer capital punishment in Israel.

The evidence and testimony at the Eichmann trial brought a shock revelation to young Israelis for whom the holocaust had been only history, incomprehensible, uncomprehended. It became, as it always was for older Israelis, real, meaningful, part of the umbilicus that connects the Jewish present to the Jewish past. But that was 1960, more than a decade ago, and there are many thousands of Israelis who were not born or were children then. Time, it is said, heals all wounds – perhaps not so entirely or not for all. But in time, wounds no longer bleed and there is only a scar or the memory of pain, or not even this on the mind's surface, but only, buried deep, an uneasy occasional disquiet surging upwards only when something calls it out of the depths, like the music of Wagner.

Travelling Russian-style

PHILIP SHORT   1 OCTOBER 1974

Philip Short, stationed in Moscow, had been given permission by the Soviet authorities to travel to the southern republics – but only by air or by train. He sent this account of his travel and of the hotels.

Usually if you can go somewhere by train in the Soviet Union you're also allowed to fly there, and most people do, especially over long distances. But travelling by train does have its advantages too, as I found when I went from Baku, in Azerbaijan, to Makhachkala, the Daghestanian capital, a couple of hundred miles north up the Caspian Sea coast. For one thing it's punctual. The ticket clerk tells you that train number six always leaves ten minutes late and that's exactly what it does. And it's also one of the best ways of meeting Russians, for in the south, at least, a train journey is not so much a means of reaching your destination as a social occasion, a great exercise in communal living. In the sleeping compartments, men and women are lumped indiscriminately together; unshaven figures in string vests wander up and down the corridors; music programmes from Radio Moscow blare out over the loudspeaker system and you find yourself being invited in to share someone's vodka, or to meet a village schoolmaster who says he wants to be able to tell his friends that he's had a drink with an Englishman.

Each carriage has its own *dezhurnaya*, robust ladies who bring round endless glasses of Russian tea, and who are equally capable of bouncing a drunk or of arbitrating in a dispute over who has which bunk. And at the stations along the way, peasant children sell apples and tomatoes from tin buckets.

The problems really start when you arrive wherever it is you're going to, for then you have to take on the system of Soviet hotels. The lift, for instance, with its small hand-written signs – 'no service after 11 p.m.' – and when you complain that the once-daily train doesn't arrive till midnight back comes the reply: 'Are we responsible for railway timetables?' Or your room, which turns out to be already occupied by someone else who has to move out. 'But I've booked it,' you say. And the answer to that: 'You didn't expect us to leave it empty, did you? What if you hadn't turned up?' And this, you're told, isn't sharp practice, but just raising productivity for the Five-Year Plan; and that's only the start. There's the bath you paid extra for to discover that there's only hot water on Fridays, and of course this isn't Friday; or the television set for which you also pay extra, whether you want it or not, because the town plan for television rental is badly under-fulfilled.

And what about the noise like a cross between a jet engine and an air-raid siren that wakes you up in the morning – the cleaning lady's hoover. Perhaps that all sounds just too far-fetched and vituperative; and if so I must disclaim responsibility. For it's all from a report on provincial hotels by two Soviet journalists, which appeared in the Central Government newspaper, *Izvestia*. My own experience in fact was rather better than that, but there was always some little quirk which made me realise that *Izvestia*'s description wasn't far-fetched at all. And there are plenty of things which *Izvestia* didn't mention. The practice, for instance, of charging foreigners ten times the Russian rates, so that a night's stay is twenty pounds instead of two; and if you query it, you're told with total conviction that it's the international norm and that exactly the same thing happens to Soviet tourists in Britain. They may even try to charge an extra twenty pounds as a booking fee.

And there are other differences in the way foreigners are treated too. At Yerevan, in Armenia, I watched a receptionist who'd gone out of her way to be helpful to me turning away a Russian woman, who was almost in tears because she had nowhere to stay, with a completely callous rudeness and indifference. Perhaps that was an isolated case, but certainly the system of foreigners being privileged operates all the time when you travel by air.

Flights in the Soviet Union may be astonishingly cheap; as little as six pounds for the equivalent of London to Paris. But all too often they're subject to overwhelming delays, and airports in the provinces can look like transit stations for wartime evacuees – old peasants with great shapeless bundles of belongings; whole families encamped on suitcases; a woman breast-feeding a baby. They may have been there four hours or twenty hours or two days, quietly resigned. Sometimes you're lucky and there's no delay at all, but at Yerevan I waited eighteen hours to fly to Baku, and at Baku ten hours to fly back to Yerevan. You queue at the enquiries desk and at five minutes to twelve they're still telling you, 'Yes, your plane will leave at twelve o'clock,' and then it's postponed till four, and when four o'clock comes round it's the same story again. The reason, I was told each time, was the weather, but when there were enough foreign tourists waiting, they arranged a special plane, which, for some reason, the weather didn't affect. Perhaps part of the explanation lies with the kind of incident I saw as I was waiting at Baku. Just as a group of passengers were at long last about to board their flight, a petrol lorry drove into the aircraft's tail. The passengers returned inside; lorry and plane were solemnly towed away and a little old lady with a broom appeared to sweep up the broken glass.

Italian Opera in Trouble
DAVID WILLEY   7 NOVEMBER 1974

From Rome David Willey reported that the Italian opera season had got away to a slow start. Many opera houses had been on strike as orchestras and choirs had not been paid.

The gilt and plush elegance of the eighteenth-century opera house in Venice, the Fenice, was the scene of an unusual first night the other evening. A performance of a play, not an opera, was given there by a Brazilian theatre company, which plumbed the depths of starkness. Not only was there no scenery, but the entire cast performed without clothes to emphasise the purity of the theme. The bare boards and the bare bodies were symbolic of the state of Italian opera today: the theatre had been closed by a strike for weeks, as the staff had not received their wages. But now, I'm happy to report, a belated season of opera is being organised in Venice with the help of a loan from a local bank.

It's the same story of falling artistic standards and economic crisis in the twelve other major opera houses up and down the Italian peninsula. Opera still has an enthusiastic public here and La Scala, in Milan, still enjoys an international musical reputation. But if you compare the state opera in Italy with that, say, in West Germany, where there are almost a hundred city and state opera houses, all playing to packed houses for over three hundred evenings in the year – not to mention another hundred odd theatres that also give opera performances – the situation here is pitiful. The lack of adequate musical education in Italy is perhaps partly to blame, but the major cause of the decline of Italian opera is simply maladministration.

Fifty million pounds sterling is given by the Italian State every year to keep the opera houses running. Most of this is gobbled up by salaries and wages for the small army of eight thousand singers, musicians, ballet dancers, technicians, ushers and administrators that it takes to stage this extravagant form of entertainment. A fifth of the subsidy goes on interest on bank loans. The San Carlo Opera in Naples, for example, alone is over three million pounds sterling in debt. But local politics also has to take its share of blame for the decline in opera.

In Naples, criminal proceedings are pending against a former director of the opera for granting plum contracts to mediocre performers, and for swelling the permanent staff of the opera from three hundred to six hundred in the space of a few years. The orchestra and the choir remain the same size. But an unjustifiable number of jobs at inflated salaries have been given to political appointees, whose musical skills are not immediately apparent.

Fernando Previtali, the distinguished conductor and musical director in Naples, cancelled a concert there the other day in protest against the 'administrative anarchy' reigning in the former kingdom of the Bourbons. 'How can I go on when I find an incompetent soloist in front of me, a couple of violins and a horn missing from the orchestra, and workmen hammering away in the boxes,' he complained. Similar tales of woe are heard in other parts of Italy. In Genoa, the opera house, damaged by bombing in World War Two, is still closed for restoration over thirty years later. In Rome, the opera house has been occupied by staff in protest against non-payment of wages.

Various proposals to reform state subsidies to opera have been tabled in Parliament and fallen victim to successive government crises. Most music lovers agree that either many city operas should be disbanded altogether and funds channelled to two or three main opera companies instead of the present thirteen, or a better productivity should be achieved with existing resources.

There's no repertory system. Each opera house tends to behave as if it still belonged to an independent city state, and refuses to travel with its productions. The West Germans may spend slightly more on opera than the Italians, but they manage to achieve fifteen times as many performances and of generally much higher artistic standard.

Saigon under Communism

DEREK WILSON   31 MAY 1975

Western correspondents had just been allowed to leave Saigon more than three weeks after the South Vietnamese had surrendered their capital to the Communists. The BBC's South East Asia Correspondent, Derek Wilson, was among them and he sent this report on how the population there was taking the new régime.

They're trying to adapt. A young officer friend of mine, a couple of months ago, confided he'd a hand grenade ready and would use it on himself rather than spend a day under a regime he detested. The other evening, after much agonising, he quietly announced, 'I'm going to study to become a Communist.' That's perhaps an extreme example; but like him the Saigonese are all, in their different ways, accommodating, attempting to get on the right side of a regime that demands total obedience to what it vaguely calls 'the Revolution'. The Saigonese quickly interpreted what that meant. The capital's long-haired youths went to the barber; the mini skirts disappeared, and the price of black satin trebled because of a rush on it to make and change into what maids and market-women wear – pantaloons and tunics.

In the city centre, book sales smother the pavements: Vietnamese love stories and translations from English and American, all thrown out by owners afraid they wouldn't be in line with the new revolutionary culture the cadres talk about. For the same reason, many Vietnamese are nervous now about being seen too much with foreign friends. It's a job to find an interpreter nowadays, for instance. A Vietnamese I've known for years failed to show up at the hotel one day because, he later told me over the phone, he thought two men in the lobby were watching him and might take him for a spy. I haven't seen him since.

Even so, that's nothing to the initial fears here. Suicides were reported. A general is said to have shot his six children and then himself. Teenage girls were said to have sewn phials of poison into their hems for fear of forced marriages to their conquerors' disabled. A captain I know quickly got married himself in case he was sent off for re-education. Instead, so far, nothing: no bloodbath, no reports of reprisal killings, only the occasional summary execution of thieves caught red-handed. The transition from war to the end of it has been almost unbelievably smooth and the atmosphere here is now relatively relaxed.

The banks are still closed and business is at a standstill. But the cafés are open and the streets full of people, though strangely quiet and empty because of a petrol shortage. Saigon's reverted to a bicycle city. Even the pavement black markets have spawned again, this time gorging on loot from abandoned American premises. The urchins, beggars and tarts have re-emerged too, for what seems destined to be a whining, giggling swansong in a capital perhaps in a last spasm of debauch before the nip of moral austerity.

That nip – an end to the old ways – has not come sooner, many Saigonese suspect, because quick victory took even the victors by surprise and they weren't geared up to revolutionise overnight. But the great initial calming of fears, everybody agrees, had a lot to do with the faces the dreaded North Vietnamese finally showed. They turned out to be young, naïve, wide-eyed and country boys in a big city for the first time; fascinated by tall buildings, cigarettes with filters, the bustle. It's a common sight to see them strolling about unselfconsciously hand in hand. In modern houses they've moved into, they keep the magic air-conditioning going all day long and constantly take hot showers.

Many Saigonese now have them in for meals. But is this simply a honeymoon? Nobody knows. Large foot patrols of North Vietnamese military police have now started tramping the streets, for instance, but only following the murders of a handful of troops. At the moment, though, the Saigonese are much less nervous of the Northerners than of bands of young, armed locals. They often can't make out whether they're the real Southern guerrillas, or fake ones; money has been extorted; houses taken over.

Despite the outward calm, though, you find great anxiety about what happens next. It's deepest, of course, among all those who served the old regime: servicemen, officers, civil servants, politicians. They've all had to register with the new authorities: answer questions about their past, and about what contribution they think they can now make to the revolution. Outside one reporting centre, an army doctor I talked to found comfort in recalling that after the Second World War, the Allies had punished only war criminals, not the officer class as a whole.

An official policy of leniency has been announced, but one officer said they'd been told at a long briefing they'd now have to atone for the wrong they'd done to the Vietnamese nation by abetting imperialism, and many fear re-education courses are in store for them. Then, the other day, to our mutual embarrassment, I found the same man outside a cinema with his wife and small daughter, selling the family's clothes arrayed out on the pavement. A few yards down, the wife of a naval commander was doing the same thing. Service families are already very short of cash, and they now face lengthy unemployment, though eventually, it seems, many servicemen will be called up again.

The young officer I spoke of to begin with has now been put to cleaning the street he lives in. And naturally also anxious about their future are the middle class. They reckon they'll be in for levelling. A civilian doctor found himself already described on the card index at the hospital where he works as 'small capitalist intellectual'. Bourgeois families who didn't flee abroad now tend to stay indoors, and if they do go out, they leave their big cars in the garage and go about inconspicuously on bikes.

But, inevitably, the new regime's first concern has been to revolutionise the majority, the workers, perhaps the ones with the most to gain from a new order. Who knows yet? There have been quickly organised meetings; lectures seem to be held around the clock. Cadres have the habit of knocking up people at two and three in the morning to attend them.

The other morning, it was the turn of the staff of the hotel I'm at. They were gathered in the wedding-reception room and given a long talk by a man in dark glasses about the teachings of Ho Chi Minh and how proud all Vietnamese could now be to have finally won their independence. Street committees are being set up in many districts and life's not so easy-going as it was. And what many quite ordinary people are worried about most of all is what sort of government they're to come under. They still haven't one. Saigon, at present, is run by a Military Management Committee, but when any Southern government does emerge, how long will it last in its own right, they ask? How soon will the military re-unification by Hanoi that's already taken place, be followed by political re-unification and the introduction of thoroughgoing Northern communism. The slogans are all about Vietnam being one, and cadres apparently ask people, 'What's the point of having two governments?' The hope in Saigon is that if Hanoi were to take over, the South could prove a bit difficult to absorb, not only because of its different temperament and culture, but because it's now been too exposed to a Western consumer society to forget it that easily.

In the countryside, the revolution is rumoured to be moving faster than in Saigon. But it's been opened up. People can now travel where they want. Families have been reunited, and for the rural folk – the majority – the most amazing and welcome thing must be that after thirty years of war, bombs and shells are no longer ripping into villages and rice paddies, and that it's peace at last.

Violence in American Schools
ANGUS McDERMID   21 JUNE 1975

In Washington, a Congressional sub-committee was investigating violence and vandalism in the nation's public schools, and they produced statistics which, said Angus McDermid, were plainly horrifying.

The figures read like a wartime casualty list. More children were killed in the schools, often in gun fights with other pupils, between 1970 and 1973 than soldiers died in combat in the first three years of the Vietnam war. And teachers, too, are frequently shot to death by angry children.

Crime in American schools begins at about the age of eight. Last year there were over eight thousand rapes – young women teachers are often the targets – nearly twelve thousand armed robberies, a quarter of a million burglaries and two hundred thousand major assaults on teachers and pupils. Drugs, alcohol, extortion rackets, prostitution, are all found in today's American classroom. And knives, clubs, pistols and sawn-off shotguns are more often taken to school these days, either for attack or self-defence, than an apple for the teacher.

It has to be said clearly that not all schools are in such a state. There are many where behaviour is exemplary and the products excellent. But if the wave of school crime grows – and the figures have more than doubled in many cases in five years – then good schools will soon become hard to find. Headlines in local papers like

'Drug Bust at Wooton High' – that is a narcotics raid at a secondary school – are frequent. The official Congressional report reads like a lurid paperback: in New York a seventeen-year-old boy was clubbed on the head with a pistol butt and stabbed in the spine; sixteen shootings in Kansas City schools; in Chicago, a headmaster killed and a school official wounded, and a sixteen-year-old shot dead over a gambling debt of five cents.

In North Carolina two children forced two others on pain of death to hand over one thousand dollars – their ages: nine. And in Los Angeles, where there are one hundred and fifty recognised school gangs, the biggest call themselves the Cripps because they're dedicated to crippling their victims. And there are girl Crippettes and the junior Cripps for eight to eleven-year-olds.

American schools haven't always been dismal, fearful caverns with armed police in the corridors. In 1964 only three per cent of the children had disciplinary problems. Ten years later, two-fifths of the country's teachers claim to have been assaulted. The experts can only suggest that it is a reflection of the condition of society as a whole, in which persons under twenty-five commit the majority of crimes and violent juvenile crime has increased two and a half times in thirteen years. 'The school', says one report, 'has simply become a convenient battleground.' Other experts, however, say that crime is generated in schools themselves. Vast numbers of pupils – a high proportion of them black – are suspended or drop out and eventually come back seeking revenge against authority.

And, of course, there are the drugs. It is apparently beyond the wit of the authorities to stop them. If there is a crack down, pupil riots often follow. A third of the country's eighteen million secondary school pupils habitually use drugs; in addition two-thirds get drunk at least once a month. Certainly, many of the children shot dead are mixed up in the drug trade; much of the pushing and trading takes place in the school buses that, because of the de-segregation laws, cart the children from school to school. And what about the vandalism, the thefts and the arson, which costs the Government two hundred million pounds a year? Well, if the stolen goods are saleable then the money goes for drugs. But how do you prevent youthful arsonists from burning down their schools, the hated symbols of authority? In Los Angeles alone, two and a half million pounds are spent annually on security guards and armed police, fire detectors and closed-circuit televisions. In Boston young thieves even stole three electronic burglar alarm systems.

Well, what's to be done about this terrifying educational jungle? Nothing much, it seems, about drugs. In New York, one pusher may sell two hundred and fifty pounds-worth of drugs a day to schoolchildren. Many teachers seem inclined to ignore the problem; some don't bother or dare to keep the pedlars out of the schools. And school doctors often fail to examine children for signs of addiction. But gradually the authorities are acting. In North Carolina a pupil can be sent to jail for six months for provoking violence. In San Francisco, there's automatic suspension for carrying a weapon. Yet teachers' hands are frequently tied. They're often sued by aggrieved pupils who can now demand a hearing with lawyers present if they think they've been unjustly punished. So how is an American teacher ever going to be able to teach? It's a question that won't be answered till there are solutions to the other big issues, like the decay of the cities, the state of the prisons, racial antagonisms and all the other major social problems that are central to the condition of life in America today.

Portugal: After the Revolution
CHARLES WHEELER   9 OCTOBER 1975

Charles Wheeler had left Washington to become Chief Europe Correspondent. He travelled to Lisbon where, eighteen months after the Portuguese dictatorship was abolished in a revolution, he found things still in a state of chaos.

In the bath the other morning, trying to sort out first impressions of Portugal, I started constructing a fantasy. I didn't get very far because the telephone rang, but it began like this.

The scene is not Lisbon but London, where the newspapers are full of the goings on at Wellington Barracks. There, a battalion of the Grenadier Guards has lately returned from service in Germany, radicalised by a course of instruction in the tactics and philosophy of the Baader-Meinhof gang and other groups of urban guerrillas. A red banner flies from the roof of the Guards' Chapel and occasionally the gates of the barracks open to admit fraternal delegations of rebellious soldiers from Aldershot and mutinous naval ratings from Chatham. From ten until two every day, the guardsmen hold a plenary session and put the day's programme to a vote. It's not an arduous programme, because any activity remotely connected with military training is invariably and unanimously voted down. Besides, the CO has gone on indefinite leave in disgust and his second-in-command, a Marxist major, long ago decided that his future lies with the men in politics.

Down the road at the Horse Guards, the Board of Admiralty is discussing the restoration of law and order in the armed services. In the basement is a force of eight hundred Royal Marine commandos. This is the only unit in south-east England loyal to the Government and the Board is debating whether or not to despatch the marines to disarm and disband the guards. The decision is a difficult one, because bloodshed in this part of London would be bad for tourism.

Also the Trades Union Congress, meeting at the Methodist Hall in Westminster, has adjourned to take part in a soldiers' and workers' rally at the Guards' barracks, where the acting CO has just threatened to hand out weapons to civilians if the government tries to use force to impede progress of the revolution. Eventually the Board of Admiralty decides to do nothing.

Meanwhile at Number Ten Downing Street, the Prime Minister is on the telephone to the BBC arguing with the workers' committee that has replaced the Director-General. He wants to make an appeal for law and order after the nine o'clock news on television. But his request is denied, for the news isn't what it used to be, and neither is Broadcasting House. Pointing down at Oxford Circus is a heavy machine gun, placed on the roof by a detachment of military police sent in three days before by the Government to restore editorial discipline. But the military police have been subverted by Left Wing current affairs producers and they have joined the revolt.

Out at White City in the Television Centre, the direst predictions of viewers have been fulfilled and all is anarchy. A pair of nationally-known newsreaders, tieless, in shirt sleeves and unshaven for a week, have just closed the nine o'clock news with a recording by the Progressive Soldiers' Choir entitled 'If you think your platoon commander is a fascist, spray him with machine gun fire'.

It was at this point that the telephone rang and I had to get out of the bath: end of fantasy. And yet it isn't one really, for all these

164

things have happened in the past week or two in Lisbon. I have not been here before and all my first impressions were bad ones. Lisbon reminded me of the nastier parts of the Caribbean, like Santa Domingo and Haiti. It has the same smell of anarchy and decay, and yet foreigners who know the place are happy here and, after a day or two, I began to realise why.

One comes to ignore the squalor, the truly appalling mass of political posters and spray-painted slogans on every square inch of stone, and the unswept streets and the desperate overcrowding of the city crammed with refugees from Portuguese Africa, or at least to treat these things as secondary, as just possibly even the goings on in the army are secondary. For what is significant about Portugal, or so it seems to me, is the way its people are managing to live with political and economic chaos without becoming violent. It is now a year and a half since the dictatorship was abolished in a revolution and in that time, and especially lately, there have been many occasions when a less level-headed people would have reached for their guns. All credit also to the men who are trying to run the country. Generals and admirals are not accustomed to ignoring provocation from the ranks and the temptation to make an example of a mutinous unit, for example by bombing it, must be strong. It isn't difficult to imagine what may happen for instance in Spain when the Franco regime dissolves and the opposing forces are more equal in strength than they are today.

In Portugal, of course, violence could break out at any time. In the north or the south, tonight or next week. It would be surprising if it doesn't, for the situation is highly volatile. But the record of the last eighteen months does offer some hope that if the guns do go off, the explosion will be contained and will not lead to civil war. For the Portuguese on the whole are a tolerant people, inclined to listen to their opponents instead of bashing them over the head. As the old hands among the foreigners here are always saying, 'In this country they don't kill the bulls'.

Life in North Vietnam

BRIAN BARRON   28 FEBRUARY 1976

Nearly a year after the end of fighting in Vietnam, Brian Barron was allowed to visit North Vietnam, the first BBC correspondent to do so for more than ten years.

If you arrive in Hanoi from the Western world, the atmosphere seems curiously muted and self-contained, suggesting a sense of weariness and resignation, evoking recollections of post-blitz Britain, austerity and ration cards for food. For those foreigners who arrive from Peking with visible relief, as one of my colleagues did, Hanoi seems a gay, flirtatious place of brightness and laughter where young people are less secretive about their emotions. The rationing of cloth in North Vietnam, five yards per person a year, creates the illusion that most are still in the army, small figures in pith helmets and jungle jackets. For those who have done military service can wear their old uniforms.

Hanoi has everything that Saigon had squandered. It's a community with soul, a city of colonial elegance, leafy, murmuring to the swish of a million bicycles. Hanoi is poor but honest; clean, well-behaved, almost Confucian in its frugality; not without a few beggar women who carefully avoid importuning foreigners, but thankfully lacking the soiled amputees and pimp-exploited urchins who work the pavements of disordered Saigon.

Haiphong is altogether different. I went there expecting a large port still showing signs of war. Instead, it seems more like Penarth, in South Wales, on a grey day, very small with less than a dozen ships tied up at the only quay. The port is a quartermaster's nightmare, overflowing with thousands of tons of goods from the Communist world, including crates which have been there for months if not years. So great is this vast stockpile that it has spilled over into surrounding streets. It's a damaged city that wears its scars like a very old man. The American bombing of Haiphong was so sustained that it has yet to be wiped from the collective memory. Fatigue, even resentment, is written on many faces. Still, a start is being made on the construction. The burned out wreckage of the oil depot is being strengthened and rebuilt. Outside Haiphong, dykes guarding the Red River Delta are being strengthened, roads widened. Most of this work is done laboriously, painfully by hand, without steamrollers. Women workers pound pieces of tar-covered stones into the road surface with hammers. With this absence of machinery and the bombing of many factories, no wonder North Vietnam admits that some of its important industries are still below the 1965 level.

As we left Haiphong, a train passed pulling trucks loaded with tanks and heavy artillery. It seems to complete one valid image of North Vietnam, a relatively small country, which, after immense sacrifice, won total victory with an army that is now the most toasted and perhaps effective in the world. But now a radical change of direction is needed. There's a crippling lack of experienced managers, technocrats and specialists. As a short-term measure the army has been milked for such people. But there aren't enough, and one of the problems is that, although there are many trained South Vietnamese, they've yet to prove their political reliability. After all, less than a year ago Vietnam was at war.

Will Vietnam demobilise? It's a question asked anxiously but unrealistically around South-East Asia, especially by those who respect if not fear the Vietnamese and believe that their national genius responds best to stress and struggle, if not war. The speculative answer must be that Vietnam's army of six hundred thousand will remain at that level for at least a few years. To demobilise would be economic folly at a time when there are three million unemployed south of the seventeenth parallel, and occasional security problems arise. That's why the Communists keep at least fifteen divisions inside Vietnam. For months now Hanoi has been immersed in political and constitutional matters. The decision to sprint towards formed reunification within the next three or four months is straining Vietnam's administrative abilities. Thousands of Communist soldiers who returned to their homes on rotational leave are discouraged from bringing large quantities of consumer goods.

But if the North is imposing its will on the South, there is also influence the other way. In Hanoi, women's hair styles are more frivolous; girls can be seen with lipstick; blouses are brighter; there are more cars and motorcycles – all rather superficial, but exciting in Hanoi. After the years of self-denial then victory, the expectations of the Northerners have been aroused. To a very limited extent, these are starting to be met.

Climbing Kilimanjaro

JOHN OSMAN   13 APRIL 1976

The hobbies of the correspondents are manifold, and the East Africa Correspondent, John Osman, chooses to climb mountains. He spent one holiday climbing Africa's highest peak, Kilimanjaro.

The icy summit of Africa is beautiful – and cold. Standing there at nearly 20,000 feet – to be precise, at 19,340 feet – I shivered, despite the sunshine and my mountain gear. Still, we'd made it: Uhuru Peak, *Uhuru* being the Swahili word for freedom.

The summit was renamed after Tanzanian independence. Formerly, it was Kaiser Wilhelm Point, dating back to 1889 when the first European, Hans Meyer, climbed the mountain. Tanzania then, of course, was German East Africa and such relics of old imperialism are unfashionable today. For example, from Kilimanjaro one looks down upon another fine mountain, Mount Meru. Nowadays, believe it or not, it's unromantically but officially called 'Socialist Peak'. However, there's still a memorial to the old German at the foot of Kilimanjaro near the entrance to what is now a national park. It's the starting point for the long ascent.

And it is one of the world's finest mountains – taller by some three thousand feet or so than the highest peak in the Alps, Mont Blanc. The variety of the climb is remarkable. On the first day, we pass banana and coffee plantations; walk through a splendid tropical forest; emerge into ferns and meadows; then spend the night at the first camp. This, Mandara, at 9000 feet, is the best-equipped resting place on the mountain. The next day, off we go across grassy slopes, trees disappearing and heather and alpine flowers appearing, not to mention curious botanical specimens like senecio and giant lobelia.

The second break is at Horombo, 12,000 or so feet: a squalid hut. Defying the dirt, our porters – two to each climber – produce a table-cloth at each meal. It's a touch of civilisation as the going gets harder and resting-places get scruffier. Six thousand people each year try for the top, but only a few reach it. We meet fourteen nationalities going up or down.

From Horombo we go higher: past the last running water; into rocky upland wastes; on to the saddle; and so to the last hut, at fifteen and a half thousand. We're sweaty, filthy and breathless.

168

We have headaches and the altitude is getting to us. To the east, behind us, Mawenzi is jagged and awesome; it's one of the mountain's two peaks. Above and before us looms the crater and the true summit, Kibo, which we begin to tackle at one o'clock in the morning.

Our porters stay behind; it's now just our guide, ourselves and painful effort – half a step forward, slowly, slowly. Through the darkness, hurricane lamps and torches flicker on the mountainside. A mighty African dawn breaks, scarlet and purple; and our guide, a Chagga named Fernandes, breaks into tribal song in praise of the heights. It's his three hundred and sixth ascent. We reach the top, over scree, rock, and finally snow and ice. The last lap has taken us nine hours. We feel sick; but we also feel great. Here we are: ice-blue glaciers cracking about us; the summit shrouded in legend; and snowfields shining in the sun. That's where the name comes from: 'Kilima Ngaro', 'Shining Mountain'.

The snow puzzled Africans and Europeans for centuries. Africans thought it was some sort of medicine and despotic chiefs used to order their tribesmen up the mountain to collect the snow to use as a potion. As for Europeans, when the first to see the mountain in the 1840s reported snow there, nobody believed them, not even though they were respected German missionaries. For long after that, the romance and mystery lingered; and as late as 1928, one old climber relates, his African friends didn't believe he'd got to the top simply because he didn't bring back any treasure. This was said to have belonged to Solomon's son, Menelik I of Abyssinia. Menelik chose to go up there to die: 'to sleep there for ever, like a king', as the charming African legend has it. And, it goes on, 'Menelik wore the seal ring of Solomon; whoever finds it and puts it on, will, from that moment, have the wisdom of Solomon.'

Needless to say, I found neither treasure nor wisdom. But I have acquired something. It's a one-upmanship tourist poster; and it says . . . 'I have climbed Kilimanjaro, in Tanzania. Have you?'

Special Adviser

NOEL CLARK   29 MAY 1976

Foreign correspondents spend most of their time gathering information. But – as the Vienna-based Correspondent for Eastern Europe, Noel Clark, related – they sometimes find themselves with questions to answer.

There are, for example, the routine feelers put out by foreign embassies – usually Communist. Nothing particularly sinister – at least not in my experience – just a gentle probing of one's psyche over lunch: fifty or so current affairs questions, often unrelated and extremely tedious, popped, grasshopper-style, between the soup and pudding. The answers to these, if one's to believe the standard works on the subject, are designed to help somebody, somewhere, assess one's ultimate potential as a source, or, if you will, as an agent. What do you think about this or that? What's going to happen when so-and-so dies?

I am vaguely aware of having been subjected to this test a number of times in different capitals over the years, though I can't be sure. If so, I am sure I've not made the grade and must assume I've been repeatedly failed for flippancy, ignorance, or cabbage-like complacency when confronted – especially over lunch – with the evils of capitalism; for my limpet-like attachment to bourgeois values and my preference for a book at bedtime when away from home.

Possibly, too, I make a mistake by setting out for any lunch, the motivation of which is the teeniest bit suspect, armed with a copy of 'London Calling', the programme schedule of the BBC World Service, which gives the best frequencies for listening wherever you happen to be. Thus I am well equipped to cope with that ever so gentle hint, occasionally dropped by my host as we're saying good-bye: 'You won't forget, will you, if you happen to hear anything interesting about such and such a person, country, situation – you know – I'd be glad of a call.' At that point I press 'London Calling' into his hand and advise him to stay tuned. His grateful smile is sometimes a trifle forced.

Often more challenging and usually more amusing are questions of another kind put by total strangers abroad, whose faith in the BBC as a source of information – broadcast and otherwise – is both touching and encouraging. Here in Vienna, one Saturday lunchtime, if you please, the office phone rang and an Austrian caller asked for an English-speaking member of my staff. This in itself was flattering since I have no staff. Said the voice: 'I am having some problem with the translation into German of an English poem. Can you help, please?' I took a deep breath, hoping it wouldn't turn out to be a couple of stanzas of the *Faerie Queene*, or a chunk of Chaucer. But no. It was a line from one of my favourite Rolf Harris numbers: 'Tie me kangaroo down, sport.' 'Please,' said the professional voice, 'in such sense what would mean 'tie me', and exactly what kind of game is it – kangaroo-down-sport?' That test I like to think I passed with flying colours for the greater glory of the Corporation. However, I didn't do so well when somebody rang me up while I was writing a piece about the Polish economy to ask what on earth the letters ZAPU stood for. 'Zambesi African Peoples' Union,' said I, quick as a flash. '*Danke schön*,' said the caller and rang off. Then it came to me that it wasn't Zambesi at all – but Zimbabwe. Only I didn't know who'd phoned; couldn't call back, and went about hot and bothered for some little time thinking how awful it would be if the unknown inquirer was about to make a fool of himself in public on the strength of having 'checked it with the BBC'.

I always feel sorry for the people I cannot help – and they are many – especially those who ring up or write in, addressing themselves to the personnel director and asking for what – in a one-man office – is, in fact, my job. Nor could I help the lady who asked on the telephone for a list of London hospitals prepared to carry out abortions at short notice. At this time of the year, numerous callers seek places for their children on the English language courses which they apparently believe me to be organising in various parts of Britain. Others would simply like to know what shows to see in London. A distraught Austrian mother phoned one afternoon to know whether I could cause to be broadcast an immediate appeal to her runaway teenage son, thought to be in London, to contact his parents at once and let them know how he was faring. Fortunately, while I was still trying to get some expert advice on how to help the poor woman, she rang again – incoherent with relief – to say he'd just been traced, still in Austria and not to worry.

Many calls are made to my number because the initials BBC happen to coincide with those of a commercial enterprise specialising in electrical goods. One such came from a chief inspector of the Austrian CID, which perturbed me slightly until it became clear to both of us that the man he thought might possibly be able to help with his inquiries was not after all a member of my non-existent staff. The bulk of requests, however, including one from a man who was convinced I must be in a position to get him two tickets for the Wembley Cup Final, are further gratifying evidence in their way that people listen to London. And that, after all, is what matters.

Welsh Americans
ANGUS McDERMID   3 JULY 1976

The United States was celebrating its two hundredth anniversary.
A nation of immigrants from every part of the world was united in its rejoicing. Washington Correspondent, Angus McDermid, comes from a part of North Wales which sent its quota of skilled immigrants who helped to build America.

Not far from here, deep in the green Virginia countryside, there's a little graveyard just off the main road. It's neat and well tended; the blue-grey headstones bear names like Williams, Evans, Thomas and Jones. The inscriptions are in a language which the local people now can neither read nor identify. But beneath the stones lie the remains of the founders of the little community which they named Arvonia, after the District of Arvon, in what is now the County of Gwynedd. And they were slate quarrymen and their wives and their children who came to blast and work and split the blue slate of Virginia into handy sizes. Their gravestones are of that same flaky but durable material that their fathers had quarried to roof the new industrial towns of Lancashire and the Midlands, and they were in America to provide roofs for the growing suburbs of Washington and Baltimore.

Why did they leave home? Was life in Wales really so miserable then? Was it a dream of riches? Perhaps, for Wales was full of tales of emigrants' successes. Were they dissatisfied, exploited? Well, quarrying was a hard life; fortunes were made but not by the men on the rockface. Was it because they, like some of their contemporaries who went to South America, dreamed of a land where they might speak their own language and yet not be thought uncouth for doing

172

so? Well, for whatever reason, they left to try their luck in the new country. Other slate quarrymen went to upstate New York, to Vermont, to Pennsylvania, places where indeed Welsh may still be heard.

By 1900 there were two hundred and sixty-seven thousand Welsh immigrants and their children in America. Most would be Welsh speaking; Welsh churches and newspapers proliferated. Yet their impact on America has not been as identifiable as that of some comparable groups of immigrants. Perhaps the Welsh were too ready to lose their identities in the melting pot of the peoples, too ready to become good Americans. And also, unlike some immigrants, they were literate; they were skilled craftsmen; they spoke English for the most part, and so they were readily absorbed. But to this day there are distinguishable areas of Welshness. In Pennsylvania the Welsh coalminers and the slate quarrymen were superimposed on a much earlier Welsh-American culture, already Americanised by the 1800s but including Welshmen who once had wanted to found a Welsh state with its own legal code and official language. They were quickly told that was not possible under the principles of the American Revolution.

In some parts of the United States, in the Middle West – and in Ohio, in particular – the Welsh do still stick together. Later this year they'll celebrate the bicentennial with a mass hymn-singing festival in Philadelphia. Perhaps, mercifully, no one in America makes jokes about the Welsh as they do about the Poles and the Italians.

The American way of life may not have suited all Welsh immigrants. Some went back to Wales and for generations they and their families would inevitably bear nicknames like Bob Chicago or Mrs Jones America. To some of them the 'American Dream' may have proved too elusive. I once asked an elderly Anglesey man who'd left for the Middle West half a century earlier with a group of youths from his home village, whether any of them had really made their fortunes. He reflected. No, well he himself hadn't done so badly: he'd started as a farmhand, he'd eventually bought his own farm, and then he'd retired to town life comfortably off. Had anyone of them made his pile? 'Oh, yes,' he said, 'there was John Jones; he ended up well, a rich man.' 'Oh, he was a farmer, too?' 'No, no,' he said, a shade cryptically, 'he became the Chief of Police.'

What the slate quarrymen of Arvonia, Virginia, may have found was that life was pretty hard. The dust was as bad for the lungs there as it had been at home. The headstones tell their own stories in that quiet corner of the American countryside: 'Thomas Robert Williams of Fachwen, Caernarvonshire, died aged forty.' Did he live long enough even to glimpse the 'American Dream' and did the Welsh of Arvonia sense, perhaps too late, that the Welshness of their new homes would not endure? For carved in the blue stone of another grave are the words, chosen perhaps with a hint of loneliness and disillusion, and chiselled by a perceptive fellow craftsman. They say in Welsh 'Huno Mae Yng Ngwlad Yr Estron' – 'He lies in the Land of the Foreigner'.

Among the slate quarrymen of North Wales, not yet dissipated, is a strong streak of cultural independence, of political awareness, of strength of character. Had this Welshman in America, not yet a Welsh-American, decided that he would not be assimilated, and would he have cheered this weekend? Well, yes, I think he would, but perhaps just a little grudgingly.

The Correspondent's Trade

IAN McDOUGALL   31 AUGUST 1976

Paris Correspondent, Ian McDougall, returned to Britain after twenty-seven years of service as a foreign correspondent during which he sent more than ten thousand news stories from over forty countries in four continents. Here, he recalled some of the changing aspects of his trade.

The reason why a broadcasting correspondent has an easier time now than he did in the forties is simple: it is that communications have improved. Communications are the only things that change in news. The news itself – despite what some may claim about there being more of it today, or less of it – remains remarkably the same from one decade to the next. And, in fact, the only really novel events that have happened in my time are space travel, political hijackings, mass tourism and the plastic explosion in household equipment – what one advertising man once described to me as 'the breakthrough in plastic toys for budgerigars'.

When I first started in the forties, as Number Two in the Paris office, we had to send nearly all our stories at fixed times over a microphone hook-up – a music circuit, as it's called in the trade – and only occasionally did we use the phone, because at that time for various tedious reasons the use of the phone for broadcasting in voice was forbidden. Tom Cadett, the Chief Paris Correspondent at that time, and myself used to scamper up and down a flight of stairs to a converted attic bedroom in a hotel and seclude ourselves behind a thick curtain, as if in a confessional, screaming ourselves hoarse till contact was established with London and praying that we'd emerge without dying from suffocation. It was, incidentally, the only broadcasting studio in the whole world equipped with a bidet – in that as in so much else the BBC led the field.

It wasn't until the early fifties that I recall being equipped with a portable recording machine. The first of these was unbelievably heavy and big enough to pack a fair-sized puppy in. The tape had to be wound back by hand, which is the perfect recipe for instant calamity. A two-year-old child would have been an easier travelling companion, and I once said so in a cable from Burma, which was the only message I sent from Burma that got any notice taken of it at all. Then we were issued, as a kind of over-reaction, with a sweet little machine about the size of a schoolchild's pencil box and about as robust as a piece of Dresden china. This also broke incessantly, but at least it was so small that one could forget about it, which was more than could be said for its predecessor.

As time went by, the telephone was rehabilitated as a legitimate means of sending despatches by voice, and the extension of the automatic system for international calls greatly reduced the need to maintain bad-tempered arguments with exchange operators in various languages. On the frontier between Malaya and Thailand, I once got through to London in a few seconds from a jungle telephone which was having its cord chewed by a sacred goat as I used it. And in the remotest part of the Carpathian Mountains of Romania, I was taken by a heavily-armed escort to a railway signal box half a mile away in the middle of the night – we'd been sleeping in a train while accompanying the then Soviet leader, Khrushchev – in order to receive a call from the BBC. I thought this was good staff work on the part of the Romanian Post Office. I thanked my escort, who, however, stolidly informed me that they had only been protecting me from the packs of mountain bears which infested the region. I then understood for the first time why they had made me change from my light-coloured pyjamas into something dark – a disconcerting instruction at four in the morning in a Communist country!

Broadly speaking, you can get almost anybody to a telephone these days, which is perhaps why some editors and producers think that there should be nothing very difficult about getting Ford, Carter, Giscard d'Estaing, Schmidt, Amin – or whoever – into a programme at very short notice. On one single day in Bonn I was asked to get Chancellor Brandt, then just newly-installed in office, into three different BBC slots more or less at the same time. The trouble is that foreign politicians tend to give priority, just as do British ones, to their own audiences.

However, while improved phone systems – not to mention cable and telex and satellite – have made human contacts much faster, they've also reduced the frequency of the old-fashioned scoop, by which I mean a story which no one else has got and which – and this is the crucial point – is worth having. There's no merit at all in being first with a load of boring old rubbish. My idea of a reasonable and feasible scoop today would be for a reporter to land on Mars, or authenticate the Loch Ness monster, or prove that Mao Tse-tung is already dead. But scoops cost money and editors tend to be closer and closer-fisted. When, some time ago, Henry Morton Stanley of the *New York Herald* questioned his editor about expenses for an interesting assignment he'd just been given, he received this magnificent reply: 'Draw a thousand pounds now and when you've gone through that draw another thousand: and when that is spent draw another thousand: and when you have finished that draw another thousand, and so on. But find Livingstone.' In fact, Stanley spent about £9,000 on the job, which would of course be equivalent to a far greater sum today, though still cheap at the price.

But my point is that today the editor wouldn't have put it like that. His message, probably in garbled telex, would have read, 'Find Livingstone, but remember cost-cutting has absolute priority.' Stanley's great scoop, incidentally, was fully believed in by his editor, though at the time others had doubts. A scoop today is suspect by all.

I am nonetheless proud that the profession of foreign correspondents survives. Democracy needs it, even though some people claim to be vague about what foreign correspondents do, and whether indeed they do anything at all. There is a lunatic fringe which thinks they drink champagne out of their mistress's shoes and live at the local Ritz. There is another fringe – not entirely lunatic but almost so – which believes they're on Christian-name terms with everyone in their territory from the president downwards and are occasionally called in to advise on foreign policy.

My own experience throughout twenty-seven years has been that the job is extremely arduous, both mentally and physically: that drudgery is of its essence, as in most other jobs and that the advantages of not having to keep nine to five hours are more than offset by the disadvantages of being on call at every hour of the day and night, a requirement which correspondents share with, almost uniquely, medical general practitioners.

When all is said and done, however, it also seems to me a profession which teaches you to cope with literally any situation without flapping and without yielding to the pressures of interested parties. Over a very long time, and on a day-to-day basis, this is harder than it sounds. It defines, too, the frontiers of your powers of endurance and rubs in the valuable lesson that the way things appear on the spot are nearly always different from the way they are visualised by the reader or listener in an armchair. Now this has nothing to do with inaccurate reporting. It has to do with the human imagination, which seems unable to cope with anything smaller than twice life-size. I don't remember being seriously frightened on a story I was actually covering, but I was often terrified when I read other people's reports of it afterwards.

Sortie in Shanghai
PHILIP SHORT   24 NOVEMBER 1977

Philip Short had been appointed the BBC's first Correspondent based in Peking. He visited Shanghai at a period when, after a decade of radical dominance, cultural life in China was beginning to return to normal.

A few weeks ago, the pavement outside the Art Gallery in Shanghai was jammed with long lines of people each morning queuing for an exhibition of nineteenth-century Romanian paintings. That's now been followed by a show of ancient Chinese art, earlier obstructed by radical opposition. At the cinemas there are feature films of the late fifties and early sixties, last screened a dozen years ago: and romance off the screen as well as on it is no longer quite as taboo as it was. You may even find, as I did at the Shanghai City Theatre the other day, that the couple in the row behind are far more interested in each other than in what's going on on the stage.

Before October last year, when Mao's widow, Chiang Ching, and the other radical leaders were arrested, most of this would have been impossible. For them, culture and the arts were in the crudest sense an instrument of politics. Consider, for instance, the so-called snail incident as it was related to me by a senior city official. Four years ago a Chinese delegation visited America to discuss colour television, and while there was presented by the American company concerned with a set of glass snails as a memento. Chiang Ching, the official said, saw this as a jibe at China's slow rate of development, a view for which she was sharply criticised by Premier Chou En-lai. Soon afterwards, a short story appeared in a Shanghai literary magazine, inserted by her supporters. It, too, dealt with a delegation which was given glass snails as mementoes, but in this version a heroic female factory worker, representing, of course, Chiang Ching, forced the delegation leader to confess his error in accepting them. And, incredible though it may seem, that kind of thing was very far from being an exception. Out of thirty-six films in preparation last year, thirty-two, all now scrapped, were barely fictionalised attacks on so-called capitalist leaders, in other words, on the veteran politicians now in power.

However, it wasn't just political heavy-handedness that laid waste to Chinese culture under the radicals. It was also Chiang Ching's highly personalised view of the arts. She extolled her own model Peking operas and condemned or banned almost everything else, including Shanghai's famous Shao Hsing Opera. Like many others, this has now been revived, and earlier this month it restaged the story called 'The New Year's Sacrifice' by the writer Luhsun, China's Gorky. It's the tale of a widowed peasant woman in the early 1920s who loses everything she has and eventually goes half mad. Her fate is drawn with humour as well as pathos, and there's no attempt at a positive ending. She dies a pauper in the street, by which time, at least on the night I went, half the audience had

178

rushed forward to the edge of the stage to get a better view, waiting there for the leading actress to return alone and take her bow.

The two most famous Shao Hsing singers, each of whom has a following of tens of millions, were forbidden to appear on stage for ten years while the radicals were in power, and both spent time in detention or doing physical labour. One, Yuaw Hsueh-fen, was later allowed to give singing lessons, but not to tell her pupils her name: while the other, Wang Wen-chuan, a soft-spoken unassuming lady in her fifties, managed to stay on, supposedly as a conductor. Another member of the company, a young technical adviser, described to me how he'd been detained in the autumn of 1975. Three men from the Public Security Bureau came to the theatre, he said, handcuffed him and drove him away in a jeep. His crime was that he'd complained about radical interference and for the next ten months he was held, not in an ordinary prison, but in what he called a special building in the city, in a cell with an iron door and bars across the window. As a political prisoner still under investigation, he said, he'd had a radio and newspapers, but only half-an-hour's exercise once or twice a week.

Now, it may seem from all this that the changes in the past year have been enormous, and in some ways they have. Shakespeare is to be republished. Beethoven is back in favour, no longer denounced as a bourgeois romantic. You see women with feminine curls and lipstick in the streets, and the slogan of the day is 'Let the old serve the new, let foreign things serve China'. But it's not happening overnight. Beethoven's works are still hardly ever performed. In Shanghai, the main bookshop couldn't find me a single work of foreign literature in Chinese or any other language. The arts are still being used, though less bluntly than before, for overt politics, and Chinese officials insist there'll be no bourgeois liberalisation. But what is certainly taking place is a relaxation, albeit relative and, for the most part, controlled.

The US/Israeli Lobby
CLIVE SMALL   24 NOVEMBER 1977

President Sadat of Egypt had visited Israel to inaugurate a new effort to bring about peace between the two countries. This had led to some urgent rethinking in the American-Jewish community, which was exerting a strong influence on American policy makers. Washington Correspondent, Clive Small, examined the tactics and power of the Israeli lobby.

Early in the morning of 25 July this year, a bomb went off in a quiet suburban street outside Washington. It wrecked the home of the Director of the American/Israeli Public Affairs Committee. That's the officially registered lobbying organisation for Israel, known throughout Washington as AIPAC. The bomb attack showed that the Israeli lobby has enemies, but it also has many friends, a pervasive influence and a power that's difficult to assess. Some American-Jewish leaders say there's a good deal of myth about the strength that the lobby can exert, but at certain moments and on particular issues its power can be extraordinarily effective. AIPAC operates from an office in central Washington with a staff of about eighteen. It has some eleven thousand members who each pay £20 to belong. To make sure Israel's case is heard at all times, it uses techniques that are accepted as part of the American democratic process, methods used by most lobbying groups. Stored in a computer, the lobby has a list of key people connected with each member of Congress: his constituents who are especially influential, his friends, his business and professional acquaintances.

When AIPAC wants a pro-Israeli point made strongly to a Congressman, the lobby contacts people on the list and, within hours, phone calls start flooding in and letters begin to arrive from his home state. An example of this, that's been quoted before, is the case of Congressman Thomas Downey. He's looked on as a liberal and a good friend of Israel, but last year he had some doubts about voting for a Foreign Aid Bill that included about a billion pounds for Israel. Mail from his constituents on Long Island had been running against the general principle of America providing large-scale foreign aid. A group of concerned American Jews saw Mr Downey to pursuade him of the need to vote the money for Israel. He told them he'd reconsider if there was a strong show of support

180

for Israel from his constituency, where only about five per cent of the voters are Jewish. The lobbying group went away and within two days Mr Downey had received three thousand telegrams from back home: so he voted 'Yes' to the money for Israel.

The lobby generally is so effective because it has a uniquely loyal and dedicated community behind it. Almost all America's six million Jews believe fervently in Israel and its future. American Jews have a strong social commitment. Their participation in all levels of politics is unequalled. Proportionately they go to the polls in greater numbers than any other group. In the important states – New York, Florida, California – they wield significant influence and hold the balance of power. They offer articulate and helpful support to politicians of whom they approve. They contribute money generously to those who share their concern and, more directly, they back the American/Israeli Public Affairs Committee. AIPAC says it has no formal links with the Israeli Embassy, but draws its strength from American Jews, and not only from them but from many other Americans, too.

Support in the United States springs from what most Americans see as the merits of Israel's case, but there is another factor worth noting in the background. Among many non-Jewish Americans there is a lingering sense of guilt about anti-Semitism and what it did in Europe in the thirties and the early forties. According to some American politicians, the Israeli lobby is well aware of this and they criticise the lobby for making use of it. One of these critics is Senator James Abourezk of South Dakota. He's of Lebanese descent, and he's one of the few Senators who consistently speaks for the Arab and Palestinian cause. He accuses the lobby of subjecting him to 'intellectual terrorism' and using the stigma of anti-Semitism to inhibit debate. Senator Abourezk says: 'It's easier to criticise the Government of the United States than the Government of Israel', and there are complaints from one or two Congressional staff members about occasionally abrasive tactics by the American/Israeli Committee. One Congressional assistant described a lobbyist shouting down the phone and saying he'd contact all the Jewish groups in a large industrial state and tell them that Senator So-and-So was wavering on Israel unless the Senator voted for a particular measure. Another staff member on Capitol Hill described how a Congressman, who usually supported Israel, had failed to appear when a vote was due to be taken on an important issue. A member of the Israeli lobby phoned up and ordered the Congressman's staff to, and I quote, 'Get up there and rattle his cage and bring him down here to vote!'

If there are instances where the zeal and passion of the lobbyists get the better of them, other observers say the members of the American/Israeli Committee pursue their aims politely and informatively, but by the nature of their organisation their lobbying has been almost single-mindedly partisan. Now, after President Sadat's visit, many of Israel's supporters in the United States will probably be taking a rather wider view. They'll see the prospect of Israel no longer being a lonely and embattled nation, but one which has a chance to fit into the context of the Middle East. And that change of climate may alter the style of the Israeli lobby, perhaps reduce its impact, but it'll still be a force to be reckoned with in Washington because the special link between the two nations will remain.

Hopes for the New Year
KEVIN RUANE   31 DECEMBER 1977

On the eve of 1978, this programme was devoted to the hopes of people in various countries for the New Year. One of the contributors was Moscow Correspondent, Kevin Ruane.

I was walking down one of Moscow's main streets during the rush hour, between five and six in the evening. The icy pavements were crowded with people. Many of them, as usual, were doing their shopping on the way home. The windows of the stores were all lit up and some were steamed over against the bitter cold outside. With me was a young woman and we'd been wandering about for some time in a vain search for a small restaurant or café in which to sit for a while in the warmth and have a chat. We found a restaurant but it was serving only dinner. 'I'd love a cup of coffee,' I said. 'Wouldn't we all,' my friend replied. 'We haven't seen any coffee for some time.'

My companion was a scientist, a member of the intelligentsia, someone with highly developed critical faculties, and when I asked what she thought the ordinary people wanted in 1978, her reply slightly surprised me. 'They want nothing very much,' she said, 'except peace. They don't want any more wars. They want to be left alone to get on with their lives without interference or trouble from anyone.' 'But what about all the shortages?' I asked. 'What about all the frustrations, all the queues that people have to stand in for hours? Don't they want an end to them?' 'Maybe,' I was told, 'but they can put up with them: they can survive. But war is different.'

Everyone here does echo the stock wish for continued peace, which says a lot, perhaps, for the propaganda about the threat to peace from outside.

It was repeated to me by another, youngish woman, but she added, jokingly, I think, that she wanted another lover. For some people, though, this isn't such a joke. I remember reading a letter to one of the weekly papers, not long ago, from an unmarried mother. She described how, in her first job, she'd fallen in love with her boss, a married man, and had an affair. She'd had a son, now twelve, with whom she was living alone. She complained of the moral burden she now had to carry; of the contemptuous looks she thought she detected in the eyes of men who knew her past; the discovery that neighbours didn't like their daughters to play with her son in case they got into trouble. The paper thought this was very unfair. It pointed to the hard fact that for every one hundred and seventy available females in the Soviet Union, there are only a hundred potential husbands. It stated rather boldly that, whereas one can live without education, possibly, without one's own car, and without a full collection of the works of one's favourite writer on the book shelves, one cannot live without love. And while the lucky ones, it said, can find happiness by following the straight highways ordained by society, is it surprising or to be condemned if some women have to use the back stairs? Love, like many other less important things, is also what they call here a deficit commodity.

In contrast, I've just got to know a man whose dearest wish for 1978 is to leave his wife. Volodya, to give him a name, told me that he and his wife are already divorced but simply can't get away from each other. Like many people in Moscow, and in spite of the huge housing programme, they've been living in a communal flat –that's to say, they share an apartment with other families. They have one room but the lavatory, bathroom and kitchen are used by all. Life in those circumstances can be difficult, but now, he says, it's worse. The authorities can't provide Volodya with alternative accommodation. So the two former spouses are living apart in one room, separated by a curtain.

Volodya is just one of the people behind the statistics which tell us that one out of three marriages break down in the big cities of the USSR. The communal flats must contain, in concentrated form, a mass of such human stories: of people searching for peace and quiet, for privacy, love and family happiness. I visited one the other day, and saw a woman who has no particular wish for 1978. She's ninety years old and her grandson says she's dying. She lay asleep in a silent sunlit room with a green potted plant at the foot of her bed, and on the coverlet, keeping watch, sat a golden cat. The old woman's arm was white, and the bedclothes hardly moved with her breathing. A Communist since 1919, she had worked with Lenin's wife, Krupskaya, and she'd taken an active part in the country's collectivisation programme. The grandson didn't approve of that, but he thought she'd earned the right not to end her days forgotten by the Party. 'On the sixtieth anniversary of the Revolution,' he said, 'they sent her a wrist-watch.'

President Carter's Foreign Tour
CLIVE SMALL   9 JANUARY 1978

President Carter of the United States had been on a lightning foreign tour. Clive Small was one of the one hundred and seventy members of the White House press corps who accompanied him and after getting back to Washington was able to look back on some of the lesser moments.

We assembled at Andrews Air Force Base before dawn, some time last year I think it was. The start of the journey already seems lost in the mists of time. A cross-section of American journalism from television stars, like Barbara Walters, to small town newspaper men, plus a few foreign newsmen. The two 707s lumbered off into the darkness and we were off on a whirlwind tour that gathered speed all the way, leaving behind a series of blurred images.

Warsaw: The trip began and almost ended there. The Polish security police, all of whom had clearly read *Catch 22*, refused to let us off the airport. We sat and fumed in our buses at the gate. The windows steamed up as the curses got louder. Newsmen saw deadlines getting deader by the minute. In desperation, one scrawled a messaged on the window: 'Help, I'm being held prisoner.' Eventually we were released by American Embassy mediators.

Tehran: We glide past the snow-caps of the Elbruz Mountains and into the rich brown smog that's the city's trademark. It boasts that it's got a better smog than Los Angeles. The man from the *Los Angeles Times* agreed. We emerged from the plane to be greeted by scores of bullet-headed young men in dark-blue raincoats. So you thought Polish security was strict. Crowds lined the streets, as the time-honoured cliché goes. Only here they were all in uniform and carried automatic weapons: though at one point a bus careered past, full of what looked like bald schoolboys waving paper American flags. Each floor of the hotel is decorated by three or four policemen in jeans and leather jackets. One sits in a comfortable armchair right outside my door. For some reason they keep their guns in an airline travel bag next to one of the potted palms. I feel extremely safe, I think. The Press Centre is a-buzz. They say Mr Carter's making a detour and going to Aswan to see President Sadat. Where did the news come from? Well, the CBS staff, like all the television battalions here, have their walkie-talkies going non-stop and they overheard NBC say, on their walkie-talkies, that their man in Cairo had been told by President Sadat that Mr Carter was going to meet him: and that's how news is spread. All the newsmen rushed to pump out the Aswan story. In the meantime, 1977 slides unnoticed into 1978. That was the year that was. The plane takes off into the smog again, climbing high into the wild brown yonder.

Delhi: Clear skies, sunshine, happy crowds, smiles and clapping for the President. American newsmen delighted by India, though officials in the party more practical. They issue an order that the water must not be drunk and pass out the address and phone number of the American Embassy doctor. Newcomers to India are bemused by Delhi. Taxi drivers display images of gods who watch over them, and they need divine guidance, because they spend most of their time on the wrong side of the road. On tree-lined streets, notice small groups deep in what seem religious rituals. Several have transistor radios clapped to their ears. As I pass, one of them removes radio from his ear for a moment, and I catch a fruity English-accented voice intoning 'It's wide of the off and Gavaskar goes back to it and glides it safely down the gully. Two runs.' Realise Carter is competing with India/Australia cricket match for India's attention. The airliner is above the sands of Arabia now and half way down the aisle the White House duplicating machine is spewing out another clutch of hand-outs.

Riyadh: Saudi Arabia. A royal reception for the President. Fountains play; revelry confined to fruit juice and non-alcoholic beer. Extremely wealthy sheiks circulate among the guests. One of them asks an American television newsman: 'Is it true that Barbara Walters earns a million dollars a month?' 'No,' he's told, 'it's a million dollars a year.' 'Oh,' says the Sheik, and turns away disappointed at the poor salary scales offered by the television networks.

Everything's relative, including time. If it's six in the morning, it must be Aswan. The schedule is relentless. A colleague starts chatting to some Egyptian officials at the airport. He's so absorbed, he fails to notice an increasingly loud roar in the background. He glances round to see an airliner zooming up into the sky. 'But that's my plane!' he shouts, appalled at the prospect of spending the rest of his working life at the airport at Aswan. Fortunately, he's given room on the second press plane and gets to Paris only a little behind the President.

And so to Brussels, and so across the Atlantic. The aircraft cabins loud with snores. The duplicating machine pouring out press releases to the last.

The Secret Tongues of Europe
ANGUS McDERMID 29 SEPTEMBER 1978

Angus McDermid had been appointed Chief Europe
Correspondent and, as himself a member of a linguistic minority, he
looked at the linguistic patchwork quilt of Europe.

Some European languages are almost secret tongues. How many tourists driving through north-east Italy realise that all around them the daily language of six hundred thousand people is Friulian. Or when in southern France do they know that two million French people, as well as some Spaniards and Italians, regularly use the beautiful language of Oc, which is a long, long way from modern French? These and many other languages may be obscure, but increasingly their speakers are demanding their own cultural and educational rights and sometimes getting them.

Western Europe has some fifty of these linguistic minorities, some minute and inevitably disappearing, others sturdy and bent on survival, resisting economic and political pressures. The French Government may frown on Breton and Corsican, but in Germany the Danish-speakers of southern Schleswig enjoy every good will. Perhaps the richest load of linguistic variety lies on either side of a line running south-east from, say, Antwerp on the Belgian/Dutch border, down through Switzerland, with its three official languages and one major unofficial one, to the German, French, Slovene and other linguistic groups of northern Italy. The road signs change abruptly from Dutch to French about fifteen miles south of Brussels. They remain French for hundreds of more miles, but the people of the roadside towns and villages may sound anything but French, at least when they speak to each other. All true Luxemburgers, for instance, speak Letzeburgisch, which has the status of a language rather than a dialect. But French is the governmental language of the Grand Duchy and German is used in many official publications. The word for this curious but happy relationship is *schizoglossia*. The motorway cuts through Alsace, which is now France but used to be Germany, so everyone speaks German there as well, and it crosses the River Saar, which is rather a disappointment for such a linguistically disputed river. In the French town of Strasbourg you will see posters in Alsatian and then you'll drive south over the Alps to the Dolomites where fifteen thousand Italians speak Ladin as well as German and Italian, to the fascinating territory of Friuli where the local language is Friulian, but with little islands like the one where the eight hundred villagers of a parish speak a southern Bavarian dialect of German among themselves, use Italian in church and school, and address themselves in a variety of Friulian to the strangers from down the road. Confusing?

Why should there be a different language for each circumstance? Well, of course, in modern times people often speak the language they're obliged by the authorities or by economic circumstances to learn. In earlier days, the authority might well have been the Lord of the Manor who spoke French, or the princeling who spoke German. Perhaps that's why the people of Thionville, in France, and Bitburg, in Germany, speak the local language of Luxemburg which is many miles away.

Linguistic experts have a lot to say about the influence of radio and television. In Belgium, however, where it sometimes seems language is the whole basis of politics, the Dutch-speakers of Flanders have welcomed television as a standardising influence, so numerous were the dialects, the accents and the impurities. Many dialects exist in Belgian/French, known as Walloon, too, and here the broadcasting authorities in Brussels have met local demands by supplying programmes in dialects which few Parisians could follow. Just to complicate the Belgian linguistic picture there are districts where German is the official language. It might be reasonable to expect that a small country like Belgium might become really bi-lingual but, alas, there is constant bickering expressing itself, whether in Parliamentary debates or in the defacing of traffic signs between the two communities. A bilingual solution has never really been considered, even though many individuals speak both French and Dutch with admirable fluency. As a result Belgium may soon have a federal-style government based on language, demon-strating that language does go right to the heart of a people. But that so many obscure tongues do survive is a tribute to those who loyally persist in speaking the language they love.

The Children of India

MARK TULLY   29 DECEMBER 1978

The coming year was to be the International Year of the Child, and Mark Tully, in New Delhi, discussed what might be best for the children of India.

Were I an Indian child with the gift of foresight, I know what I would ask as my present for the International Year of the Child – it would be the loosening of some bonds of family. Well, that's a polite way of putting it. More accurate would be to say quite simply – less selfish parents. That might seem quite odd when we read so much about the ill effects of the decline of family life in the West. But many of those who write and preach about our declining standards forget the tyranny of Victorian family life – a tyranny very much alive still here.

Looked at from a distance the way families live in India seems most laudable. It's still very much a cradle-to-the-grave institution guaranteeing to the children security, and to their grandparents respect as well – the thing which old people in capitalist societies lack most. But that security and respect is paid for very dearly by young children as they grow up.

I've two friends, very prominent businessmen in Bombay. Both were clever when at school, but they were brought up in the claustrophobic atmosphere of a joint family, with grandparents, parents, uncles, aunts, cousins, brothers and sisters, all scrambling around like fish caught in an ever-tightening net, feebly flapping their fins to try and avoid suffocation. Those two young boys never did break out of the net. Instead of going to university, father ordered them straight into the family business; arranged their marriages for them and their accommodation within the family house. Some twenty-five years after they left school, they are still in the family business and the family house. But they don't run the business or the house and they certainly don't run their own little bit of the family. When I visit them in their old-fashioned office, they are clearly ill at ease because in the far corner looking out from his glass cabin sits the patriarch. He's never been rude enough to ask them who I am or what I'm doing, so long as I'm there, but they assure me that as soon as I've gone he calls them up and asks what they were doing wasting their time and setting a bad example to the clerks by talking to someone who couldn't possibly increase their business. When they come to my hotel room, however, they're different people, anxious for liquor they are not allowed to drink at home; wanting to read all the magazines that are banned from the family house; and keen to enjoy all the other pleasures that India's most sophisticated city offers. In short, in their mid-forties they are as excitable and irrepressible as public schoolboys enjoying their first night on the town. I often wonder whether, when the old bully who has dominated their lives does eventually die, they'll have the courage to break the mould and at least allow their children to recast their own lives, or whether, by then, the flame which still flickers will have died out and they'll follow their father's way.

This is only one example of the tyranny of an Indian family. Every day there are reports of young brides committing suicide. They'd been married – sold might be a better word – to men whose family background and status appear quite suitable, but who are in every other way totally unsuitable. It's not always the bridegroom's fault. Many young girls who've never been outside their families before are driven to suicide by loneliness and bullying by their mothers-in-law. In poorer families the children are frequently deliberately stunted educationally too. Go to a village and ask the schoolmaster what percentage of children attend the school and you'll be lucky to be given a figure of even fifty per cent. Ask him why and he'll say because their parents are illiterate and they are afraid that if their children learn to read and write they won't be able to control them. I remember asking a mother once why her young daughter was helping her cook the meal instead of going to school. She said, 'Who'd marry my daughter if she could read and write?' The poor don't see literacy as something to be encouraged – they see it as something to be feared.

Very close family ties which still survive here can also work the other way round, with unscrupulous sons using their peculiarly exalted status in the family to embarrass weak or indulgent fathers. So the tyranny of the family can work both ways. Of course, things are changing amongst some but by no means all of the urban élite families, for instance. But that is a very small section of society indeed. In fact the family is strongest amongst the powerful urban middle classes. The only other section of society where you notice some weakening of the family is amongst the very poor in the cities where economic desperation often forces people to forget their loyalties and launch out on their own. But for most Indians, family still comes first. Laudable, you'd have thought, but I doubt it unless this Year of the Child can persuade Indian parents and grand-parents to be less selfish and more imaginative in the way they bring up their loyal children.

China Reaches Out

PHILIP SHORT   29 JANUARY 1979

The Chinese Vice-Premier, Deng Xiao-ping, had begun the first official visit to the United States by a Chinese leader since the Communist victory thirty years before. From Peking, Philip Short pondered on its implications.

Everyone from President Carter to Dr Brzezinski to the editorial writers of the Chinese press has been describing Deng's trip as a historic visit. But history, above all in China, takes a long view of things. And it's fair to ask amid all the euphoria that's been building up around the visit, whether China's current opening up to outside influences represents the beginning of a new chapter in the Middle Kingdom's view of the world, or whether it's just a footnote, a zig-zag in the continuity of China's historical isolation. The legacy of two thousand years in which China's emperors were the sons of heaven ruling over the human world has left a deep imprint on the way it conducts its affairs. Mao's system of rule was so different from that in the Soviet Union and Eastern Europe partly because it was in the Confucian tradition under which society should be regulated, not by laws and institutions, but by a collective moral order, spreading down from the ruler to the humblest of his subjects. And China's view of foreigners still revolves to some extent about the notion of Chinese-ness.

So, one finds no less a person than the Mayor of Peking issuing a statement last week which warned Chinese against fraternising too much with foreigners and accepting dinner invitations from them. Such people, he was quoted as saying, are forgetting their national character. In other words, as one Chinese wryly interpreted it to me, they're forgetting that they're Chinese which is a measure of the sense of apartness China has to surmount in coming to terms with the rest of the world. And at least some sections of China's leadership recognise that fact.

On the night of Vice-Premier Deng's departure, Chinese tele-vision screened a documentary programme about America which included an interview with a young Chinese bride at her wedding party in a Chinese restaurant in New York. Her husband was American, and she spoke of her hopes that relations between the two countries would prosper in the same way as her own new Chinese–American family. This may sound corny, but in China, until very recently, weddings between Chinese and foreigners were effectively banned. And only last year, when I asked a Chinese journalist what he thought of the possibility of mixed marriages resuming, he snorted and said the very idea was simply ridiculous.

That same television documentary administered shock treatment to Chinese viewers in other ways. It showed what it described as an American worker earning sixteen thousand pounds a year, which is just twice as much as most Chinese workers earn in their lifetimes.

And the cameras spent perhaps ten minutes looking round the house, room by room – the electric train set for the children, the deep freeze and the washing machine, all the paraphernalia that are so much taken for granted as a part of Western life, but which are beyond the wildest imaginings of most Chinese. The shock was all the greater because, until a month or so ago, the press here was depicting American life in terms of alcoholism and divorce, strikes and racial tension, and such events as the mass suicide of the People's Temple followers in Guyana, which the party newspaper, the *People's Daily*, said reflected the decadence and emptiness of capitalist society. The decision to acknowledge openly to the Chinese people how far China's development does lag behind the advanced countries, and to show them how affluent American capitalist society is, is the strongest evidence so far that China's opening up will continue; that this is a historic turning-point.

Over the centuries, the influence of foreign states was never quite enough to overturn the concept of the Middle Kingdom. The Holy Roman Empire, which China admired, was too far away for any but tenuous contact. Persia and India, while closer, were much weaker states, and the countries of the West, when they came, came to exploit and invade. But now the world is a much smaller place, and interdependence is harder to avoid. As the *People's Daily* put it in its New Year editorial, 'today no country can modernise with the door closed against the world'. And one of the more difficult adjustments China will face in the years ahead is to accommodate the traditions of its isolated past to the demands of a new world role.

Germany Faces up to the Holocaust
GRAHAM LEACH   19 FEBRUARY 1979

When it was known that the controversial American television series, Holocaust, was to be shown in the Federal German Republic, there was considerable interest in how the West Germans would react to it. How they did was decribed by Graham Leach.

So maybe some of the uniforms were not exact down to their finest detail. Perhaps the series was too one-sided with no account taken of those Germans who did try to help the Jews; and maybe there were elements of soap opera. But for many people here these criticisms paled into insignificance beside the enormity of the horror and the brutality the programme depicted. The series had its faults, people are saying, but was not nearly as bad as had been expected. It may have been because the programme was dubbed into German that much of the Hollywood-style melodrama didn't seem quite as sickly as we'd been led to believe. Corny American accents were replaced by real German voices. I did not see the series in Britain with the American soundtrack, but the voice of Erich Dorf, the young lawyer who turns into one of the Nazi Party's most evil creatures, could not have been more chilling than that of the actor who dubbed his voice into German. The impact that this series has made here has been shattering.

A few days ago I was out walking in the woods with my wife when we met three of our neighbours who never before had discussed politics or the past with us. For three-quarters of an hour on a bitter winter's afternoon they tried to impress upon us that they really had not known anything about what had taken place under the Nazis. Another acquaintance of ours had rung me up just before *Holocaust* began, having seen excerpts from the series. She said she couldn't possibly watch it if it was all so melodramtic. In the end she did tune in and last week she telephoned me again to say she'd completely changed her mind about the series. 'It was one of the best things that could have happened,' she said.

With the series now over, one of the country's newspapers is serialising the book on which the television series is based and book shops are cashing in by featuring displays of books about the Jews under the Third Reich. Political institutions have been inundated with requests for written material about the extermination programme, and polling organizations have carried out a survey on the effects of the series. But what the opinion polls do not show are the stories behind the figures – those private, anguished moments in individual families when embarrassing questions about the past have been asked. The figures do not recount the details of the many thousands of telephone calls which came in from those people wishing to take part in the phone-in programme which followed each episode. They don't recount how switchboard operators had to listen to people crying and sobbing and just asking the question, 'How could it have happened?' Figures cannot convey the story recounted by one German friend whose cleaning lady came in one morning so shocked after the previous night's episode that my acquaintance had to sit her down and talk to her for half-an-hour about how the new Germans were trying to make sure the mistakes of the past should never happen again.

So what has all this amounted to? One spin-off from the series is that the television companies, by their own admission, have been given a sharp lesson in how to reach out to an audience. For years, the Germans have been fed on a diet of very worthy but stiflingly boring documentaries about their past, most of which passed straight over their heads. This American series has shown how to handle the past by identifying with the fate of one family. People who never before knew or wanted to know about the Nazi era have been completely caught up in this series. In that sense it's been a real breakthrough. But perhaps more importantly, *Holocaust* has led to the first real debate in thirty years about what went on under the Nazis. There are endless stories of wives turning on their husbands and asking, 'Exactly what did you do in the war?' Questions are being asked which have not been posed in a generation. Will this great debate have any long-term effects? Well, this year West Germany has to decide whether or not to raise or extend the Statute of Limitations, the law which ends all new Nazi prosecutions after December. The reaction to this series at home, coupled with the international demands coming in from, among others, the European Parliament, American Congressmen, the Israelis, the East Europeans – demands not to end the prosecutions – make it seem likely that West Germany will find it impossible to call it a day and draw a line under the past.

A Parisian Sunday

STEPHEN JESSEL   16 APRIL 1979

Sunday in Paris, and how to face it – a problem confronting Paris Correspondent, Stephen Jessel.

There are, of course, the British Sunday papers, providing they haven't been held up by bad weather or by strikes on one side of the Channel or the other; if they've been printed at all, that is – the one that for some reason puts the sport in the business news which costs a trifling sixty-five pence, and the one that's the same on Sunday as it is on weekdays, yours for a mere ten shillings. Shopping's possible: markets and most food shops remain open until around 12.30. But, tempting as it might fleetingly be to spend the day eating, sleeping and reading the Sunday papers, to do so would be frivolous. Paris is, after all, rich in museums, galleries and exhibitions. The trouble is that they tend to be free on Sunday and therefore packed and so not very enjoyable. This is not to overlook the ancillary sights though: Japanese tourists, for example, relentlessly photographing each other all over town; the bus-loads of pink, scrubbed Germans heading for Montmartre and the murky delights of Pigalle; the British huddled on park benches, lunching frugally off bread, paté and many litres of cheap red wine.

Paris, though, is a city that can create claustrophobia and Sunday is the time to leave it in search of the countryside. The maps suggest that there are big parks to the west and east of the city – the Bois de Boulogne and the Bois de Vincennes – but these are no more the countryside than our Kensington Gardens. They are tired, tame stretches of greenery, regulated, ordered, full of slowly promenading families. On weekdays and after dark they are full of people engaged in old-established but unmentionable activities, and even on a sunny Sunday afternoon there's a certain tattiness about them. The seeker after more authentic sights and sounds will have to go further afield – but where?

The Ile de France, the region around Paris, has some of the dullest, flattest and most heavily populated country in France. The poet Rimbaud once wrote a stunning short poem about walking along a footpath through fields of corn on blue summer evenings. Not in the Ile de France you don't, unless you wish to be shot at, shouted at or gnawed to death by half-trained mastiffs. Private property in France is private property.

It's too far for the Loire, especially if you have to face Sunday evening traffic coming back. And so one ends up, lunched or unlunched, in one of the forests that ring Paris – Chantilly to the north, or Rambouillet to the west, or Fontainbleau to the south. Do not be put off by the discovery that the edges of the forest are, on a fine Sunday, solid with parked cars. Ten yards from the forest edge – well, twenty maximum – each family will have set up its table, chairs and picnic. There's the playing of the merry transistor. The family dog will be making a pest of itself, and those not themselves engaged in preparing a large and elaborate picnic will be playing one of the world's deeply pointless games, a sort of bowls with steel balls, but thrown, not rolled. Make your way into the wood or forest along the neat avenues and the sound of the radios, the barking and disputes about the picnic fade away.

I should not give the impression that the Parisians regard the countryside simply as a place for picnicking. It is there, too, to be looted. In the spring, the woods are stripped of bluebells, a curious exercise given the lifespan of the bluebell once picked. Whole families hunt for dandelion leaves for salads – very good with bacon – and in autumn, great battalions of Parisians move across the landscape in pursuit of mushrooms.

One should not exaggerate. Even within half-an-hour's drive of Paris, along the valley of the Chevreuse, for example, forgotten corners exist. Next to a wood populated chiefly by abandoned cars, a meadow full of coltsfoot and cowslips, a copse full of nuthatches. And if footpaths are deplorably lacking around Paris, France has many great trails, some hundreds of kilometres long, criss-crossing the entire country, marked by red and white flashes along the way, taking the walker through some of the most magnificent country in Europe. One of these days, I'm going to take Trail 4 from Saint-Flour in the Cantal, north to the Puy de Dômes, across the roof of the Auvergne, through the volcanic moonscape up there. One of these days – one of these Sundays.

The Pirates of the China Seas
JIM BIDDULPH   10 AUGUST 1979

For most people, the China Sea pirates were, until recently, just a part of history – a bunch of brigands who had been swept away from the seas. In fact, said Far East Correspondent Jim Biddulph, they never really disappeared.

Until recently the pirates had to be content with attacking fishing boats and over the past few years there have been repeated reports of fishing boats from all over the region being fired on; the fishermen robbed and maybe killed; their boats damaged or sunk. In the past couple of years, for example, there were five pirates killed in a clash with an Indonesian sea patrol after a Singapore trawler had appealed for help. Another clash, this time off the Thai coast, resulted in one policeman being killed and two others wounded after their police boat tangled with a pirate junk armed with M-79 grenade launchers and automatic weapons. Eighteen months ago Philippine airforce planes had to go into action to free a grounded Panamanian freighter which was under attack by more than a hundred pirates.

But on the whole the pickings were small. Then, along came the Vietnamese refugees. No longer did the pirates have to take on tough fishermen from Hong Kong and Singapore, or venture into coastal waters where there was the danger of attack by coastal patrols. Here instead were the refugees; they're packed into small boats, perhaps forty or fifty in the size of boat that normally half a dozen people might use for a day's pleasure cruise. Their boats are either underpowered or have no power at all; the people on board have often been at sea for a fortnight heading for the Thai or Malaysian coast from South Vietnam.

What is going on now in the South China Sea is pillage on a huge scale. Some boats reach land having been intercepted more than once. One boat that reached Malaysia had been caught by pirates eight times. And of course we only know about the boats that manage to sail to shore. It's a fair assumption that many have sunk. The pattern seems usually to be the same: the refugees see a junk approaching and think help is at hand; the pirates board the refugee boat, rape the women and search and beat the men.

This is very profitable villainy, because, certainly at the beginning of the exodus, the refugees were the rich merchants of Vietnam, carrying their savings with them in gold pieces. As the tales of piracy spread, the refugees found the obvious hiding places on their bodies for the gold; the pirates found it. In some cases women are taken away on board the pirate boats and seldom seen again. Sometimes men are taken on board, beaten up, presumably to try and make them say where the gold is hidden, and then thrown into the sea. On one occasion the pirates drained the freshwater tank of a refugee boat, suspecting that there were gold pieces hidden at the bottom. There weren't . . . but there wasn't any water left either.

The pirates, using very highly-powered craft, seem to be operating out of the creeks and inlets of the coast of Thailand. Nobody knows how many there are or whether there is any controlling figure like the China Sea pirate Ching Yi of a century and a half ago, who had four hundred pirate craft and twenty thousand men. Some evidence suggests that there is a pirate chief, an organiser, behind the looting of what must be many millions of pounds worth of gold. For example, a fortnight ago pirates held the captain and crew of a Thai oil tanker at gunpoint while a second tanker syphoned off three hundred and twenty thousand litres of diesel fuel. Now that could not have been the operation of some Thai corsaire with a fast junk and half a dozen men.

It's difficult to see what can be done about piracy. The raids are on the high seas in international waters; the victims are Vietnamese who have fled Vietnam. Now a hundred years ago, when Chinese pirates were raiding western vessels, combined operations by the British and American Navies attacked the pirates' strongholds. But in this instance, Hanoi is hardly likely to send a gun boat. And even if the pirates do refuel their ships in the creeks of the long Thailand coast, there is only so much the Thai forces can do. There are, after all, tens of thousands of perfectly legitimate boats doing the same thing. There are reports that some refugees are arming themselves before taking to sea. But an occasional burst of automatic fire will hardly stop a determined pirate. It looks as though the misery of the South China Sea will continue.

The Powerlessness of the Great Powers

JOHN SIMPSON　30 NOVEMBER 1979

John Simpson looked back on the seventies and what had happened to the power of the Great Powers.

Throughout the seventies, the decade we'll be saying goodbye to with some relief in five weeks' time, there's run a continuing paradox: the powerlessness of Great Powers – the strength of weak ones. Egypt, Romania, Yugoslavia, have all poked sticks through the bars at the Russian bear in the last ten years; and though it could flatten them with a blow of its paw, it has to be content with growling. The American eagle had its feathers plucked by North Vietnam in the early part of the decade, and now, right at the end of it, the Ayatollah is pulling out the rest.

It was different in the fifties and sixties. Then, a Great Power really was great. If Washington disliked what was happening in the Dominican Republic or the Lebanon, it sent the Marines in. When the Shah of Iran was toppled by the Ayatollah's friends in 1953, the CIA put him back on the Peacock Throne in a matter of days. In 1979 it didn't even try.

The reasons for the change are obvious enough: the United States isn't what it was, in world supremacy, or in wealth, or even in self-confidence. In 1953, Third World opinion meant nothing to anyone, since the Third World scarcely existed independently of the big power blocs. The raw materials, the minerals and the fossil fuels of the Third World, were still mostly in the control of the colonial powers. Nowadays, what the chancelleries of Africa or Asia think and do matters; not perhaps individually, but as members of a group. And of course the North-South divide can be seriously affected by the East-West one. Now that the United States and the Soviet Union are finely balanced in terms of power, Washington feels it can't afford to lose a single client state. A Guatemala or a Grenada may be insignificant as a piece of geographical real-estate – until it starts getting into the wrong hands. 'It's time for America to show its real strength,' says Mr Ronald Reagan; but when politicians say that kind of thing, it's the best sign that the real strength has fled. The world has changed from the days when Washington could play king-maker; and the last time it tried, in Chile in 1973, it burned its fingers badly.

We are, then, in an era when the Great Powers have been shackled and nothing has yet taken their place – certainly not some form of international government. Three centuries ago, Thomas Hobbes wrote: 'During the time men live without a common power to keep them all in awe, they are in that condition which is called war; and such a war as is of every man against every man.'

The depressing discovery of the twentieth century has been that 'common power' doesn't last if it's built on idealistic foundations – nations coming together in equality to solve their mutual problems harmoniously. The history of the League of Nations and the United Nations alike shows that. Sadly, things are best arranged when the common power flows from a single government, and the tougher the government the better. Squabbling in the Balkans brought the developed world to catastrophe in 1914; but since the last war, the

Balkans have mostly been under the control of the Soviet Union, and there's been no squabbling. Now that super-power influence is waning, the Balkans may represent once again a potential threat to the peace of the world. In General Hackett's recent book about a possible Third World War, the super-powers come to nuclear blows over a post-Tito Yugoslavia.

With an American flotilla in Iranian waters, General Hackett might now think Iran was an even more plausible flashpoint for a world war. In fact this crisis, like so many previous ones, will probably be sorted out. Academics in the United States and the Soviet Union spend their lives theorising about crisis management, and the White House and the Kremlin have profited from their theories. But the depressing pattern is there, just as it was before 1914: powerless Great Powers getting caught up in the irresponsible squabbling of small, weak nations, which draw their paradoxical strength from the ability to carry the Great Powers along with them. From the 1890s onwards, journalists and generals used to write books about the Great War they felt was coming. Their predictions always got the circumstances and usually the date of the war wrong, and they often got the wrong participants; but they were right about the war itself. Quite apart from Iran, and all the other small-scale conflicts around the Third World, from Kampuchea to the Middle East and Southern Africa, the most ominous thing of all may be that generals and journalists are starting to predict a world war once again.

The Irish Pub

PHILIP WHITFIELD   1 JANUARY 1980

From Dublin, Philip Whitfield discussed one of Ireland's most notable characteristics

In Ireland, the pub is one of the pivots of society, second only to the Church, and when, as in our neighbourhood, the pub faces the church, the two great institutions complement each other. One of our Christmas cards was addressed to 'Number 6 in the houses behind Gleeson's pub opposite the Church'. Of course it arrived on time. You give directions in Dublin by referring to churches and pubs.

To those who drink in Ireland, the pub is a second parlour; it opens in the morning and stays open until late at night. In Dublin the pubs are supposed to close for an hour in the afternoon – the so-called 'Holy Hour' – but the presence of a cheese sandwich or a bowl of soup seems to keep the police happy, and anyway it seems such a chore to clear everyone out of the bar only to let them in a few minutes later. It's not surprising, then, that the pub becomes the centre of local intercourse and commerce. Never stand beside the telephone in an Irish bar. It rings continually with people looking for Seamus or Michael or whoever. To the stranger, everything is confusion particularly in the morning. There's a man with a load of turf at the back door looking for payment; the barman seems to be arranging for a delivery of milk and tea, bread, ham and cheese, while boiling a kettle of water for the first 'hot Irish' of the day. For the uninitiated, a 'hot Irish' is a measure of Irish whiskey poured on to a bed of sugar, flavoured with a clove and then topped up with piping hot water. The barman, who commands considerable respect, is acknowledged to be an authority on all matters of politics, horses, Gaelic football and the eligibility of any unmarried person under forty within a ten-mile radius.

The problem is Irish pubs are just too seductive. Last year the Irish spent more on drink than any other country in the Common Market – one and a quarter million pounds a day, or three pounds a week for every man, woman and child in the Republic. In recent years the number of people seeking hospital treatment for alcoholism has trebled. According to the Prime Minister, Mr Haughey, alcoholism is as great a threat to the national well-being today as tuberculosis thirty or forty years ago. The Government's Health Education Bureau has begun a campaign to dissuade people from heavy drinking, and now the Irish Brewers Association is spending half a million pounds to educate people 'not to misuse their products', as their promotion literature puts it. The new Irish Prime Minister has given up smoking and is said to be a modest social drinker these days. He's expected to put a new impetus behind the non-drinking lobby in the medical profession. But Mr Haughey knows he can't change a way of life with a few television commercials.

Out in the west of Ireland, it's still traditional to go visiting neighbours in the country up to midnight and to sit around the fire talking and drinking until two or three in the morning. There, it's likely the drink will be poteen – the original home-brew – crystal-clear alcohol distilled from potatoes or corn. You won't find a pub where a woman will be served with a pint of beer or stout in Ireland – pints are regarded as unladylike. Most Irish pubs have a men's bar; women, it seems to me, are allowed into many pubs on sufferance. But then attitudes are changing rapidly in Irish society to cope with the times. Take the traditional pint of stout. Here a pint is poured with a love and a gentleness seldom associated with barmen. The pint has to stand for several minutes as the head of beer settles into a dark, black stout. Then it's topped up and allowed to stand for another few minutes before the final creamy head is poured into the glass. Now they tell me, scientists in the brewery in Dublin have developed a way of putting the head on in a trice with a syringe. It would be a brave man who'd launch that on the Irish market.

Russian Exile

KEVIN RUANE   30 JANUARY 1980

Soviet Academician Andrei Sakharov had been seized by the police in Moscow and flown out to live under surveillance in the city of Gorky, two hundred and fifty miles away. Kevin Ruane looked at the traditions and the practice of what's known as internal exile.

Once upon a time before the Revolution, when Russia was still ruled by a Tsar, a man later to become famous was sent away into exile in a small village called Shushenskoye, at the foot of the Sayan mountain range in Siberia. It was 1897; the man spent three years there as a punishment for his political activities. He carried on his political writing in spite of police surveillance, and was joined by a young woman also under sentence, and they got married. The man's name was Lenin. Their story as shown by a Soviet television programme this week has a definite romantic appeal, but their experience is not unique to the days before the Revolution. Exile to Siberia is part of Soviet reality. About a year ago a young man from Moscow, sentenced for anti-Soviet slander, went off into Siberian exile. He was followed by a Moscow girl all the way to a settlement called Ust-Nera in Yakutiya in the far north-east, famed as the coldest place on the earth. They, too, got married, and last month their first child was born – a boy they call Mark. Her name is Alla, her husband is Sasha Podrabinek, a dissident sentenced for publicising allegations that authorities have used psychiatry for political purposes.

His name perhaps will not be remembered as long as those of Lenin or Sakharov, but his experience is more typical of the severity of a form of punishment first mentioned here in the sixteenth century. At first those condemned to internal exile, disgraced noblemen as well as ordinary people, were sent to remote parts of European Russia and then to the Caucasus in the south. Then, in the last century, Siberia became the place to despatch political exiles, many of whom made a significant contribution to the cultural and economic awakening of that vast and forbidding place. Today the regulations governing internal exile are laid out in the Russian 'Code of Corrective Labour', and it's under those, in recent years, that many political dissidents as well as common criminals have been sentenced and punished. The most common form of exile ordains that a convict be sent away and confined to a strictly prescribed area, to live and work like anyone else there, but under police surveillance, obliged to report to the authorities at regular intervals. He travels there under escort, but as a concession to the ordeal involved in the journey, the code says that one day under escort counts for three days off his sentence. Last century, before the construction of the Trans-Siberian railway, condemned men had to cover large tracts on foot; today the journey east, known as '*etapirovaniye*' or 'staging', is still feared perhaps most of all. One modern exile has said it took him more than sixty days to travel five thousand miles. The journey was split up between stops at local prisons on the way, and stages by train lasting three or four days, with more than twenty prisoners crammed into one compartment designed at most for six. On reaching his destination, the exile can in theory choose his job or his own accommodation, but since he arrives with little or no money and in the clothes he was sentenced in, he's largely dependent on the local police for help in finding somewhere to sleep and to work. He also has to let his family and friends know where he is and where to send parcels of warm clothing.

Sasha Podrabinek says he's living in the coldest place on this planet with temperatures of sixty below. But he is working at his usual job as a doctor's assistant. Others with higher qualifications have not been so fortunate, being forced to sleep at night in freezing wooden dormitories with no indoor plumbing, while doing heavy manual work at logging camps during the day. Others are more fortunate. One woman, two years ago, bought her own wooden house and worked a vegetable garden with the villagers, and read or wrote in her spare time. It was so peaceful, she says she could almost have stayed.

Academician Sakharov's position is quite different. For one thing he was not sentenced; for another he was flown in a short time to his destination under an escort of ten. A furnished flat, with housekeeper provided, awaited him. As regards comfort, this is clearly much better, but in terms of isolation it could be considered much worse. Ordinary exiles can be visited and write letters. Dr Sakharov, under much closer surveillance, apparently cannot. It's what he calls 'living in a gilded cage'. It's a unique situation, but there is a link with the past. His wife says her mother, besides being a veteran of the camps, was also once in exile near Gorky. So there are family connections. But another connection is also interesting. The Sakharovs' new home is in a district of the city where a prominent Soviet leader is the chosen candidate for next month's elections to the Russian Supreme Soviet. His name is Yuri Andropov, Chairman of the State Security Committee – the KGB.

My Meeting with Tito

KENNETH MATTHEWS   29 FEBRUARY 1980

President Tito was dying. During World War Two, Kenneth Matthews, as a BBC war correspondent, was attached to Middle East Command. By them, he was smuggled into German-occupied Yugoslavia to join Tito's partisans, and he was the first journalist from the West to interview Tito.

When I first heard Tito's name I certainly never expected to meet him. Did he even exist? At my briefing before I left London my last instruction was – 'And find out who Tito is if there is such a person.' There were these odd reports of a shadowy bandit, or Communist chieftain of partisans, fighting a war of his own in the Yugoslav mountains. One branch of British Intelligence decided that 'Tito' was simply the initials of a revolutionary organisation, 'Terrorists International', and one widely circulated rumour had it that Tito was a woman.

But the truth began to dawn that Tito was real enough, and soon every journalist in the Middle East was hoping to make contact with these mysterious partisans. It was my luck, when we drew lots, to pick up the number 2 ticket – very special luck as it happened because the number 1 was taken prisoner as soon as he set foot on occupied territory. So I flew in one dark night to a little improvised airstrip in a basin of the mountains and joined a company of men and women who'd broken all their ties with homes and families and depended for their lives on the loyalty of the local populations among whom they moved. I quickly realised that their leader was a man of no ordinary quality. His army was disciplined and he'd fired the imagination of his people. Communist he might be, but he was no narrow fanatic. He had great personal magnetism. I remember Lindsay Rogers, the New Zealand surgeon who operated on more than a thousand partisan wounded, telling me, 'Nobody can refuse Tito anything – he just smiles at you and that's the end of the matter.' When it came to my turn to see Tito he smiled at me too, though by that time his relations with Britain were going fast downhill.

It was perhaps inevitable that Tito should gravitate towards Russia after the War. There was the Communist faith; there was the racial pull of another more powerful Slav nation; above all there was the delusion, not confined to the Yugoslavs of course, that the Soviet Union had found the way to the earthly paradise. But Tito had also quarrelled with the Western Allies: the British Eighth Army had blocked his claim to the city of Trieste. So he walked into Stalin's arms and a period began when all the worst features of the Soviet system appeared in Yugoslavia: liquidation of political opponents; staged treason trials; suppression of religion – the lot. This state of affairs looked from the outside as if it might go on for ever. In fact it lasted about three years. Then came the break with Russia – the international sensation of 1948. The Russians had been treating Yugoslavia like conquered territory and Tito had not fought the Italians and Germans in order to become a tame appendage of the Soviet Empire. But to cut loose from Russia altogether – wasn't that a form of suicide? Tito stood alone; the onlookers waited for the thunderbolt to fall on his head. But week after week, then month after month, he survived. He showed the world what courage in politics could achieve against all predictions of disaster.

It was too much to expect that Tito would change sides – the Communist ideology had gone too deeply for that. He accepted some aid from the West when the Russians imposed an economic blockade on him, but he declared that a future Yugoslavia would join no great power bloc, and that was a foreign policy which came to be known as 'non-alignment'.

Tito's lifestyle came in for some criticism at this time. The partisan chieftain, accessible to every caller, had become the closely guarded potentate, hedged about with security men and motorcycle outriders wherever he moved. But it was understandable that some extraordinary precautions were necessary to protect him from assassination, and his popularity didn't noticeably suffer. His people were recovering from the ravages of war and the effects of the Russian boycott. The democratic freedoms were reappearing.

There was one more test of Tito's statesmanship – one more major confrontation with the Russians – the 1968 invasion of Czechoslovakia. Tito had put his full weight behind the Czechoslovak attempt to break free from the Russian embrace; he immediately denounced the Russian use of force, and all Yugoslavia seethed with indignation. They were re-living at one remove the experiences they themselves had been through twenty years before. The Czechs were not so lucky. But the upheaval gave Tito the chance to tell the Russians once again that every State had the right to choose its own way of development – a thing which might be finding echoes in Afghanistan today.

I think Tito will be best remembered for standing up to the Russians at a time when Stalin's tyranny seemed irresistible. He changed the course of European history. But he also saw his country rebuilt out of ruins, restored to moderate prosperity, and with its awkward mixture of races and cultures more united than it had ever been before.

Zimbabwe

DAVID McNEIL   28 MARCH 1980

Rhodesia was about to become Zimbabwe. A new black government had been elected, many of whose members had spent years in detention as part of their struggle for power. Southern Africa Correspondent, David McNeil, described the prize they had won.

Enormous! That's what it is: enormous. In the history of British colonialism there can have been no greater reward for nationalist struggle, for this is a country that works. The basic infrastructure is sound; it has survived years of war; it's damaged, yes, but it can be repaired. The new Zimbabwe does have the potential to become one of the richest African states. Years ago, the then Minister of Agriculture, Mr David Smith, now a member of Robert Mugabe's Cabinet, declared that if white agriculture collapsed, millions of people in Central Africa would starve. These days it's put in a less arrogant way. This country can provide enough food for its own people with plenty over for its neighbours – but only if the white infrastructure remains. The senior members of the new government realise this. Privately they'll tell you they want the whites to stay, but only the right sort of whites. The shopkeepers, the junior civil servants can go as far as they're concerned – it'll make more room for blacks. But they want the experts to stay – the teachers, the surgeons, the technologists, the farmers – those with expertise who can use it and can pass it on.

Eighty per cent of Zimbabwe's population will need to be propped up for some time to come. That's the percentage that live in the tribal trustlands – the least productive parts of the country. Until now they've existed at subsistence level and it won't be easy to get them to change. The former white regime tried to change them; they tried to regulate the use of land; they tried to limit the population growth rate of more than three and a half per cent – one of the highest in the world – and it didn't work. The blacks in the tribal trustlands were given land according to the size of their families and told: 'That's it, there'll be no more.' And the agricultural experts arrived. 'You're growing seven bags of maize on this land,' they said. 'We can show you how to be more productive – how to grow twenty-seven bags.' And the black farmers said, 'No. We're growing enough for our families' needs.

What do we do with the rest? We'll have to harvest it; bag it; take it to the markets; sell it. And what do we do with the money? Banks? No – that's too much trouble.'

Robert Mugabe talks about collective farming. That means organisation and marketing on a scale never before attempted in this country, and the people installed on the land will need money to buy machinery and fertiliser. There'll have to be extensive capital investment by the government and further educational support until the new farmers have gained the required skills.

There are between four and seven million acres of usable empty land immediately available to resettle blacks uprooted by the war – under-utilised land that belongs to the state. Beyond that there's plenty more if the government wants to carry out its threat to acquire land from farmers who aren't making a go of it.

But the future of this country does not hinge on the availability of land or natural resources. The wealth is there to be tapped. It lies in the ability of the new government to tap it. Without any doubt, the real strength of Zimbabwe will be the infrastructure built by white Rhodesians, especially during the years since UDI. In 1965 tobacco accounted for a large percentage of the country's export earnings. Sanctions meant diversification into groundnuts and cotton; it meant ingenuity in the manufacturing sector. If Rhodesia didn't have it she made it herself. And she succeeded to such an extent that she was able to sell hi-fi equipment on the South African market at a price that was less than it cost the South Africans to make it. And beneath all the war rhetoric the deals with Rhodesia's neighbours were struck: maize seed to Mozambique, and maize itself to Zambia throughout the war.

So you have a thriving farming sector; a burgeoning secondary industry; enormous potential from tourism in what must be one of the most stunning countries it's possible to visit – there'll never be anything to equal the Victoria Falls in my experience. And you have a great base on which to build. But Zimbabwe owes nearly everything to white entrepreneurial skills, cheap black labour not withstanding. And in the short term at least it will stand or fall on the retention of those skills. The riches of Rhodesia have been carved out of the bush, and the bush is waiting to reclaim them.